# NOTES ON CONTRIBUTORS

*Philip Adey* is Professor of Cognition, Science, and Education at King's College, London. He started his professional life as a chemistry teacher but soon became interested in the issue of 'difficulty': why do some students find some concepts more difficult than others, and what can be done about it? The present book is his most recent contribution towards an answer to this problem.

*Mundher Adhami* studied geophysics at Moscow and Durham universities, and worked in computer dynamic modelling before switching to teaching mathematics in London schools. He then moved into curriculum development for GAIM at King's College, London and the London examination board. Since 1993 he has been a King's College research worker in the CAME series of research and associated teachers' professional development programmes.

*Ken Gouge* has twenty-six years experience as an arts educator, local authority adviser and consultant to national arts organizations. For the last ten years he was General Adviser (visual and performing arts) for Wigan LEA, leading a team of advisers working in dance, drama, music, the visual arts and media education. He is currently leading the Wigan Arts Reasoning and Thinking Skills Project. He runs his own independent arts education consultancy.

*Jeremy Hodgen* is a lecturer in mathematics education in the Department of Education and Professional Studies at King's College, London. He has taught in both primary and secondary schools. His current research interests include primary teachers' mathematical subject knowledge and teacher education.

*Shirley Larkin* is a doctoral research student attached to the CASE@KS1 project at King's College, London. She has a background in arts and literature and has taught in parent organized community schools and in further education. Her research interests cover language and cognition and she is currently researching the development of metacognition in 5- and 6-year-old children.

*Anne Robertson* is a primary teacher who trained in Edinburgh in the early 1970s. Having worked in Edinburgh for several years, she moved to London and taught in Haringey and Newham. She then took an advisory post in Barking and Dagenham helping teachers to address special needs issues in primary classrooms. In 1998 she began work in Hammersmith and Fulham on the new CASE@KS1 project in Year 1 classrooms.

*Michael Shayer* is Professor of Applied Psychology at King's College, London. He met the '12-year gap' (between the best and the worst of entrants to secondary school) full in the face in Peckham in the mid 1960s, and has tried his best ever since, first to understand it and then to change it.

*Grady J. Venville* has taught science, English as a second language and science education in primary, secondary and tertiary institutions in Australia and Japan. She also has been involved with several large research projects in Australia and England, particularly in science education. Grady completed her doctorate on pupils' understanding in genetics in 1998. She is currently a lecturer in science education at Curtin University of Technology in Perth, Western Australia and her current research interest is pupils' cognitive development and their understanding in science.

*Kevin Wall* has taught in a variety of schools across the age range for nearly 18 years. In 1999 he took an MA in psychology and special educational needs and is currently completing his PhD, which has focused on gestural and verbal communication among 5–6-year-olds. His research interests include communication, motivation and peer interactions.

*Carolyn Yates* is Director of Cognitive Acceleration Programmes Scotland. Her particular interests are in training and development and thinking skills. She has advised and led projects with overseas ministries of education as well as councils in England, Scotland and Wales. She was co-author, with Philip Adey and Michael Shayer, of *Thinking Science*, the materials of the CASE project.

# LEARNING INTELLIGENCE

# LEARNING INTELLIGENCE

## Cognitive Acceleration across the curriculum from 5 to 15 years

Edited by

**MICHAEL SHAYER AND PHILIP ADEY**

LEARNING RESOURCES
CENTRE

Havering College
of Further and Higher Education

**OPEN UNIVERSITY PRESS**
Buckingham • Philadelphia

Open University Press
Celtic Court
22 Ballmoor
Buckingham
MK18 1XW

email: enquiries@openup.co.uk
world wide web: www.openup.co.uk

and
325 Chestnut Street
Philadelphia, PA 19106, USA

First Published 2002

A catalogue record of this book is available from the British Library

ISBN   0 335 21136 4 (pb)   0 335 21137 2 (hb)

**Library of Congress Cataloging-in-Publication Data**
Learning intelligence : cognitive acceleration across the curriculum from 5 to
15 years / edited by Michael Shayer and Philip Adey.
      p. cm.
   Includes bibliographical references and index.
   ISBN 0–335–21136–4 (pb) — ISBN 0–335–21137–2 (hb)
   1. Educational psychology. 2. Cognitive learning. I. Shayer, Michael, 1928–
II. Adey, Philip.

   LB1062 .L38 2002
   370.15′2—dc21
                                                                    2002024617

Typeset by Graphicraft Limited, Hong Kong
Printed in Great Britain by Biddles Limited, Guildford and King's Lynn

# CONTENTS

# 1 COGNITIVE ACCELERATION COMES OF AGE

## Philip Adey and Michael Shayer

## Introduction

Cognitive Acceleration (CA) has come of age in the sense of growing out from its roots in secondary school science into all areas of the curriculum and across the school age range. We may claim immodestly that this proliferation has come about through the efforts of the authors represented in this volume and others, but must recognize also that the current political and social climate is generally friendly to the growth of programmes which develop higher level thinking abilities. It has become a truism that modern society has very little place for unthinking manual labour and that every school leaver needs to be equipped with flexible thinking skills developed to their maximum capacity, and this is now a tenet of the British Government's educational policy. Although Nisbet's (1993) prediction that 'before the century is out, no curriculum will be regarded as acceptable unless it can be shown to make a contribution to the teaching of thinking' has not quite been fulfilled, it is the case that the National Curriculum (NC) for England now does include the development of thinking as a central requirement. We may quibble about the particularities of the 'thinking skills' specified, but it would be churlish not to recognize the real political will that schools should be required to attend directly to students' intellectual development, beyond the requirements of mastering particular bodies of information. We are convinced that some 80 per cent of the school population currently perform academically well below their potential, yet by means of suitable intervention virtually all can function at levels where presently only the top 20 per cent lie.

In this book we will show how such interventions are being worked out in a wide variety of curricula and age contexts. Our original context-delivered interventions were aimed at the 12- to 14-year-old group and were focused on the two most cognitively demanding of the school subjects: science and mathematics. In discussion of their pedagogies, understandably the emphasis was on promoting thinking. Yet one has only to hear an already skilled child musician, or see the drawings of a child with an artistic gift, to realize that the ability to exhibit a high degree of integrated processing of reality is in no way confined to the context of mathematics or science. Without buying Gardner's (1993) model of Multiple Intelligences, it is easily possible to view in these sophisticated performances 'intelligence-in-action', just as much as in the performance of a child with good mathematical ability. Chapter 9 will describe the Wigan Arts, Reasoning and Thinking Skills (ARTS) project, where the emphasis is on promoting those aspects of superior performance that Arts specialists habitually use to judge and differentiate the performances of their pupils. The recent Cognitive Acceleration in Technology Education (CATE) project, described briefly at the end of this chapter, promotes intelligence-in-action in the context of design and technology.

Evidence suggests that the differential between children's potential and their performance is already present at the age of 5, so one of the interventions to be described (CASE@KS1, Chapters 2–6) addresses 5- to 6-year-olds. At this age, school subjects are not so differentiated as they are by the end of primary school, so the CASE@KS1 intervention is rooted in general mental abilities and not set in a particular subject context.

Chapters 7 and 8 will describe the working out of CA principles in mathematics in Years 5 and 6, where the requirements of the particular subject need to be delivered within a primary school setting, that is by a class teacher rather than a specialist mathematician.

Chapter 10 will take a slightly different perspective, showing how some of the skills involved in intervention teaching can be applied usefully to regular science lessons with a benefit to pupils' comprehension, and possibly also to their motivation. Although this seems like blurring the model, it can also be looked on as giving teachers more conscious control of their professional skills in general. Finally, Chapter 11 offers a theoretical integration of the Piagetian and Vygotskyan foundation on which the whole CA enterprise is founded.

In the remainder of this chapter we will revisit the psychological roots of CA and the 'six pillars' of CA which arise from its underlying theory, and recapitulate some of the evidence for the effect of the methods on students. This is partly for the benefit of readers new to CA, but we hope that old CA groupies will benefit from seeing the most recent expression of these fundamental principles. We will finish the chapter by raising the possibility that CA actually offers a new paradigm for education.

## Theory base

Here are three basic hypotheses on which all CA interventions are based:

1 it is valid to work on the basis of some *general* intellectual function in children which underlies any particular context (subject)-dependent component;
2 this general intellectual function develops with age; and
3 the development of this general intellectual function is influenced both by the environment and by maturation.

Let us provide a little more detail to justify each of these hypotheses.

## *A general processor?*

The question of 'general' versus 'special' cognitive processing turns out to be one which exercises educators far more than it does psychologists. Psychologists know from the predictive power of IQ scores on a wide range of academic achievements (Anderson 1992), from factor analytical studies (Carroll 1993), and from studies on working memory capacity (Pascual-Leone 1976; Baddeley 1990; Kyllonen and Christal 1990; Towse et al. 1998; Logie 1999), that it is not just useful but empirically justified to posit a general cognitive processing capacity which underlies any more particular abilities which may be identified. Duncan (2001) has recently claimed to have found a location on the pre-frontal cortex for such a general processor. As educators are concerned more with the practicalities of a curriculum which aim to address many facets of a child's learning and development – in other words because they are more concerned with the trees than with the forest – they are more likely to focus on children's differential abilities in different fields. Measurement supports the existence of special abilities in language, numerical, spatial, logical, musical and other spheres which have some independence from one another, but measurement does not support the *exclusive* existence of such special abilities. Whether we model the underlying general intellectual function in terms of IQ, working memory capacity or Piaget's *structures d'ensemble* is a matter of fine-tuning.

## *Cognitive development*

That intellectual functioning develops with age is probably a commonplace of cognitive psychology, established empirically by the work of Jean Piaget, Bärbel Inhelder and their colleagues in Geneva from the 1930s to the 1970s. Now neurophysiological studies provide detailed descriptions of brain growth from the first formation of the neural tube in the foetus some 12 days after conception, through massive growth in the number of neurones during the next 36 weeks, and then an explosion of synaptic connections (and associated myelination) between neurones immediately after birth (Johnson 1997). During the next 13 to 15 years, and through a series of critical periods of growth (Epstein 1986; Hudspeth and Pribram 1990) the brain becomes increasingly well organized, culminating with the finalization of the main structures in the pre-frontal lobes – an important site for logical and control systems – during adolescence.

A similar story emerges from the IQ camp. Measures of fluid intelligence (here-and-now cognitive processing ability) grow steadily (but not uniformly) from the earliest years when measurements can be made to a plateau at about 16 years of age, and then starts to decline from the early 20s (Cattell 1963: 167–74). Studies of language development also provide evidence for development and for critical windows, and give an insight into the complexities of trying to provide explanations in terms of localized brain functions. Johnson and Newport (1993) have shown how the mechanisms we use to acquire a second language after we reach maturity are very different from those used to acquire our first language.

### Influences on cognitive development

You may accept that there is such a thing as general intelligence, and that it develops with age. But if you do not accept the third of our hypotheses, that this development can be influenced by the environment (and that as parents and teachers we have some control over the environment), then you condemn humankind to a deterministic world in which IQ is some sort of fixed function of an individual and the whole educational enterprise is called into question. Since IQ at birth predicts no more than 20 per cent of IQ at maturity (Plomin 2001), this would obviously be an untenable position. The most direct evidence for the impact of environment on cognition comes, necessarily, from animal studies. Greenhough et al. (1987), for example, have shown that the brains of rats reared in natural-like conditions where they have to search for food, escape dangers and generally exercise their cognitive processing, develop significantly more dendritic growth than those of rats reared in unstimulating laboratory cages.

There remains the question of just what sort of environment is likely to provide maximal stimulation to the intellect, and answering this question is essential if we are to describe effective cognitive intervention. We sought answers from two sources: the developmental psychology of Jean Piaget and the socio-cultural psychology of Lev Vygotsky. In designing what we supposed to be maximally stimulating activities, we drew from these bodies of theory a series of working principles commonly referred to as the 'pillars' of cognitive acceleration. Here we offer you six pillars. (Experienced CA-ers may be surprised at six, not the usual five, but you will find that this is just a re-formulation, not the radical invention of any new principle.)

## Six pillars

### 1 Schema theory

A schema (pl. schemata) is a general way of thinking which can be applied to many different contexts. The original work of the Cognitive Acceleration through Science Education (CASE) project in secondary schools used the schemata of formal operations described by Inhelder and Piaget (1958), such as control of variables, equilibrium, probability and formal modelling, as a framework within which each activity is developed. For the CASE@KS1 (and upcoming CASE@KS2) work the schemata of concrete operations such as seriation, simple classification, causality, perspective-taking and various conservations (Piaget and Inhelder 1974, 1976) played the same role. Whether or not the questions which have been raised by, for instance, Donaldson (1978) or Goswami (1998) about the Piagetian notion of 'stages' and the ages at which children can perform certain intellectual tasks are justified, the descriptions of schemata provide a clear set of types of thinking which can readily be operationalized into teaching and assessment activities.

For the CAME intervention the schemata were sought by abstracting underlying 'strands' of thinking in mathematics such as 'multiplicative relations' (including ratio and proportion), 'algebraic expression', and 'functions'. More detail of these are provided in Chapter 7.

## 2 Concrete preparation

In educational practice, students need some sort of introduction to any intellectual problem they will encounter. They need to know the context of the problem and something of the vocabulary they are going to require to think and talk about it. Thus, the first phase of any CA intervention is designed in such a way that all the students can engage with the task. Unlike an ordinary instructional lesson, however, it needs to start to induce in the students the learning behaviour they are to work with in the second (construction) phase of the activity.

## 3 Cognitive conflict

Here we draw on the Piagetian idea of equilibration and the Vygotskyan idea of a Zone of Proximal Development (ZPD). Equilibration is the process by which cognitive processing mechanisms in the mind accommodate to events which cannot readily be assimilated and which create some sort of cognitive conflict. The ZPD is the difference between what a child can achieve unaided and what she can achieve with the assistance of a more able peer or adult. Both of these notions lead us to suppose that cognition can be stimulated by the presentation of intellectual challenges of moderate difficulty. This must be accompanied by support (scaffolding) in the form of leading questions, invitations to discuss difficulties encountered, suggestions to look at the problem from different angles, and so on. Newman et al. (1989) have described such challenge-plus-support as 'working in the construction zone'.

## 4 Social construction

Vygotsky established that the construction of knowledge and understanding is pre-eminently a social process. Understanding appears first in the social space that learners share, and then becomes internalized by individuals (Vygotsky 1978). But Piaget also was clear that the environment which creates the cognitive conflict and which stimulates cognitive growth is importantly a social environment as much as a physical one. The activities of talking around new ideas, exploring them through group discussion, and asking for explanations and justifications, are all part of the process of building individual knowledge. CA interventions in any subject area and at any age encourage students to describe and explain their ideas, to feel unafraid of getting things wrong, and to engage in constructive polylogue with colleagues while teasing out a group understanding. The techniques for generating reasoned discussion promoted by the Philosophy for Children movement (Lipman et al. 1980) offer much the same promise, and Wegerif et al. (1999) have shown how explicit attention to the development of co-operative talk in children leads to gains in scores on Raven's Matrices, a language-free measure of general logical processing.

### 5 Metacognition

Vygotsky's emphasis on language as a mediator of learning suggests not only that meaning is constructed as children talk amongst themselves and discuss with adults, but also that language provides the tools for thought. The notion of metacognition, although somewhat over used (Brown 1987), emphasizes the value to the developing thinker of becoming conscious of their own thinking and developing and practising the technical vocabulary necessary for describing different thinking actions. The requirement for consciousness means that it is a process that must take place *after* a thinking act, since at the time a student is engaging in a problem-solving activity their consciousness must be devoted to that. There is a substantial literature (for a small sample, see Klauer 1989; Perkins and Saloman 1989; De Corte 1990; McGuinness 1990) which testifies to the value of this type of metacognition in making general thinking processes explicit, and thus more readily available for use on other occasions.

### 6 Bridging

Finally, to be generally useful, new thought processes must be made available across a wide range of contexts. Thus there is a phase in any CA activity where students are invited to think of other contexts where that schema might be used. For example, following an activity in which objects have been classified in two ways, students may see that as a useful general way of organizing their music collection, their clothes or food in a larder.

### Integrating the pillars

The way in which a typical CA lesson incorporates the six pillars is through a three-Act model of the whole activity. Act 1 is 'Concrete Preparation' with the whole class, as described, although a little construction may be initiated with a few 'seeding' questions from the teacher. In Act 2 the class splits up into groups – each somewhere between two and five in number – and the groups work on the problem with the aim of having some insights to offer when the time comes for Act 3. Act 2 is where the main construction occurs due to the pupils' collaborative work. Here also cognitive conflict should occur, either spontaneously when the students realize their ideas are inadequate to produce a solution, or when the passing teacher drops in the right question which makes them realize their ideas have contradictions. Act 3, a session for whole-class discussion, is initiated by the teacher when he realizes that enough ideas have been generated around the class in Act 2, even though not all groups may have achieved a solution. To begin with, each group shows quickly – either on the apparatus or on the board – the problems they have met, and how they worked to solve them. At this point, further construction occurs within individual pupils as they see or hear others going just that much further than they did on the task. Metacognition occurs when the teacher asks the whole class to find some way of describing, in words that make sense to them and hence are more easily stored for later recall, the most important insights that the class has achieved and how it has achieved them. An optional Act 4 may be suggested by the teacher where he asks the class for possible bridging to other contexts. But the place where bridging also takes place is in Act 1, Concrete Preparation, when the teacher asks the members of the class to remember what ideas they have met before which might be useful for working on the problem which has been presented (see Chapter 10 for finer detail of the process). In practice, these three or four Acts may not be so strictly demarcated. Metacognitive questions may arise at any time, and during the constructive group work the teacher may call the whole class together either for an extra bit of Concrete Preparation or to generate some cognitive conflict by allowing groups to hear ideas that have tentatively been developed so far.

To summarize the basic principles, behind all CA interventions lies the assumption that the ability to process many aspects of reality simultaneously is the key to high performance in any sphere, and conversely any context-related intervention is likely to affect the learning ability of a child generally, and not just in that specific context, provided the intervention activity is conducted 'with an eye on the Towers of the Eternal City'[1] and not just on verbal learning or unthinking techniques. There are two common themes which run through all CA interventions: one is derived from Piaget and the other from Vygotsky. The 'Eternal City' is framed by the teacher viewing the particular subject that provides the context for the intervention in hierarchical terms (the Piagetian aspect). Thus, in any one class he can see different levels in the hierarchy exhibited in the pupils' performance, while presenting the activity knowing that many different steps in the hierarchy can be promoted by it. The 'Towers' represent a distant aim toward which the teacher can aspire vicariously for his students. The

Vygotskyan aspect, common to groups of six 5-year-olds working at a common task in CASE@KS1, and to 13-year-olds in whole class discussion or small group collaboration in CASE and CAME, is that 'the collective' is not some remnant of communist mysticism but is a true description of where most child development lies. No one child has the whole of the world to invent and construct for themselves; in any activity most of their gains will come from appropriating a higher level of performance they have witnessed in a member of their 'collective'. However, they too have contributed to the thinking or the action in the group that has crystallized – perhaps in one child only for the moment – the new higher level performance or insight. So it is not as simple as to say that the less able are being mediated by the more able. All are contributing. In all these interventions a learning 'collective' is being created for the purpose of enhancing the development of all. The teacher's art here lies in knowing how to promote the collaborative learning that generates the 'collective'.

## Realizing the model

We now turn to the educational issue of translating a psychological model into educational practice. It will be clear that intervention for cognitive acceleration requires a significant shift in teaching methods compared with even high-quality conceptual teaching aimed at the development of understanding of (and love for) a subject. No one involved in real curriculum change (as opposed to the printing of a new revised edition of a textbook or a National Curriculum[2]) is under any illusion that changing teaching approaches on a large scale is an extraordinarily difficult task. It is perfectly obvious that printed materials alone will never do the job, and we are convinced also that no non-human resources (interactive video, ICT and so on) can ever replicate the type of subtly nuanced questioning, exploring and responsiveness to verbal and non-verbal clues, which characterize teaching designed to maximize cognitive growth.

From the start of CA programmes in the early 1980s at Chelsea College, we have taken the two-pronged approach of (a) trying to explicate as clearly as possible in printed materials and video the underlying principles and the classroom practice of intervention; and (b) providing extensive professional development programmes for departments and local authorities that wish to implement cognitive acceleration. An important part of the professional development is coaching work in teachers' own classrooms to demonstrate how the methods work in almost any school environment. If in this book we do not dwell at length on the mechanisms of professional development which have been developed for CA programmes it is because it is a subject so large as to be worthy of a book in its own right. However, we hope that no reader will get the impression that implementing CA with any age group or in any subject area is a simple process.

## Evidence of effects

### *CASE*

Over the years, we have published evidence of the effects of cognitive acceleration on students' cognitive growth and academic achievement. For CASE, the most accessible summaries are probably Shayer (1999a) and Adey and Shayer (1994). In our original CASE experiment (1984–87) we used an experimental/control pre-test, post-test and delayed post-test design to show that CASE in Years 7 and 8 produced accelerated cognitive development immediately and, as predicted by the hypothesis of a general intellectual processor amenable to cognitive stimulation, improvements in GCSE grades not only in science but also in mathematics and English. In other words, the CA intervention produced a long-term effect (3 years after the end of the intervention) and a far transfer effect (from the context of delivery, science, into very different subject areas such as English). Effect sizes were in the range from 0.3 to 1.0 standard deviations, which translates to between a half and one GCSE grade, as described in Adey and Shayer (1994).

Yet these were very small-scale research data, with only about 130 students in each of the experimental and control groups. Far more important are the subsequent data we have been able to collect from successive cohorts of schools which have participated in CASE Professional Development (PD) programmes since 1991. These show what can be achieved in schools generally, not just those enthusiastic about taking part in a new research project. The data presented here is based on over 2000 pupils from 11 schools whose teachers had been trained on the 1994–96 PD course (Shayer 1999b).

Figure 1.1 shows the long-term effect of the CASE intervention on GCSE 1999 science results in schools which had used the CASE intervention 5 years earlier in Years 7 and 8. Each point represents one school. Each school administered a test of cognitive development to the whole of its Year 7 cohort when they entered the school. From national data on the means and distribution of levels of cognitive development for the 9–16 year age range (Shayer and Adey 1981; Shayer et al. 1976; Shayer and Wylam 1978) this enables schools to be placed on a scale (the *x* axis in Figure 1.1) according to the mean level of cognitive development of their intake. This is shown as a percentile such that, for instance, a school at the 30th percentile has a higher mean intake than 30 per cent of schools in England and Wales, and a lower mean intake than 70 per cent of schools. The *y* axis shows the mean grade attained by students at that school at GCSE science. The control schools did not use the CASE intervention. Unsurprisingly, there is a strong relationship between a school's mean intake level and its success at science GCSE. By definition, the national average is at the 50th percentile, and it can be seen that the regression line for the control schools passes through the national average, and hence the sample of schools is representative. The important point is the CASE schools score consistently higher grades at GCSE than control schools with the same intake level. The magnitude of this added-value effect can be seen visually as the vertical distance between the

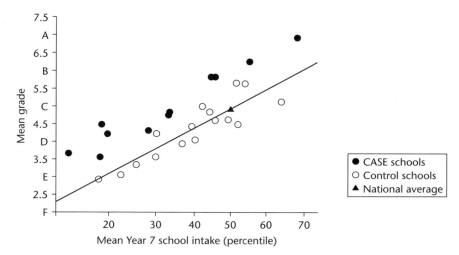

**Figure 1.1** GCSE 1999 science added-value
*Source*: Shayer 1999b.

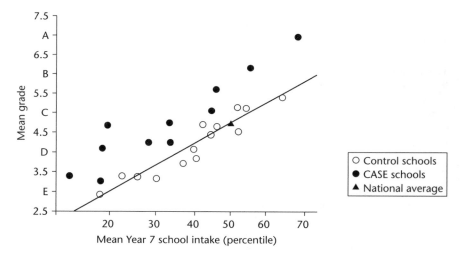

**Figure 1.2** GCSE 1999 mathematics added-value
*Source*: Shayer 1999b.

school's point and the regression line for the control schools: the average was 1.05 grades (0.6 standard deviations). This shows that the size of the long-term effects on pupils justifies the effort by teachers to apply new teaching skills.

Yet has the general thinking ability of the pupils been affected? For this we need to turn to the effects in the other school subjects. Figure 1.2 shows the effects for GCSE mathematics. Here the mean added-value was 0.95 grades

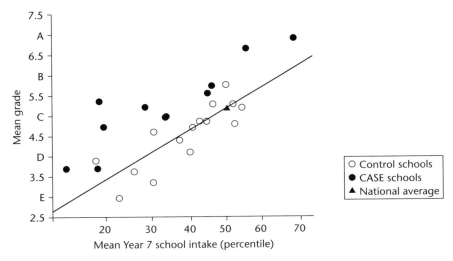

**Figure 1.3**   GCSE 1999 English added-value
*Source*: Shayer 1999b.

(0.5 standard deviations) – almost as large as for science, suggesting a more general effect on pupils' thinking. But the sceptic may argue that mathematics has a lot in common with science, so these results may have been expected. A more stringent test is the English results, shown in Figure 1.3. Here there is more variation between schools, but the mean added-value is still 0.90 grades (0.57 standard deviations). This is the evidence that the effect of the CASE intervention on pupils' thinking is quite general, and their general intellectual development has been enhanced.

## *CAME*

The research phase of CAME only ended in 1997, so there are no data yet for GCSE. However we do have Key Stage (KS) 3 results for the original CAME research schools. These data are analysed in a similar way to those for science, but here the performance used is not the average but the percentage of the year group who achieved NC level 6 or above in the KS3 tests. In Figures 1.4, 1.5 and 1.6 the added-values for all three subjects are shown.

   It can be seen immediately that the effects are a little smaller than for the CASE GCSE in 1999, although it can be seen that three schools lie over 20 percentile points above the regression line for the control schools. On the other hand, they are of the same order as obtained from tests conducted at the end of Year 9 with the original CASE research results, as reported in Adey and Shayer (1994). The comparison between the control schools mean and the CAME schools was statistically significant with all subjects, and were in fact higher in English than mathematics. The greater variation in the English results was due to the low reliability of the KS3 English assessments. This

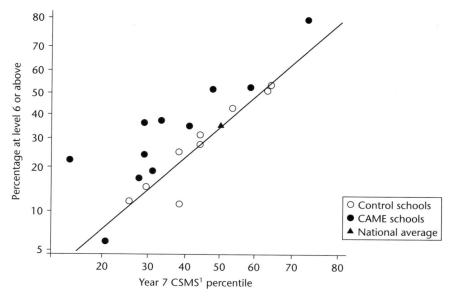

**Figure 1.4** KS3 1998: percentage at level 6 or above in mathematics
*Note*: CSMS is the 'Concepts in Secondary Maths and Science Programme', funded 1974–9 at Chelsea College by the SSRC.

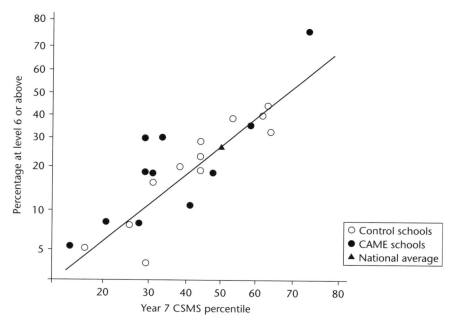

**Figure 1.5** KS3 1998: percentage at level 6 or above in science

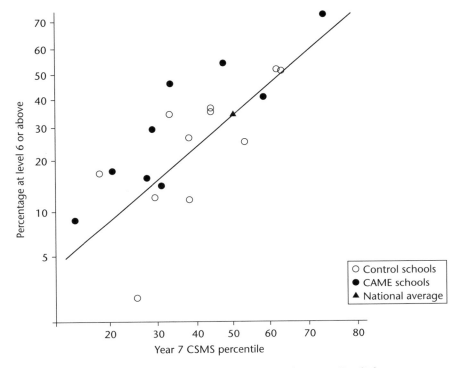

**Figure 1.6**   KS3 1998: percentage at level 6 or above in English

indicates a general effect of the CAME intervention rather than one just confined to mathematics.

When those schools that have had the full CAME PD programme from King's College report their GCSE results, it will be possible to make a fuller comparison with the effects of CASE.

## A chronology of CA programmes

In Table 1.1 an outline of the various CA Projects is shown. Most of the underlying CA methodology was developed during both the research and development (R&D) phase of CASE and in subsequent experience of the running of PD programmes. By 1993 there seemed no reason why the same six pillars of Piagetian/Vygotksian theory should not be equally applicable to mathematics as to science, and so the next phase of applied research was the secondary CAME project. CAME Primary was offered as one of the five projects within the Leverhulme Numeracy Programme (King's College 1997–2002).

Note that there are also many international extensions and applications of CA methods. Amongst the ones we know about (and we hear rumour of

Table 1.1  Timing of Cognitive Acceleration Projects

| | CASE | CAME | CATE | Wigan ARTS | CAME Primary | CASE @KS1 | CASE @KS2 | CAME @KS1 |
|---|---|---|---|---|---|---|---|---|
| **Pupil age range** | Y7–Y8 12–14 yrs | Y7–Y8 12–14 yrs | Y7–Y9 or Y10/Y11 | Y7–Y8 12–14 yrs | Y5–Y6 9–11 yrs | Y1 5–6 yrs | Y3 7–8 yrs | Y1/Y2 5–7 yrs |
| **R&D phase** | 1984–87 | 1993–97 | 1994–96 for Y10/11 1996–2000 for Y7–Y9 | 1999–2002 | 1997–2000 | 1998–2001 | 2000–02 | 2001–04 |
| **Funding** | SSRC | Leverhulme Esmée Fairbairn, ESRC | Greenwich LEA | Wigan LEA | Leverhulme Trust | Hammersmith LEA | Astra Zeneca Science | ESRC |
| **PD phase** | 1991 onwards | 1997 onwards | 2001 onwards | Late 2001 | 2001 onwards | 2001 onwards | | |
| **Published materials** | *Thinking Science*, Nelson 1989 3rd edn. 2001 | *Thinking Maths*, Heinemann 1998 | under negotiation | | BEAM, 2002 | *Let's Think!*, NFER Nelson 2001 | | |
| **Added-value assessment** | GCSE 1995 onwards | GCSE 2002 onwards | KS3 2001 | KS3 2002 | KS2 2003 onwards | KS1 2001 and 2002 | | |
| **Main researchers** | Shayer, Adey, Yates | Shayer, Adhami, Johnson | Hamaker, Backwell | Googe, Yates | Johnson, Adhami, Shayer, Hafeez | Adey, Robertson, Venville | Adey, Wilson | Shayer, Adhami, Adey, Robertson |

many others) we could mention work by Jarkko Hautamaki and colleagues at the University of Helsinki, Finland; a translation in preparation by Poul Thompson, University of Aarhus, Denmark; Carola Hauk at the University of Bremen, Germany; Martin van Os in Utrecht, Holland; Dusan Krnel in Slovenia; work initiated by Carolyn Yates in Palestine, Nellie Mbano in Malawi, Choi Byung-Soon at the Korea National University of Education, Trevor Bond at the James Cook University of North Queensland and also in Oregon, USA, with Jolene Hinrichson.

## The CATE project

All of the CA projects mentioned are featured in chapters in this book, with the exception of CATE (Cognitive Acceleration in Technology Education) and CASE@KS2 and CAME@KS1. The last two are too recently initiated to have much to report yet, but we should say something about CATE.

As part of their work as Advisers at the Greenwich local education authority (LEA), Tony Hamaker and John Backwell were asked to look at the problems of some Year 10/Year 11 students in Technology. Perhaps asking students to collaborate in CA mode in their work on design and technology (the school subject least regarded by pupils as 'academic') and being challenged to develop their own confidence in their ability to learn, would help? As with the CAME projects, the Piagetian aspect drew only indirectly from the work of Piaget, but used the Statements of Attainment contained in the NC to describe the strands of student cognitive deficits which were to be addressed through the CATE activities. This R&D was funded as a Technological and Vocational Education Initiative (TVEI) project and evaluated by a pre-test, post-test design (Hamaker et al. 1997). Those students who at pre-test on a Piagetian test were below the Early Formal level had an added-value – compared with controls – of over 0.7 standard deviations in GCSE technology, and also significant effects in science and mathematics as well. Although the CA methodology used here was intended more to affect student's motivation and achievement than cognitive development, an effect-size of 0.8 standard deviations was reported on a Piagetian post-test. This result, incidentally, does raise the question of whether there is still, at ages 14–16, potential for further cognitive development. There is a final brain-growth at 14–15 years of age, so it may be that this is responsible for the effects found at this first trial with older students.

Subsequently Hamaker and Backwell, as part of their work as consultants delivering various PD programmes to schools, decided to develop the work on CATE activities to make it a regular part of the whole of KS3 work in Year 7 to Year 9 technology, and for this age-range placed the emphasis on the cognitive acceleration aspect. It is planned that the published materials will contain, in addition to the Teacher's Guide, an evaluation pack for the monitoring of the effects of the intervention and a series of teacher in-service education and training (INSET) activities, to allow for the continuing professional development (CPD) of the teachers.

## A new paradigm?

We now raise the question: does the pedagogic method of cognitive acceleration, based as it is on psychological theory, exemplified in many different forms and recognized in national curricula, now constitute a new paradigm for 'normal education'? This is by analogy with Thomas Kuhn's (1962) notion that scientific revolutions cause 'normal science' to be questioned and eventually rejected in favour of the new paradigm, which then becomes the new normal science. The claim is not that CA methods have become universally practised, but that they may offer a model that could substantially influence national-level curriculum development. We cannot provide a substantive answer to this question, but invite the reader to consider the advantages and disadvantages of such a paradigm-shift. We are talking here about re-focusing the main aim of the whole enterprise of education from being primarily concerned with content – knowledge, understanding, skills and attitudes – towards a primary concern for intellectual development per se. Common to the experience of all the projects described in this book is that the feature many primary and secondary teachers welcomed most was the opportunity it offered them to think again about the teaching skills they were using already, and the provision of a language-of-the-art which would help them reflect about and then extend their own practice. Chapter 10 gives some detail of science teachers collaborating in just such a process – here extending some of their intervention teaching skills to enrich the conduct of their 'ordinary' science lessons. This implies that teaching for intellectual stimulation as well as for knowledge and skills, far from being the dilution of academic standards (as Chris Woodhead for one sees it), in fact takes students deeper into the learning specific to each subject, and at the same time broadens their understanding so that their experience of each subject contributes better to their general education.

Such a shift would go a long way towards meeting the needs of a knowledge society, an economy based on services managed by sophisticated IT systems but requiring intelligent use, interpretation and development by humans. It could go some way towards countering current trends towards narrowing the curriculum. Where strong emphases on specific content such as numeracy and literacy, rather narrowly conceived, have served to push the Arts and social development out of the primary school curriculum (if it ain't tested, don't teach it), a reappraisal of education in terms of intellectual development would open the curriculum to a far wider range of content experiences.

Might a move away from just considering NC content increase the amount of uncertainty faced by headteachers and teachers in their curriculum planning? We think not. All the evidence we have gathered indicates that when a sufficient proportion of teaching time is allocated to CA activities, the achievement of pupils as assessed by external indicators such as Key Stage testing and GCSE actually improves. We have seen examples where headteachers specifically create time within the school week for the CPD of their teachers as school policy, with a benefit to teachers and pupils alike. Concern for intellectual rigour then shifts from promoting unreflective competence to realizing that there are always further depths beyond one's present understanding.

Perhaps it is ambitious to envisage such a paradigm shift at present. Indeed, in our PD programmes we have seen some advantage in keeping CA lessons distinct from the regular curriculum, in that the contrasts are clear and so the art of intervention can be developed by teachers in a safe capsule without worrying at the same time about the demands of the NC. Later they can go further in integrating all their teaching skills.

But there is still great scope for further CA type interventions in the existing curriculum. As a thought experiment imagine the effect on pupils entering a comprehensive school where the Arts, technology, maths and science departments are all using CA methods as described in this book. Might this not remove at a stroke the turn-off that so many children experience in their first 2 years' transition between primary and secondary schooling? The theory base is established and well-articulated, the practice has been worked out in a variety of contexts and the academic advantages have been clearly demonstrated. We hope that this book will encourage many more teachers, schools, local authorities and national educational bodies to take CA seriously, and stimulate more research into effects, into methods of implementation and into PD.

## Notes

1 St Augustine, City of God, and Dante, Purgatorio, XVI, 94–6.
2 It is, incidentally, encouraging to note that after decades of trying to bring about curriculum change by publishing National Curricula with statutory obligations and painfully detailed work schemes, the government is now beginning to accept that no real change to teaching methods is likely without an element of coaching (Department for Education and Employment 2001).

# 2  COGNITIVE ACCELERATION WITH 5-YEAR-OLDS

## Philip Adey

### Introduction and context

This project arose out of a desire by the Education Authority of the London Borough of Hammersmith and Fulham to explore the possibility of increasing the life chances of children in its more disadvantaged areas by enhancing their cognitive development at the start of their school careers. Having heard of the CASE project, which had reported effects on cognitive development and academic achievement of 12- to 14-year-old students, the Chief Inspector of the LEA approached us and together we planned, executed and evaluated a cognitive intervention programme for Year 1[1] classes in ten schools. We called the project CASE@KS1.H&F, but commonly refer to it as CASE@KS1.

Hammersmith and Fulham is a medium-sized borough which contains a wide diversity of social cultures. In the south of the borough, a terraced house may fetch half a million pounds and be occupied by an architect or an accountant who commutes to the City. The north of the Borough contains a high proportion of social housing and a wide variety of ethnic minorities, some British of many generations but many new arrivals, new immigrants or refugees. There is also a substantial traveller population.

The Education Authority had obtained a Single Regeneration Budget from the national government to enhance the economy and employment prospects in the north of the borough and was able to allocate part of this to an educational effort in KS1, the first period of formal education in the UK when children are 5 to 7 years old. The hope was that targeting the cognitive development of children at the start of their formal schooling would have long-term effects on their academic achievement, social variables and eventually on their employment prospects. Justification for this hope lies in the relationships between (a) cognitive development and academic achievement and (b) academic achievement and social effects such as employment, drop-out, drugs misuse and early pregnancies. For (a) the evidence is fairly clear cut. An important factor in success in school-valued achievements such as progress through NC levels and test and examination results is the ability to process effectively information provided by teachers, books, and other sources. Better information-processing capability is a function of working memory capacity (Kyllonen and Christal 1990; Logie 1999) and the development of working memory is one way of describing cognitive development (Pascual-Leone 1988). The promotion of cognitive development may not lead to immediate effects on school measures of achievement since, as Shayer and Beasley (1987) have argued, the better processing ability must have time to be applied to new learning before academic gains become apparent.

The effect on social variables ((b), above) of enhanced cognitive development is less certain. Reports from the Head Start programme of reduced school drop-out, crime rates, teenage pregnancies and arrests of teenagers who experienced the programme in their pre-school years have been questioned. On the other hand, social problems are frequently associated with low self-esteem, and Ames (1986) and Dweck and Bempechat (1983) have shown how children's perceptions of self-efficacy rise in response to academic success. It seems at least worth exploring the possibility that higher academic success might lead to a reduction in socially disruptive behaviour.

This chapter will describe only the initial effects of the programme on cognitive development. Longer-term effects are not available at the time of writing.

## Bases of the intervention

The main theoretical bases of all CA programmes have been outlined in Chapter 1. Other, more pragmatic, considerations also served to frame the development and delivery of this intervention programme.

### Duration

The original CASE programme in Years 7 and 8 had operated over 2 years on the grounds that significant previous successful interventions such as that of Feuerstein et al. (1980) had shown no effects in less than 2 years. A supplementary reason was the time required to change the teaching practice of secondary science teachers. For the KS1 intervention it was supposed that with much younger children effects could be achieved in a shorter time and that a 1-year intervention should be tried – after all, 1 year is 20 per cent of a 5-year-old's life. We also recognized that teachers of young children are more focused on pedagogy than on subject matter as compared with their secondary school counterparts and so supposed that introduction of new methods would not involve such a radical change in pedagogic outlook for Year 1 teachers as it did with subject-based teachers of Years 7 and 8.

### *Curriculum context*

The English NC, even in Year 1, is wedded to the notion of 'subjects', in the sense of content areas such as English, mathematics and science. Given the perceived pressure on curriculum time, it is necessary at least to pay lip-service to the idea of such 'subjects'. In fact, we based the intervention activities firmly on the schemata of concrete operations as described by Piaget, but were able to link each activity to a curriculum area such as science, numeracy, spatial awareness or social points of view.

### *Practicality*

Most importantly, this intervention programme was framed by the practicality of the origin of funding, which dictated that the methods to be tried must be practicable in a normal educational setting of ordinary schools with ordinary teachers and classes of at least 30 children. This could not be a laboratory study with experts providing a few children with one-to-one cognitive stimulation.

## Experimental design

The experimental hypothesis which emerges from this theoretical framework and the practical constraints may be formulated as follows:

> 'Within a formal educational setting, the development of concrete operational thinking, as characterized by Piaget and Inhelder, can be accelerated in children aged 5 or 6 years with an intervention programme which provides well-managed cognitive conflict and structured opportunities for social construction, including the encouragement of metacognition.'

This is the hypothesis which guided the design of the experiment and the development of the intervention programme.

The main first test of this hypothesis described in this chapter used a quasi-experimental design with pre-tests of cognitive development administered near the start of the school year to all of the Year 1 children in ten experimental (CA) schools and five control schools. At the end of the school year, the same tests were administered to the same children. During the year, the children in CA schools experienced an intervention programme designed on the theoretical bases outlined in Chapter 1 and in the last section of this chapter.

### *CA and control groups*

The intervention programme was implemented in ten schools which between them had 14 Year 1 classes and teachers. These were all of those schools falling within an area of the London Borough of Hammersmith and

**Table 2.1** Some social and ethnic data on the children in the study

|  | CA | Control |
|---|---|---|
| Nos of children for whom these data were available: | 338 | 206 |
| % eligible for free school meals | 20.1 | 22.8 |
| **Ethnic composition (%)** | | |
| White | 41.4 | 48.5 |
| Black African | 14.8 | 9.2 |
| Black Caribbean | 16.6 | 8.3 |
| Black other | 8.3 | 10.7 |
| Indian | 0.6 | 1.9 |
| Pakistani | 2.4 | 0.0 |
| Bangladeshi | 1.8 | 1.0 |
| Chinese | 0.9 | 0.0 |
| Other | 13.3 | 20.4 |

Fulham for which the Single Regeneration Budget funding was available. During the year under study, two of the original 14 teachers left the sample and were replaced. A control group of five schools, with eight Year 1 classes, was also selected from adjacent areas as being as similar as possible in social and demographic character to the CA schools. All of the teachers were female and very few of them had more than 5 years of teaching experience at the time of the study. Table 2.1 provides some basic demographic data about the children in these 22 classes.

This shows that the populations were similar with respect to ethnicity and social status as measured by entitlement to free school meals, although there are somewhat more children designated as White in the control schools, and somewhat fewer designated as Black Caribbean or Black African.

Further comparisons between the CA and control schools are available from the 'baseline testing'. This is a series of assessments made of every child within 4 months of them entering the reception class (during the year before Year 1). In Hammersmith the 'Signposts' (Birmingham City Council 1997) scheme is used as the baseline test. Teachers, through observation and some individual task-setting, assess each child individually on a number of scales including three relating to language and three relating to number. For the purpose of comparing CA and control groups, two composite scores – one for language and one for numeracy – were computed for each child. Mean scores and differences for the children in this study are given in Table 2.2.

It appears that the children in the CA classes score significantly higher on the baseline testing than did those in the control classes, but caution should be exercised in interpreting these results. At the time these data were collected, baseline tests were administered by teachers with little special training in their administration and without independent verification (the tests are now moderated more closely). It is also the case that a school's popularity in its locality (and hence its funding) is influenced by perceptions of the academic

**Table 2.2** Comparison of baseline test means for language and for number for CA and control children

|  |  | *Language* | *Number* |
|---|---|---|---|
| CA | N | 339 | 339 |
|  | M | **3.88** | **4.23** |
|  | σ | 1.72 | 1.93 |
| Control | N | 206 | 206 |
|  | M | **2.96** | **2.74** |
|  | σ | 1.48 | 1.66 |
| t-test CASE-control |  | 6.61 | 9.53 |
|  | p< | .001 | .001 |

**Table 2.3** Experimental design

| *Condition* | *No. schools* | *No. classes* | *Approx no. children* | *Pre-test Sept 1999* | *Intervention* | *Post-test July 2000* |
|---|---|---|---|---|---|---|
| CA | 10 | 14 | 400 | Conservation; Drawing | CA intervention | Conservation; Drawing |
| Control | 5 | 8 | 240 | Conservation; Drawing | None | Conservation; Drawing |

value added between the baseline on entry and subsequent Key Stage NC test scores, so there are advantages in reporting low baseline test scores. It will be seen later that cognitive assessments made by the research team under controlled and cross-validated conditions, with nothing at stake for the schools' reputations, showed no difference between the CA and control schools.

In summary, the experimental design is shown in Table 2.3.

### The cognitive development tests

Two tests were used. Items in the first test ('Conservation') covered many of the classic Piagetian conservations: number, liquid amount, solid amount and weight. For example, the researcher would place one counter on the table and invite the child to place her own, of a different colour, opposite it until there were two rows of six counters equally spaced. One row is now expanded and the other pushed together and the child asked if there are still the same number of counters in both rows. For liquid volume, three small measures are poured into a tall vessel, then another three into a short, wide glass. The question is whether there is now the same amount of water in each. The procedure followed a careful protocol to ensure that no weighting was given to one answer or another and to probe for the stability of the child's concept and for her reasons. Conservation was only acceded if the right answer was given together with an adequate reason.

Donaldson (1978) has claimed that the standard Piagetian protocol under-estimates children's real ability by imposing the authority of an adult on non-conserving responses, and a similar argument is used by Dasen (1972) with respect to assessments made in non-Western cultures. On the other hand Eames et al. (1990) showed that when properly administered with an appropriate mixture of pro- and anti-conservation prompts and counter-suggestions, the results were reliable and much as originally reported by Piaget and his co-workers, given due allowance for the non-representative nature of the Genevan sample. In this case the tests proved to have good internal consistency (Cronbach alpha 0.85 to which all items contributed positively) and discrimination.

The conservation test had to be administered individually and as it was impractical to do this for over 500 children, we chose a one-third stratified sample on the basis of baseline test scores, choosing from each class a sample which included high scorers, low scorers and mid-range scorers. We also ensured that the sample had virtually the same numbers of boys and girls.

The second test ('Drawing') probed spatial awareness, also being based on original Piagetian protocols (Piaget and Inhelder 1976) and on a group version developed by Shayer et al. (1978). It assesses children's ability to perceive the horizontality of the surface of water in a bottle as the bottle is tilted, and the verticality of a plumb line under similar circumstances. Children were required to draw in the level in ready-drawn bottles both in anticipation of the bottle being tilted and after they had seen it. Scoring depended on both anticipation and the perceptual learning which occurred when they saw the tilt. The Cronbach alpha internal consistency measure for this with a pilot sample of 114 children was 0.74. This is not high, but acceptable for a six-item test. Discrimination was satisfactory.

The Drawing test could be administered by one person to six children at a time, so the whole sample of the CA and control groups received this test at pre- and post-occasions.

## The intervention

### Activities

The intervention consisted of a series of activities designed to provide cognitive conflict to 5- and 6-year-olds, to be delivered in a way which maximized opportunities for social construction, including metacognition (see the 'six pillars of CA' in Chapter 1). With young children it would be difficult to maximize social construction in whole-class settings so the activities were designed to be used with groups of six children. The total programme for this experiment consisted of 26 CA activities plus three 'listening' activities intended to introduce children to the working methods of the activities (listening to others, respecting others' views, finding ways of disagreeing constructively, and so on). The materials have now been published as *Let's Think!* (Adey et al. 2001). In practice, the teachers would do the CA activity with one group of six children on Monday, while the rest of the class would carry on with other work set from the 'task board', sometimes with the help of a teacher assistant. Each day of the week a different group would get the CA activity, so that a whole class of 30 children could be covered in each week. The activities typically took 30 to 40 minutes.

Each activity related to one of the schemata of concrete operations described in detail by Piaget and Inhelder, and scaled by Shayer et al. (1988). This latter work, especially, provides comprehensive data from a large international study on the relative difficulty of each schema. One set of concrete schemata, however, was specifically excluded from the intervention programme for this experiment, namely those related to conservation. This was in order to provide an opportunity to measure transfer effects. Since conservation formed one of the pre- and post-tests, the absence of intervention activities relating to conservation would allow any general development of concrete operations to be assessed, distinct from more direct learning effects on schema included in the intervention programme.

One example of a CA activity will be described to illustrate these phases, and two others outlined to show the application of the concrete schemata.

### Activity 1

This relates to the schema of seriation. The teacher and six children are seated around a table. The teacher puts a stick on the table, and they discuss what to call it. She puts a second stick on the table, and the phrases 'shorter than' and 'longer than' are introduced and practised as necessary. A third stick allows the idea that one stick may be both 'shorter than' and 'longer than' at the same time. So far, this is all concrete preparation. Now the teacher produces ten sticks of different lengths. The children's task is to place them in order, with the longest at one end and the shortest at the other. This proves to be quite difficult, and the teacher must work hard to ensure that all participate, that they listen to each other, and that they explain and justify their actions to each other (also, that the bottom ends of the sticks are kept level!). When the ten sticks are in order, and all are agreed that the order is good, the teacher gives out more sticks to each child. These are of intermediate lengths, and have to be fitted in the right place in the sequence, again with justifications, and with more successful children explaining their strategy to less successful ones. This has been the main conflict/construction phase. There may now be a specific metacognitive phase, reflecting on how they solved the problem, what was difficult, and how difficulties were overcome in both cognitive and social contexts. Finally, the teacher will ask bridging questions to elicit where else they might use the idea of putting things in order.

### Activity 8

This concerns the schema of classification. A collection of dinosaurs are introduced, and the children sort them in simple, one variable, ways such as by colour or by type. The teacher now invites them to put all T Rexes in one hoop and all blues ones in another. Conflict arises about the blue T Rex. The resolution constructed eventually is to overlap the hoops.

*Activity 18*
In this activity (spatial perception), the children have a model crossroads with various buildings, cars, bus shelters and other urban furniture. They are seated two at each of three sides of the table, so no pair can see all of the objects. They have to select from a set of pictures, firstly the one that represents what they can see, and then what another pair of children can see.

### Teacher PD

Effective delivery of these activities depends on the teachers having a good understanding of the underlying theory and much practice in generating cognitive conflict and encouraging social construction and metacognition involving each child. Such pedagogical skill cannot be delivered by printed materials alone, but requires a carefully designed PD programme. The research team on this project had extensive experience of working with practising teachers to support the development of their pedagogy and we drew both on this experience and on research on effective staff development (for example Joyce and Showers 1995) to design a course of six INSET days and three or four coaching visits to each teacher to help them develop the necessary skills. The programme introduced the basic theory of cognitive acceleration, allowed the teachers to experience the specific activities, and gave them plenty of opportunity to share their experiences of using the activities with each other. Teaching methods on the PD programme mirrored the methods of cognitive acceleration, especially with respect to social construction and metacognition.

## Effects

### Overall

The simplest question to ask about the effect of the intervention is 'Did it work, in the sense of increasing the rate of cognitive development in the CA classes relative to the control classes?' The answer is 'Yes, it did.'

Our method of analysis is based on the gains made by each child in scores on the two tests of cognitive development, that is, for each child, their score on the drawing post-test minus their score on drawing pre-test, and their score on the conservation post-test minus their score on the conservation pre-test. To get an overall picture of the effect of various factors on these two gain scores, we did an analysis of covariance (ANCOVA) of the following factors with each of the gain scores:

1 experimental or control group (CA/CTRL) to test the main hypothesis that the intervention impacts on gain in cognitive development;

2 teacher (tchr) to test whether the cognitive gains of children are significantly affected by their teachers;

3 gender to test whether boys and girls make different cognitive gains during Year 1;

4 baseline test scores, composite for language (b'line lang.) to test whether cognitive gains are related to a starting achievement level in language;

5 baseline test scores, composite for number (b'line numb.) to test whether cognitive gains are related to starting achievement level in number; baseline tests scores were included because of the apparent significant difference in these between CA and control classes (see Table 2.2); and

6 English language proficiency of child (Engl.) to test whether cognitive gains are related to the child's proficiency with English.

We tested also all of the two-way interactions, except for (teacher * CA/ CTRL), as each teacher had to be either CA or control, so there could be no interaction.

Table 2.4 shows the result of this analysis for the gain scores on the drawing test, and Table 2.5 the same analysis for the gain scores on the conservation test.

**Table 2.4**   Analysis of covariance of various factors with gains in drawing scores (n = 445)

| Source | df | $\Sigma$ squares | Mean sq. | F-ratio | Prob. |
|---|---|---|---|---|---|
| Const. | 1 | 13041 | 13041 | 585 | $\leq 0.0001$ |
| CA/CTRL | 1 | 691 | 691 | 31.04 | $\leq 0.0001$ |
| Tchr | 20 | 919 | 45.95 | 2.06 | 0.006 |
| Gender | 1 | 7.88 | 7.88 | 0.35 | 0.552 |
| CA/CTRL*Gender | 1 | 24.52 | 24.52 | 1.10 | 0.295 |
| Tchr*Gender | 20 | 466.3 | 23.32 | 1.05 | 0.407 |
| b'line lang. | 1 | 40.34 | 40.34 | 1.81 | 0.180 |
| CA/CTRL*b'line lang. | 1 | 27.29 | 27.29 | 1.23 | 0.269 |
| Tchr*b'line lang. | 20 | 574.2 | 28.71 | 1.29 | 0.185 |
| Gender*b'line lang. | 1 | 11.22 | 11.22 | 0.50 | 0.479 |
| b'line numb. | 1 | 6.62 | 6.62 | 0.30 | 0.586 |
| CA/CTRL*b'line num | 1 | 1.68 | 1.68 | 0.08 | 0.784 |
| Tchr*b'line numb. | 20 | 459.8 | 22.99 | 1.03 | 0.424 |
| Gender*b'line numb. | 1 | 67.18 | 67.18 | 3.02 | 0.084 |
| b'line lang.*bline numb. | 1 | 119.1 | 119.1 | 5.35 | 0.022 |
| English | 4 | 128.1 | 32.02 | 1.44 | 0.222 |
| CA/CTRL*Engl. | 4 | 181.7 | 45.43 | 2.04 | 0.089 |
| Tchr*Engl. | 55 | 1067 | 19.40 | 0.87 | 0.727 |
| Gender*Engl. | 4 | 206.6 | 51.66 | 2.32 | 0.057 |
| b'line lang.*Engl. | 4 | 65.17 | 16.29 | 0.73 | 0.571 |
| b'line numb.*Engl. | 4 | 24.53 | 6.13 | 0.28 | 0.894 |
| Error | 279 | 6214 | 22.27 | | |
| Total | 444 | 11304 | | | |

**Table 2.5** Analysis of Covariance of various factors with gains in conservation scores (n = 188)

| Source | df | Σ squares | Mean sq. | F-ratio | Prob. |
|---|---|---|---|---|---|
| Const. | 1 | 531.1 | 531.1 | 135.0 | ≤ 0.0001 |
| CA/CTRL | 1 | 39.13 | 39.13 | 9.94 | 0.003 |
| Tchr | 20 | 233.5 | 11.67 | 2.97 | 0.001 |
| Gender | 1 | 0.020 | 0.020 | 0.005 | 0.943 |
| CA/CTRL*Gender | 1 | 4.03 | 4.03 | 1.02 | 0.316 |
| Tchr*Gender | 19 | 124.5 | 6.55 | 1.67 | 0.072 |
| b'line lang. | 1 | 18.60 | 18.60 | 4.73 | 0.034 |
| CA/CTRL*b'line lang. | 1 | 18.54 | 18.54 | 4.71 | 0.034 |
| Tchr*b'line lang. | 20 | 203.1 | 10.16 | 2.58 | 0.003 |
| Gender*b'line lang. | 1 | 0.95 | 0.95 | 0.24 | 0.626 |
| b'line numb. | 1 | 1.58 | 1.58 | 0.40 | 0.529 |
| CA/CTRL*b'line numb. | 1 | 0.30 | 0.30 | 0.08 | 0.785 |
| Tchr*b'line numb. | 19 | 68.63 | 3.61 | 0.92 | 0.565 |
| Gender*b'line numb. | 1 | 2.93 | 2.93 | 0.74 | 0.392 |
| b'line lang.*b'line numb. | 1 | 2.30 | 2.30 | 0.59 | 0.448 |
| English | 4 | 7.69 | 1.92 | 0.49 | 0.744 |
| CA/CTRL*Engl. | 4 | 2.04 | 0.51 | 0.13 | 0.971 |
| Tchr*Engl. | 25 | 164.5 | 6.58 | 1.67 | 0.057 |
| Gender*Engl. | 4 | 56.02 | 14.01 | 3.56 | 0.012 |
| b'line lang.*Engl. | 4 | 25.29 | 6.32 | 1.61 | 0.186 |
| b'line numb.*Engl. | 3 | 24.82 | 8.27 | 2.10 | 0.110 |
| Error | 55 | 216.4 | 3.93 | | |
| Total | 187 | 1214 | | | |

This first analysis suggests that there is a strong effect on both gain scores of being in a CA or control class, with CA classes having significantly greater cognitive gains than controls and a strong effect of the individual teacher, but no other significant effects and no strong interactions.

The fact that there is no interaction with baseline test scores discounts any possible differential effect arising from the fact that the CA and control groups had significantly different mean baseline test scores. The issue of gender is not as simple as it appears from this global analysis and we will need to look at it further.

The main CA/control effect will be now considered in more detail, followed by further analyses looking at effects by gender and by individual class (that is by teacher).

### CA versus control

The ANCOVA shows that there is a significant effect for CA classes over control classes, but it does not show the effect size. We obtained this from an analysis of gain scores for the control and CA children separately. Table 2.6

**Table 2.6** Significance and effect sizes of differences between CA and control pupils

|  |  | Conservation | | | Drawing | | |
|---|---|---|---|---|---|---|---|
|  |  | pre | post | gain | pre | post | gain |
| CA | N | 122 | 122 | 122 | 302 | 302 | 302 |
|  | M | 2.03 | 4.05 | 2.02 | 7.53 | 13.93 | 6.40 |
|  | σ | 2.25 | 2.95 | 2.83 | 5.55 | 4.58 | 4.65 |
| Control | N | 66 | 66 | 66 | 166 | 166 | 166 |
|  | M | 1.47 | 2.53 | 1.06 | 8.40 | 12.17 | 3.77 |
|  | σ | 2.11 | 2.25 | 1.77 | 5.62 | 5.50 | 5.28 |
|  | overall σ | 2.21 |  |  | 5.59 |  |  |
|  | Diff. CA-Ctrl |  |  | 0.956 |  |  | 2.636 |
|  | t |  |  | 3.73 |  |  | 9.85 |
|  | p< |  |  | 0.001 |  |  | 0.001 |
|  | Effect size |  |  | 0.43 |  |  | 0.47 |

provides details of mean pre-test and post-test scores and mean gain scores (post minus pre for each child) with standard deviations for each on the two cognitive tests for CA and control pupils.

As established by the ANCOVA, there are significant effects on the CA pupils compared with the control children, but this analysis shows that the effect sizes are 0.43 and 0.47 standard deviations on conservation and drawing respectively, values which can be considered to be substantial.

### Gains by gender

Table 2.7 shows the gains made separately by girls and boys in the CA and control groups. This data suggests that in control classes, boys made somewhat greater gains in cognitive development over the year than girls did, although this difference does not reach significance on either test (and hence did not show in the ANCOVA). In the CA classes, girls made the same gains as boys, and both boys and girls made greater gains than their peers in control classes, although not reaching significance for boys on the conservation test, where the number of control boys was only 33.

### Teacher/class

It will be clear from the description of the intervention given earlier that the teacher plays a central role in delivery of effective cognitive stimulation. As described, all teachers in the 14 CA classes participated in a PD programme, including in-class support.

The analyses of covariance shown in Tables 2.4 and 2.5 reveal, unsurprisingly, a main effect for teacher on the post-test scores on cognitive tests. In order to investigate the effect in each teacher's class separately, the mean of the

**Table 2.7**   Gains on conservation and drawing tests by CA and control boys and girls

| | | Conservation | | | Drawing | | |
|---|---|---|---|---|---|---|---|
| | | pre | post | gain | pre | post | gain |
| CA girls | N | 63 | 63 | 63 | 150 | 150 | 150 |
| | M | 2.13 | 4.24 | 2.11 | 7.79 | 14.11 | 6.33 |
| | σ | 2.39 | 3.16 | 3.06 | 5.42 | 4.43 | 4.43 |
| Control girls | N | 36 | 36 | 36 | 80 | 80 | 80 |
| | M | 1.72 | 2.53 | 0.81 | 8.40 | 11.60 | 3.20 |
| | σ | 2.35 | 2.04 | 1.65 | 5.12 | 5.45 | 4.66 |
| | σ overall | 2.37 | | | 5.31 | | |
| | CA-Ctrl diffs | | | 1.30 | | | 3.13 |
| | t | | | 2.76 | | | 4.93 |
| | p< | | | 0.01 | | | 0.001 |
| | effect size | | | 0.55 | | | 0.59 |
| CA boys | N | 59 | 59 | 59 | 143 | 143 | 143 |
| | M | 1.93 | 3.85 | 1.92 | 7.33 | 13.71 | 6.38 |
| | σ | 2.11 | 2.72 | 2.60 | 5.81 | 4.72 | 4.85 |
| Control boys | N | 33 | 33 | 33 | 83 | 83 | 83 |
| | M | 1.21 | 2.39 | 1.18 | 8.40 | 12.72 | 4.33 |
| | σ | 1.85 | 2.46 | 1.96 | 6.11 | 5.58 | 5.75 |
| | σ overall | 2.04 | | | 5.93 | | |
| | CA-Ctrl diffs | | | 0.74 | | | 2.05 |
| | t | | | 1.53 | | | 2.74 |
| | p< | | | n.s. | | | 0.01 |
| | effect size | | | 0.36 | | | 0.35 |

'residualized gain' scores of each of the children in each class was calculated for both the drawing and conservation tests. The residualized gain for each child is calculated by subtracting from their raw gain score (post-test minus pre-test) the mean gain score of the whole control group. This is a measure of the extent to which each child's gain score is greater or less than would have been expected had they been no different from an average control group child. Mean residualized gains of all control children together must be 0 by definition.

Figure 2.1 shows the mean residualized gain scores for each class, for drawing and conservation tests, by class with CA classes on the left, and control classes on the right. Within the groups, classes are arbitrarily ordered by the magnitude of the class mean drawing residualized gain score. The number of children contributing to each mean residualized gain score is shown below Figure 2.1.

If the CA intervention is to be shown to be effective, it is necessary to demonstrate that it can be effective in the hands of a high proportion of the teachers who have been introduced to it. If the overall effects described earlier proved to be attributable to just 3 or 4 excellent teachers out of the 14

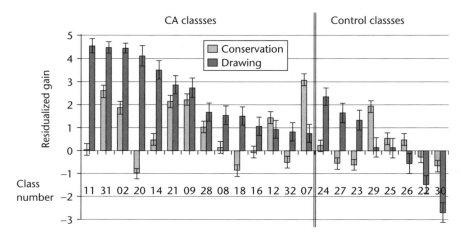

Numbers contributing to each class mean residualized gain score:

| Class | 11 | 31 | 02 | 20 | 14 | 21 | 09 | 28 | 08 | 18 | 16 | 12 | 32 | 07 | 24 | 27 | 23 | 29 | 25 | 26 | 22 | 30 |
|---|---|---|---|---|---|---|---|---|---|---|---|---|---|---|---|---|---|---|---|---|---|---|
| Conservation | 9 | 9 | 16 | 10 | 9 | 9 | 10 | 11 | 5 | 10 | 4 | 4 | 9 | 7 | 7 | 6 | 9 | 3 | 10 | 11 | 10 | 10 |
| Drawing | | 23 | 23 | 24 | 27 | 24 | 22 | 22 | 24 | 13 | 22 | 23 | 13 | 27 | 15 | 17 | 19 | 25 | 11 | 27 | 18 | 26 | 23 |

**Figure 2.1**   Mean residualized gain scores by class

who participated in the experiment, that would not be convincing of the effect of the general method of cognitive acceleration. Now, at the class level of data the numbers of children per group are small and the relative influence of uncontrolled error sources of variation increases. Thus, class level data must be treated with considerable caution – especially with respect to the conservation tests given to one-third of the total sample. Yet even with this caution in mind, Figure 2.1 shows that the effect is not limited to just a few special teachers. Out of the 14 CA classes, 5 show greater gains on the drawing task than the best control class, and 12 CA classes show greater gains on drawing than 5 out of the 8 control classes (beyond the limits shown by standard error bars). Mention should be made of class 29. We have good reason to believe that the three children tested for conservation here had inadvertently been 'coached' by their teacher to give conservation answers. Because of the semi-anecdotal nature of our information here, we have not excluded class 29 data from the whole analysis but will exclude class 29 from the conclusion from Figure 2.1 that, for conservation gains, 7 out of the 14 CA classes scored higher than any of the 7 remaining control classes.

## Discussion

Year 1 classes that participated in a CA programme made greater cognitive gains over 1 school year than pupils in similar classes who did not experience the intervention, but there are a number of issues which are worth exploring a little further, namely the distinction between acceleration of general cognitive development and instruction in specific types of thinking, the generalizability of the results, the longevity of the effects, the relationship of the results to the theoretical principles, and the implications of the effects for the model of acceleration adopted.

## CA versus instruction

The distinction between learning and development has been discussed in Chapter 1, where transfer was cited as part of the evidence needed for claims of enhanced development. In this study cognitive development over the year of the experiment was assessed by two different tests, each relating to a different schema of concrete operations. The drawing test taps the schema of spatial perception. The intervention programme did have a number of activities related to spatial perception (see the outline of Activity 18), but none of them referred even remotely to the subject matter of the drawing test. Greater gains in drawing scores by CA over control classes may be taken as evidence of near transfer. It may be argued that this effect has been one of instruction in the general principles of spatial perception, although that would require a more specific abstraction of such principles from the particular activities than did occur in the delivery of the activities.

More convincing is the effect on the conservation scores. There were no activities relating to conservation in the intervention programmes precisely because it was proposed to look for far transfer. The significant effects on conservation scores of the intervention programme provides evidence for the intervention having very general effects on children's cognitive development, and is consistent with acceleration of general cognitive development.

## Generalizability

To what extent can we generalize from the results reported here? For one thing, they refer to work with one limited age group, 5- and 6-year-olds. Whilst work with 12- to 14-year-olds has been shown to be effective for the promotion of formal operations, these results give us no reason to suppose that CA would work at any age. Indeed, in terms of the ages of transition in CA (Shayer et al. 1976; Shayer and Wylam 1978; Shayer et al. 1988) and of brain growth spurts (Epstein 1986, 1990) one would not expect the same effect to be attainable at ages intermediate between those already established. Current work with 7- and 8-year-olds is designed partly with a view to falsifying this 'critical window' hypothesis.

Secondly, the social environment in which this study was conducted was specifically one of inner city disadvantage. It may turn out that such effects would not be attained with children whose home lives had already provided them with adequate cognitive stimulation. This needs further work.

In contrast with these possible limitations to generality, no interaction was found between the effects of the intervention on cognitive development and a number of social variables, including ethnicity, English language proficiency and receipt of free school meals. In other words, no particular social or language group appeared to make greater or fewer gains than any other as a result of the intervention. The evidence discussed under 'Teacher/class' above also supports the contention that the intervention effect can be generalized across a range of teachers and that a limited PD programme was sufficient to introduce the CA teachers to the principle of cognitive stimulation and make them generally more effective than the control teachers in terms of generating well-managed cognitive conflict and scaffolding social construction. Qualitative support for this assertion is provided in Chapters 3–6 of this volume.

### Longevity of the effects

The effects reported here were attained at the immediate end of the intervention programme. A further test of their stability and depth (in the sense of impact upon development) will be made when the children who experienced this intervention (and the controls) are assessed for NC levels at the end of Year 2, 1 year after the end of the intervention programme. Experience with secondary-age children showed that CA effects lasted for at least 3 years after the intervention, but it will need to be shown that a similar effect can be obtained with much younger children.

### What conclusions can be drawn about the theoretical bases of the intervention?

As described in Chapter 1, the CA intervention rests on four theoretical principles: cognitive conflict, social construction, metacognition and schema theory. Do the results reported here confirm the importance of each of these theory bases? No, in principle unless one conducted a controlled experiment in which each of these four bases was independently varied, one cannot conclude unambiguously that all four are necessary or that they contribute equally to the overall effect. However, we are dealing here with a real-life large-scale educational investigation funded by an Education Authority, the main concern of which is the improvement of the life-chances of its students rather than the theoretical investigation of sources of cognitive growth. In that context, we need to consider the intervention programme as a whole, building pragmatically on theory bases established in other contexts as providing plausible grounds for optimism in the search for cognitive stimulation. The results reported here indicate that this intervention package can be effective, even if we cannot be certain about the several contributions of each of its elements.

Having said that, it may be useful to consider what a series of experiments designed to tease apart the four elements might look like. To start with, we would argue that it is not practically possible to separate cognitive conflict and social construction. We may be able to characterize each separately and point to somewhat different (but overlapping) origins in Piagetian and Vygotskyan psychology (see Chapter 11), but in the practice of teaching one cannot have one without the other. They are two sides of the same coin – the hammer and anvil of Hegelean dialectic from which intellectual growth is shaped. A puzzle (the conflict) generates questions, questions are directed at others, tentative suggestions are offered, and the group feels its way towards some resolution of the conflict, with the teacher forestalling premature closure on inadequate solutions. All of this constitutes social construction and a group doing this generates cognitive conflict in its members. The very act of sharing a puzzle, of asking a question, of inviting a partner to contribute to the solution, creates challenge.

Of the other theoretical bases, one could imagine investigating the effect of metacognitive reflection by managing two intervention groups both employing conflict/construction, but only one of which paid attention to metacognition. There might be practical difficulties in managing such groups to ensure clear separation of methodology, but in principle it could be done. Shirley Larkin explores the nature of metacognition in 5-year-olds in detail in Chapter 5.

The role of schema theory in the formulation of the intervention is somewhat different. The schemata of concrete operations adopted from Geneva are no more than convenient and well-worked-out descriptions of various types of thinking which underpin all rational thought. We are making no special claims for Piagetian schemata as the only way of describing reasoning and could well imagine a set of interventions based on conflict/construction, with or without metacognition, being devised with reference to other classifications of reasoning. For example, Klauer (1989) has shown positive general effects on problem-solving ability of teaching inductive reasoning.

### Implications for the model of acceleration

Even if we consider the intervention method as an integrated whole, to what extent do the positive results reported here validate the model of CA proposed? On the basis of this experiment alone, the best one could say is that the model has provided a useful framework for the development of a stimulating intervention, and that the construct has survived an attempt at falsification. If the intervention had had no effect, and could be shown to be a reliable practical interpretation of the theory, then that would have called the theory into question.

But when one considers this study as part of a series – all of the CA work in science and mathematics with older children referenced earlier, work described later in this book, as well as studies such as those of Wegerif et al. (1999) showing the effect of high-quality social interaction on cognitive functioning – then one can become somewhat stronger in asserting that the theory base is becoming validated. Such support is strengthened when, as in the present study, the same theoretical constructs appear to produce positive effects when imported into a very new context.

### Conclusion

The experiment described here has demonstrated that a cognitive intervention programme based on Piagetian ideas of cognitive conflict and the schemata of concrete operations and on Vygotskyan ideas of social construction and scaffolding can have a significant effect on the rate of cognitive development of 5- and six-year-old children in Year 1 classes in a disadvantaged inner city environment. While there are some limitations to the generalizability of the findings, even within these limits we would claim that the effects have real social and educational potential. Anything that can be done to increase the intellectual-processing capability of young children from disadvantaged backgrounds must be of general value in a society which has moved rapidly from one needing much thoughtless manual labour to one requiring independent and individual thought-in-action from a far higher proportion of the populace than ever before.

## Note

1 'Year 1' is the first year of formal schooling in England, when children are 5+ years old. Many will have been in a 'Reception' class for at least part of the previous year, but some will not.

# 3 ENHANCING THE QUALITY OF THINKING IN YEAR 1 CLASSES

## Grady J. Venville

## Introduction

Although there is a wide array of educational literature aimed at enhancing teachers' awareness of the importance of fostering thinking skills in their pupils, Kuhn (1999) points out that 'teachers have been offered remarkably little in the way of concrete examples of what these skills are – what forms they take' (p. 17). In this chapter I aim to address this problem by presenting research conducted in Year 1 classrooms cultivated through a programme of PD and curriculum activities specifically devised to foster cognitive acceleration (see Chapter 2). The theme explored is how 'good thinking' materializes in the very early years of schooling. The research presented focuses on the behaviour of the children and the way they interact with their peers, the teacher and the activities to offer specific, concrete examples of good thinking. This study utilized the CASE@KS1 activities being taught in regular Year 1 classrooms as a context for exploring the notion of good thinking. A general assumption was that CASE@KS1 activities were more likely to provide an environment conducive to good thinking than regular Year 1 lessons. The results presented in Chapter 2 demonstrate that the PD and intervention implemented as part of the project had a significant effect on the rate of cognitive development of the 5- and 6-year-old children, therefore this assumption is now supported.

The purpose of this study was two-fold. The first was to describe and investigate concrete examples of Year 1 pupils engaged in good thinking in their classroom. The second was to use the examples from the classroom to generate more general assertions about ways teachers can foster habits of good thinking in the early years of schooling. More specifically the research questions were:

1 How are CASE@KS1 lessons different from regular lessons in terms of how Year 1 pupils are engaged in thinking?
2 Do the behaviours that pupils are engaged in during CASE@KS1 lessons constitute good thinking?
3 What pupil behaviours can teachers encourage to foster good thinking in Year 1?

What is thinking? Hamers and Csapó (1999) point to the nature–nurture debate on thinking where there are ongoing arguments about intelligence being either inherited or acquired. They define intelligence as 'a person's "rough" intellectual power, and thinking as the "skilled" use of that power' (p. 25). This definition indicates that thinking can be taught or trained and that improvement in thinking can realize the greater intellectual potential of a person. The links between teaching thinking and academic achievement have been well established (Nisbet 1993; Adey and Shayer 1994; McGuinness 1999; Shayer 1999a) and these studies support this definition of thinking. Therefore, 'good' thinking can be considered as the process in which people are engaged when they are able to solve a difficult or challenging task and which results in an improvement in a person's intellectual power. This chapter aims to give a rich and contexualized description of good thinking.

Early in the 1990s, Nisbet (1993) claimed that 'before the century is out, no curriculum will be regarded as acceptable unless it can be shown to make a contribution to the teaching of thinking'. Although we now know that this is not the case, support for the teaching of thinking from research and political arenas is strong (Department for Education and Employment 1999; McGuinness 1999). There is a significant body of research about the teaching of thinking and these ideas have been investigated in secondary and upper primary classrooms. See Hamers et al.'s (1999) and McGuinness' (1999) recent reviews. There is, however, little classroom-based research that investigates thinking in the very early years of formal education. The significance of our work with 5-year-olds is that it provides early childhood teachers with concrete examples of behaviours that, if encouraged in the classroom, are likely to foster habits of good thinking that are applicable not only in science and mathematics, but across the curriculum.

The theoretical underpinnings of this study have been described in Chapters 1 and 2 and the interplay between its Piagetian and Vygotskyan roots is explored in Chapter 11. Vygotsky's ZPD has been described by Barbara Rogoff (1991: 68) as 'a dynamic region of sensitivity to learning experiences in which children develop, guided by social interaction'. In terms of ideal conditions for enhanced thinking, research from Vygotsky's perspective suggests that it is critical that children verbalize their reasoning and accept reasoning at a higher level than that with which they started out. Furthermore, the more children are involved in tasks as a joint endeavour and come to shared understandings, the more likely it seems that they will learn (O'Donnell and King 1999). Vygotsky argued that social interaction was important for children's development from birth, whereas Piaget, in contrast, argued that the greatest benefits of peer collaboration would be achieved when children had reached the concrete operational stage (Hogan and Tudge 1999). Research has been inconclusive on this issue, but in this study a social environment was used as the context for the investigation of thinking even though many of the children at the ages of 5 and 6 years were still likely to be thinking predominantly in pre-operational ways. Thus, the particular focus of the CA theory base to be explored in this chapter is the nature of the social interaction in small groups. I aim to capture, describe and make available for analysis such interaction as one critical facet of 'social construction'.

## The context

The CASE@KS1 activities have been developed within Piagetian schema of concrete operations such as seriation, classification, spatial perception, causality and transitivity (Piaget 1930; Piaget and Inhelder 1974, 1976). All activities begin with 'concrete preparation', where the pupils and teacher negotiate common language for the materials to be used and establish familiarity with the situation in which the task will be set. 'Cognitive challenge' is another important aspect of each activity. A situation that causes dissonance in the pupils' mind is created so that they are challenged to think of possible solutions beyond that which they already know. Pupils are challenged in various ways depending on the schema in which the task has been developed. Some examples of the activities are outlined in Chapter 2. The activities are distinct from earlier so-called 'child-centred' innovations in that they are firmly rooted in psychological theory, and they recognize fully the critical role played by the teacher in their implementation. They are also unusual in that they require no reading or writing, since the emphasis is on developing thinking through cognitive conflict and construction induced verbally (but see Chapter 6 for an account of non-verbal interactions).

The CASE@KS1 activities provide the vehicle through which teachers are able to implement the theory, but implementation depends critically on the PD programme. The PD for the CASE@KS1 teachers in the experimental year consisted of nine PD days held out of class as well as a number of in-class demonstrations and coaching sessions (Joyce and Showers, 1995). The out-of-class days were used to:

1 familiarize the teachers with the activities;
2 explore the underlying theory of CASE@KS1 and relate that to the teachers' practice;
3 develop professional camaraderie;
4 support the teachers with general management and teaching issues related to the implementation of CASE@KS1; and
5 gather feedback about the activities.

## Design and procedure

In order to gain an in-depth and contextualized description and understanding of Year 1 pupils engaged in thinking, qualitative research methods were used with a total of 32 lessons included in the analysis of this multiple case study. Several members of the research team assisted me in collecting data for this study. A lesson was considered to be a discrete session of work that lasted between 30 minutes and 1 hour. The three phases of the research are outlined below.

### Phase 1: general observation

Fourteen classes in ten schools trialed thinking activities over the period from January 1999 to July 1999. We visited each of the classes several times during the trialing period to observe the teachers' delivery of the activities, the pupils' responses to the activities and their interaction with the teacher and the other children. Field notes were taken during all observations. This general observation played a significant role in developing ideas about the focus of this study, that is the kind of behaviours the children were involved in that demonstrated good thinking. A preliminary list of behaviours that we felt were important in helping the pupils to think in appropriate ways in order to solve the problems and tasks posed by the thinking activities were identified.

### Phase 2: focused classroom observation

Each of the 11 teachers involved in this study were observed two or three times in the 6 months between September 1999 and February 2000. A total of 32 lessons were included in the analysis: 17 CASE@KS1 lessons and 15 non-CASE@KS1 lessons. The non-CASE@KS1 lessons consisted of 14 mathematics lessons and 1 history lesson and provided data for the purpose of general comparison between the kind of thinking and behaviours that happened in CASE@KS1 lessons with those that occurred in regular lessons. Detailed field notes were taken during all lessons with the guiding framework of the list of behaviours generated from the first phase of the observation. All field notes were typed and returned to the teachers for verification, except those from the non-CASE@KS1 lessons. As the non-CASE@KS1 classes were control classes for the larger CASE@KS1 experiment, observation notes were not returned to the teachers so that the feedback did not influence their teaching during the data collection period.

### Phase 3: analysis and generating assertions

Preliminary analysis during typing and reading of the lesson transcripts resulted in the consolidation of 16 behaviours that were described in more detail with examples. The descriptions of the behaviours were used by myself and two colleagues to code a lesson transcript, after which we met for discussion. The feedback resulted in some of the behaviours being coalesced into broader groupings. For example, the three original groups were (a) a child explains her idea/thinking/action; (b) a child recognizes and/or explains her own/the group's/another child's difficulty; and (c) a child helps to explain another child's good thinking/action. These three groups were all coalesced into a single group (category A in Table 3.1) of 'explaining'. This re-grouping resulted in a final set of seven behaviours, which were coded from A–G and described with examples (see Table 3.1). I then coded all the lesson transcripts and calculated the frequency of the behaviours in each of the lessons and the averages for the CASE@KS1 and non-CASE@KS1 lessons. The occurrence of a behaviour was scored when there was direct evidence in the lesson transcript that one of the behaviours had occurred. For example, if a child explained their idea for a solution to a problem this was counted as one occurrence of explaining. Examples of the coding are included in the findings so that the reader can trace the coding process themselves (Guba and Lincoln 1994). The results from the coding are simply used to present a broad picture of the differences between CASE@KS1 and non-CASE@KS1 lessons. The results were presented to the CASE@KS1 teachers as a group in February 2000 for further verification. The case study transcripts were re-read and three excerpts chosen for detailed analysis. The criterion by which these excerpts were chosen was that they were representative of the CASE@KS1 and non-CASE@KS1 lessons by showing the general frequency and patterns of behaviours established through the analysis. The excerpts were edited to improve readability. Speech in quotation marks are approximations that are as accurate as possible from the field notes. The results were utilized to generate assertions about how teachers can foster good thinking in Year 1.

## Findings

The seven broad categories of behaviour that the Year 1 children demonstrated whilst participating in a CASE@KS1 lesson were explaining, highlighting discrepancies, adopting new ideas, demonstrating, thinking and working collaboratively, asking questions and other useful strategies such as creating analogies. Brief descriptions of these categories are provided in Table 3.1. The relative frequency with which these behaviours occurred in CASE@KS1 lessons and non-CASE@KS1 lessons is documented in Table 3.2.

Three excerpts from classroom field notes are provided in these findings. Two are from the context of CASE@KS1 activities (excerpts 1 and 2) and one is from the context of a mathematics lesson on ordering conducted in a non-CASE@KS1 classroom (excerpt 3). The first two excerpts provide concrete examples of what we judged to be good thinking based on the coding of the lessons, the third is a regular lesson for the purpose of comparison.

**Table 3.1** Categories of thinking behaviours

| Category | Description |
|---|---|
| A Explains | A child explains:<br>• his idea/action;<br>• another child's idea/action;<br>• her idea for solving a problem;<br>• his/another child's misunderstanding/difficulty. |
| B Highlights discrepancy | A child:<br>• recognizes/points out his own/the group's/another child's difficulty;<br>• disagrees with another child/the teacher;<br>• accepts that another child/the teacher has different ideas. |
| C Adopts a new idea | A child adopts a new idea to:<br>• a better/agreed one when his original idea was articulated/shown;<br>• a better/agreed one when no clear original idea was articulated/shown. |
| D Demonstrates | A child demonstrates an appropriate action or his idea to other children or teacher. |
| E Thinks/works collaboratively | Children:<br>• make various suggestions about solving a problem;<br>• build on each other's ideas or use several sources of information to solve a problem;<br>• agree a problem is not solvable. |
| F Asks questions | A child asks questions to the teacher or another child to clarify task/activity/problem/ideas. |
| G Other useful strategies | A child may use other thinking behaviours such as:<br>• creating analogies with ideas from a different context or example;<br>• using a physical strategy to organize his thinking. |

**Table 3.2** Average occurrence of thinking behaviours in CASE@KS1 and non-CASE@KS1 lessons

| Category | Average occurrence in CASE@KS1 lessons (n = 17) | Average occurrence in non-CASE@KS1 lessons (n = 15) |
|---|---|---|
| A Explains | 28 | 6.9 |
| B Highlights discrepancy | 4.7 | 1.4 |
| C Adopts a new idea | 3.1 | 0.13 |
| D Demonstrates | 4.6 | 1 |
| E Thinks/works collaboratively | 1.6 | 0.53 |
| F Asks questions | 0.65 | 1.4 |
| G Other useful strategies | 0.18 | 0 |

### *Excerpt 1: the green mammoth*

This excerpt was taken from a CASE@KS1 lesson taught by Ms Gwalia in Kingswood Primary School (pseudonyms have been used for all teachers, schools and pupils in this chapter). The lesson was a classification activity where the children were asked to sort a group of plastic dinosaurs into groups by colour and then by dinosaur type. The excerpt is from the next part of the activity when the children were challenged to sort the dinosaurs into two hoops: one containing green dinosaurs and one containing mammoths. (Mammoths are not strictly dinosaurs, but for simplicity the teachers referred to the group of extinct animals in the set as dinosaurs.) The difficulty was that one dinosaur was both green and a mammoth. The children in the group were Jade, Tiffany, Melissa, Seren, Joshua and Sam.

Ms Gwalia set the task by asking the pupils to put the green dinosaurs in one hoop and the mammoths in the other hoop. The pupils set to work and sorted the dinosaurs into the correct groups. The green mammoth was in the group of green dinosaurs and not with the other mammoths.

Ms Gwalia went over the initial instructions to put green dinosaurs in one group and the mammoths in the other group and asked, 'Do you all agree that is what you have done?'

Seren pointed to the green mammoth in the green group and said, 'I want that one in the mammoth group.' (B)

Ms Gwalia asked whether it was all right for the mammoth to be in the green group.

Melissa said, 'Yes', but Seren wanted it in the mammoth group.

Sam said he wanted it in the green group, 'Because it's the same colour.' (A)

Tiffany said she wanted it in the mammoth group in such a decisive way that all the pupils agreed with her. Joshua was the only student who still asserted that it should go in the green group.

Ms Gwalia pointed out that there was a 'big problem' because the pupils clearly disagreed about where the green mammoth should go and they did not have a solution that suited everyone. She asked them, 'How can we solve this problem?'

Ms Gwalia then asked Tiffany to clarify the problem and she explained, 'All mammoths have to go here, and all green dinosaurs have to go here.' (BA)

Joshua suggested getting another green mammoth and putting it in the other group, 'So that each group would have a green mammoth.' (A)

Ms Gwalia replied, 'We haven't got another one, so what can we do? How can we solve the problem?'

Sam tried to solve the problem by isolating the green mammoth on the side of the table outside both of the hoops. (D)

Ms Gwalia explained that the dinosaurs on the outside were all not green and not mammoths and that the problem dinosaur didn't belong there.

Seren picked up the green mammoth and had a close look at it as the discussion continued.

Ms Gwalia pointed to the two groups and asked, 'How can it be part of this and part of this?' Melissa suggested a vote. (A) Ms Gwalia said, 'A good idea, but it won't solve the problem.' Seren proposed that the mammoth wanted to be with his family, pointing to the other mammoths. (A)

Ms Gwalia pointed out, 'But he's green too.'

Seren put his hands up to his head and said, 'Let me think!' (G)

Ms Gwalia added, 'You might all need to put on your thinking caps.'

Melissa suggested putting the green dinosaur in the middle of the two hoops, 'It could go in the middle.' (A) The pupils put it in the gap between the two hoops. (D)

Ms Gwalia asked whether it was actually in the hoops if they put it in the middle.

The pupils chorused, 'No.'

Melissa said, 'Put it in both of them!' (A)

Ms Gwalia pointed out that the dinosaur was not *inside* the hoop and asked the pupils, 'How can it be in both?'

Jade said, 'You have to put them both together like that and make it stay in the middle and make it think!' She pulled the two hoops so they were just touching and put the dinosaur over the edges of both hoops to demonstrate her idea. (AD)

Joshua explained that 'It wants to be here and here', indicating both groups. (A)

Seren suggested overlapping the hoops so that the animal is in both groups and showed the pupils how to do it. (ADE)

Jade said, 'It's inside both groups.' (A)

Ms Gwalia asked Jade what she was thinking when she solved the problem.

Jade replied, 'I was thinking if I get them together it will be in both of them.' (A)

Seren said, 'I was thinking that's in the small groups and the others are in the big groups', indicating the green mammoth in the small intersection of the hoops. (A)

Ms Gwalia said, 'You were able to solve the problem by thinking and that is how a group can work together to find out the solutions to problems.'

### Excerpt 2: sorting vehicles

This lesson was taught by Ms Hempsted in Oatlands Primary School. The activity involved classifying plastic vehicles of different colours. The children in the group were Cashel, Hannah, Sarah-Jane, Christy and Hossain.

Ms Hempsted set the task, 'I want you to sort them into groups that are the same, has anyone got any ideas?' She then sat back from the group and let the pupils talk and work together.

Sarah-Jane said, 'I'm getting the trucks.' (A)

Hossain said, 'I'm getting the blue ones.' (A)

There was confusion as Hossain asked Sarah-Jane for her blue truck. (F) They sorted the confusion out by each of them talking and explaining what they were doing. (A) As a result, Sarah-Jane changed to collecting the red vehicles. (C) Christy collected green, Cashel yellow and Hossain blue. All the vehicles were quickly sorted by colour.

Ms Hempsted asked Hossain, 'How did we sort them?'

The other pupils called out, 'Colour' and then Hossain said, 'By colour.'

Ms Hempsted challenged the children to find a different way of sorting and asked Hannah her idea.

Hannah said, 'I'm getting the same kind of car.' (A)

Ms Hempsted asked Hannah, 'What should the other children do?'

Hannah said, 'They should get the same cars too.' (A)

Ms Hempsted asked, 'What do you mean?'

Hannah pointed to the racing cars and jeep while she explained. (DA)

Cashel said, 'I'm getting the yellows.' (A)

Ms Hempsted asked Hannah to explain to Cashel what they were doing.

Hannah collected two trucks and showed her. (D)

Sarah-Jane said, 'She didn't understand.' (B)

Hannah explained to Cashel again and showed her two jeeps. (AD)

Ms Hempsted asked Christy to explain.

Christy collected some jeeps and said, 'They are all the same car.' (AD)

The pupils started sorting (C), but Cashel collected a mixture of cars as did Sarah-Jane.

Hannah said in a loud voice, 'They are doing it wrong, you weren't listening to me.' (B)

Cashel and Sarah-Jane watched her as she showed them the same kind of car. (D) Cashel looked a bit upset.

Ms Hempsted gave Cashel a car and asked her where it should go. She put it in the correct group with other cars of the same type. (C) Sarah-Jane still had a mixture of cars in front of her. Ms Hempsted asked Cashel to help Sarah-Jane, however, Cashel had difficulty helping Sarah-Jane because she said she thought a sports car went with the jeep because they both had no roof. (A) She then abandoned that idea and went back to the idea of putting the same coloured vehicles together.

Sarah-Jane then spontaneously gave a racing car to Hossain, who had a group of racing cars in front of him. (DC) Ms Hempsted asked her why she did that.

Sarah-Jane said, 'Because they are the same as his.' (A)

Ms Hempsted asked, 'What is the same about Hossain's cars?'

The group talked about a few features of the cars that were the same. Finally, they got around to saying that they were all racing cars. (A)

Ms Hempsted asked Cashel, 'What's the same about them?' and pointed to a group of jeeps.

Christy said, 'They are all cars.' (A)

Cashel said, 'They are all jeeps.' (A)
Ms Hempsted asked the pupils, 'How did we sort them?'
Christy said, 'groups of the same cars.' (A)
Sarah-Jane repeated Christy's words, 'groups of the same cars.'

### Excerpt 3: a dog's day

This lesson was taught by Ms Griffiths in Abbey Primary School. The numeracy lesson was about putting things in order. The children in the group were Stefan, Chaz, Teshan, Brendan, Brian and Cindy.

Ms Griffiths said, 'What we're going to do is to put someone else's day in order.' She talked about the order of the school day and explained that everyone's day goes in order. She showed the pupils a worksheet and explained that 'On the sheet is a dog and you're going to put his day in order and you're going to make a nice book and colour it in.'

Ms Griffiths asked Vanessa what the dog was doing in one of the pictures. Vanessa didn't answer and Ms Griffiths helped her by saying, 'He's eating his breakfast.' Ms Griffiths then asked the pupils what the dog was doing in the other pictures. Sometimes the pupils couldn't answer, so Ms Griffiths went to another pupil until she got the answers.

Ms Griffiths wrote on the board the six things the dog in the work-sheet was doing: (1) asleep in bed, (2) waking up, (3) yawning, (4) in the shower, (5) eating breakfast, (6) going out.

Ms Griffiths showed the pupils how to fold the paper to make a book and talked about the order of the pictures. She explained that the pupils were to fold and colour in the paper and then write words underneath. She asked the pupils, 'Is this the order of the whole day or just the morning?'

The pupils chorused, 'Just morning.'

The pupils went to their desks to start work on their book. The observer sat with one group of six children. Ms Griffiths said, 'I can't hear the tap dripping' to the whole class in order to remind the pupils to work in soft voices. The children started to fold their sheets of paper to make the book. The pupils in the observer's group helped each other with folding. Teshan showed another student in the group how to fold. Ms Griffiths went around the class saying comments such as 'Lovely' and 'Excellent' when pupils did a good job. The pupils started to write the order of the dog's day in their book. Most pupils in the observer's group had folded the book except two children, Brendan and Chaz. One pupil was colouring the pictures.

Stefan said, 'I can't see', and went over to the board so he could see the words on the board and write them down into his booklet.

Two children in the group, Cindy and Brian, talked about what they were writing.

Teshan said to Cindy, 'You can copy from me.' Then when she noticed that Ms Griffiths had come over to the desk Teshan said to Ms Griffiths,

'Cindy's copying from Brian.' Teshan then told Ms Griffiths, 'I've done it' and showed Ms Griffiths her work.

Brian and Cindy continued to write the order of the dog's day into their book from the board. Brendan said, 'I can't fold it up right.' (B)

Teshan said, 'I'll do it for you', took his sheet and folded it into a book for him.

Teshan gave the sheet back to Brendan and went through the order with him. She said, 'Start with that one and now you're going to number two. (A) Did you do that one?' (F)

Brendan replied, 'Yes.'

Teshan said, 'Now you're going to do that one', pointing out the next picture in the sequence.

Teshan helped Brendan write on his sheet by saying the words and sounding out the letters as she wrote in her book. (AD) Brendan wrote the letters in his book in unison with Teshan. (E)

Chaz asked Stefan, 'Can you fold it up for me?' (F) Stefan took Chaz's sheet and folded if for him and gave it back. Cindy and Brian continued to write.

Ms Griffiths said, 'Wonderful, what a lovely hard-working class.'

Stefan, Teshan, Chaz and Brendan started colouring their pictures. The pupils discussed pots of pencils and Cindy made sure the pot was where she could reach it.

Teshan asked, 'Have you got a red' and commented, 'They've got two reds.'

Ms Griffiths asked the pupils to pack up and put their books out the front and stand behind their chairs. The pupils started to pack up.

## Discussion

The analysis of the behaviours that children demonstrated while solving the CASE@KS1 activities included explaining, highlighting discrepancies, adopting new ideas, demonstrating, thinking and working collaboratively and asking questions (see Table 3.1). It is clear from Table 3.2 that these behaviours occurred about four times more frequently in the CASE@KS1 lessons than in the regular lessons observed as part of this study. This is not a surprising result, as the CASE@KS1 lessons were designed to be thinking lessons from their conception. The more important issue for discussion is the question of whether these behaviours observed in the CASE@KS1 lessons constitute 'good' thinking? In order to respond to this question, the following discussion will focus on: difficulty as part of a lesson; talk and action; time and effort for thinking; and evidence of 'good' thinking.

### Difficulty

Difficulty featured in each of the three excerpts, but the responses to the difficulty were markedly different. In the first excerpt, the green mammoth, the difficulty was experienced by all student members of the group. They simply did not know what to do with the green mammoth. Should they put it in the group with the other green dinosaurs, or should they put it in the group with the other (multicoloured) mammoths? In the second excerpt, sorting vehicles, the task difficulty was experienced by two members of the group, Cashel and Sarah-Jane. Once they had sorted the vehicles by colour, they found it very difficult to focus on a different feature, vehicle type, and use that as the sorting criterion. The other children in the group, while able to do the classification themselves, faced the difficulty of explaining it to Cashel and Sarah-Jane so that the whole group could accomplish the task. In both the green mammoth and the sorting vehicles activities the difficulty was something accepted as part of the lesson and the response was that it was a challenge that the pupils were to engage in and find a solution.

This challenge resulted in a variety of behaviours aimed at solving the problem. Highlighting discrepancies, brainstorming ideas, explaining, demonstrating and changing ideas all were frequently observed behaviours as the pupils attempted to solve the problem. Highlighting discrepancies occurred with a frequency of 4.7 in CASE@KS1 lessons and 1.4 in non-CASE@KS1 lessons. For example, in the green mammoth activity the difficulty was explained and clarified by Tiffany: 'All the mammoths have to go here, and all the green dinosaurs have to go here.' This resulted in a brainstorm when several pupils explained their ideas to find a potential solution to the problem. The whole group participated in finding a solution. Joshua suggested putting another green mammoth in the other group, Sam suggested isolating the green mammoth, Melissa suggested a vote and Seren suggested that being with its family of mammoths was the best solution.

Difficulty arose in the second excerpt when the children were challenged to find a second way to sort the vehicles. As with the green mammoth task, this vehicle-sorting difficulty was something that was addressed by the whole group. The teacher encouraged the children who were able to do the task to explain it to those who could not. Although it is difficult to ascertain if these pupils were really able to sort using the second criterion of vehicle type, there is strong evidence to support the idea that they were able to adopt the new idea.

In contrast, in the dog's day excerpt, difficulty was treated as something to be avoided. When a student showed or expressed difficulty, the response of the teacher and, in some cases other pupils, was to solve the problem for that child, or do the task for them. The teaching objectives of this lesson were about order, however, this did not feature as a difficulty for the pupils because the teacher wrote the answer on the board before they started their individual work. Brendan and Chaz had difficulty folding their booklets and Brendan had difficulty writing the words in his booklet. In these situations friends simply did the work for the child or helped them in a way that provided them with the answers and did not require any thoughtful effort. The contrast with typical CASE@KS1 activities is striking.

## Time and effort for thinking

A disposition of good thinkers described by Tishman et al. (1995), is the tendency to devote time and effort to thinking. An implicit expectation evident in the first and second excerpts was that the children should think, to solve problems, to contribute new ideas, to explain what they were doing and to justify their suggestions. Evidence from the green mammoth activity showed that thinking was not only expected, but explicitly encouraged. When Seren said, 'Let me think!' and put his hands up to his head, the teacher added, 'You might all need to put on your thinking caps.' This attention to thinking immediately preceded the sequence of events that led to the solution of the green mammoth problem. The expectation that pupils think for themselves by teachers asking open-ended questions and then allowing the pupils to take time to think was clearly evident in the CASE@KS1 lessons and is probably an important aspect of a thinking environment for Year 1.

## Talk and action

Work by Meloth and Deering (1999) indicates that task-related talk about facts, concepts, strategies and thinking is very important to pupils' learning and that this kind of talk occurs with low frequency unless there is direct intervention. The first two excerpts and Table 3.2 demonstrate that during CASE@KS1 lessons the children did a lot of explanatory talk, they explained the activity, the equipment, the problem, their ideas, what they were doing, each other's ideas and so on. The average number of explanations in a CASE lessons was 28, whereas the average number of explanations in a non-CASE lesson was fewer than 7 (see Table 3.2). Pupils also demonstrated more frequently with an average of 4.6 occurrences per CASE@KS1 lesson than in non-CASE@KS1 lessons, where the average was 1 (see Table 3.2). In excerpt 1, Sam explained why he wanted the green mammoth in the green group, 'Because it's the same colour', and Jade reflected in a metacognitive way, 'I was thinking if I get them together it will be in both of them.' In the excerpt 2, Christy collected a group of jeeps and explained her action by saying, 'They are all the same car.' Sarah-Jane explained why she gave a car to Hossain: 'Because it's the same as his.'

In the course of the activity, the way the pupils explained and spoke about their actions opened their thinking to the group so that they became shared ideas. This meant ideas could be evaluated by the other pupils and the teacher and discussed further and acted on accordingly. Ideas were shared, rejected or accepted and built upon until satisfactory solutions were accomplished. The teachers in the first two excerpts asked questions and spoke to the pupils in ways that encouraged them to share their ideas and to speak about what they were doing. The questions were often open-ended and, therefore, required the children to think and put together their own answers. The solution to the green mammoth problem was prompted by teacher questions such as 'So what can we do, how can we solve this problem?' The solution was found subsequently through a process of collaboration where pupils were challenged by a difficult task, explained their ideas so that they became part of the shared group knowledge and this clearly resulted in a cumulative building of knowledge until a solution was found.

Excerpt 3 of the non-CASE@KS1 lesson is in marked contrast to the first two in that little importance was placed on explanations or pupils sharing their ideas about how to complete the task. Children often talked about things unrelated to their work, for example pencil pots. Some pupils did express that they were confused or did not know what to do. However, the response to this from other pupils was to allow them to copy what they were doing without any explanation or discussion about the process. Questions from the teacher were often closed and required one 'correct' answer, for example 'What is the dog doing in this picture?'

### Evidence of good thinking

The kind of talk and action in which the pupils in the CASE@KS1 lessons were involved were of the kind which several researchers (Hogan and Tudge 1999; Meloth and Deering 1999; Wegeriff et al. 1999) have suggested is likely to result in good thinking and cognitive advance. Some of the behaviours described in the findings that helped children solve the CASE@KS1 activities can be explained by Piaget's notion of autonomy. The concrete operational child is not egocentric in the way pre-operational children are and can assume the viewpoint of others (Wadsworth 1996). Early in the sorting vehicles excerpt the children ran into problems because Hossain began sorting by colour and Sarah-Jane sorted by vehicle type. The problem was soon solved as a result of the children talking and because Sarah-Jane changed her idea and agreed to Hossain's idea of sorting by colour. This exemplifies good thinking by Sarah-Jane because she was able to use a pattern of thinking typical of the more cognitively advanced concrete operational child, that is she was able to assume Hossain's viewpoint and sort in the way he suggested. Table 3.2 shows that there was an average of about three occasions in each CASE@KS1 lesson when a pupil/pupils were able to adopt a new idea and it was very infrequent (0.13) in the non-CASE@KS1 lessons. Being able to adopt a new idea is an important part of good thinking for Year 1.

The concrete operational child also is increasingly capable of evaluating arguments rather than simply accepting pre-formed unilateral ideas (Wadsworth, 1996). It is interesting that early in the green mammoth excerpt all the pupils, except Joshua, agreed with Tiffany to simply put the green mammoth in the mammoth group. There is no evidence that Tiffany had given a good explanation as to why it should go there and not in the green group and the other pupils simply accepted this unjustified idea. From this point on in the lesson the teacher modelled and encouraged evaluative behaviour. She asked for other ideas for a solution to the problem and encouraged pupils to explain why and how. The ideas were welcomed, but the teacher modelled the process of evaluation by giving reasons why they were not suitable solutions, such as 'We haven't got another one', 'It won't solve the problem' and 'But he's green too.' This moved the children beyond the point where they unquestioningly accepted one idea. They continued to contribute new ideas until they reached a suitable solution. This kind of behaviour, encouraged by the teacher, resulted in the group as a whole being able to evaluate arguments as a concrete operational child would do rather than thinking in a pre-operational manner, simply accepting the pre-formed unilateral ideas.

The green mammoth excerpt can be viewed also through a Vygotskyian theoretical lens as the role of social activity is clearly evident. Vygotsky claimed that the child's learning can be assessed by those additional problems that a child can solve with social assistance, the notion of ZPD (Light et al. 1991). The teacher took a lead role in promoting the brainstorming activity to switch the pupils on to thinking about alternatives to putting the green mammoth in one or the other group. The teacher provided the expertise necessary to guide the pupils through the ZPD where their ability to consider alternatives was not evident and had probably not yet matured. Vygotsky claimed that teaching is only good when it addresses those functions that are in a stage of maturing, which lie in the ZPD (Vygotsky 1978: 86). This was evident in the vehicle-sorting activity. Christy, Hannah and, to a lesser extent, Hossain took on the role of the more competent peer in helping Cashel and Sarah-Jane solve the problem they faced.

## Conclusions

This study used the context of a CA intervention project, CASE@KS1, to investigate the notion of good thinking in Year 1. The CASE@KS1 lessons observed as part of this research were different from the regular lessons in several ways. Children in CASE@KS1 lessons more frequently explained ideas, actions, difficulties and made suggestions for solving problems. During the CASE@KS1 lessons the children also more frequently highlighted discrepancies, adopted new ideas, demonstrated their ideas and actions and worked collaboratively with other children. These behaviours are thought to be an important part of 'good' thinking for Year 1 pupils. CASE@KS1 lessons also were different from the regular lessons observed, in that difficulty was an accepted part of the lesson and children were expected to dedicate time and effort to thinking in order to solve the difficulty.

From both Vygotskian and Piagetian perspectives, the kind of thinking that occurred in the CASE@KS1 lessons did provide potential for enhanced cognitive development. Children were stimulated to develop concrete operational thought patterns during the course of the activities. For example, some children showed less tendency to egocentricity and increased tendency to evaluate arguments. The role of social activity was prominent in the CASE@KS1 lessons and evidence of Year 1 children building on each other's ideas to find a solution to a problem was demonstrated. Children were able to solve problems that they were initially unable to solve through interaction with more knowledgeable peers and with their teachers.

The results of this study indicate that the Year 1 children were engaged in 'good thinking' whilst participating in the CASE@KS1 activities. Although the focus was on the children, many of the children's behaviours were induced by the teacher. It is possible, therefore, to extract salient information from the findings presented in this study to make three assertions about how teachers can foster good thinking in Year 1. First, difficulty should be an accepted part of the classroom. Children should be encouraged to undertake challenging problems and helped with strategies for solving the problems. The challenge should be at a level just beyond that which the children have already achieved so that it is possible for them to use new ideas to find solutions. Second, talk that explores and explains the task at hand is a critical aspect of good thinking in Year 1. Teachers should encourage children to explain problems, their ideas, actions, misunderstandings, agreements, questions and possible solutions. Finally, thinking needs to be a discernible part of the classroom environment. Children should be given time to think, teachers should model thinking out loud, talk about their thinking and encourage children to do the same. Teachers should use open-ended questions that require the pupils to engage in original thought before they are able to answer.

# 4 PUPILS' UNDERSTANDING OF WHAT HELPS THEM LEARN

## Anne Robertson

### Introduction

The pupil is the central focus of the learning situation and to understand pupils' learning and behaviour it is necessary to understand how pupils construct learning. Understanding pupils' constructs could enable teachers to address pupils' learning needs more effectively and thus raise attainment.

Several initiatives currently taking place in schools are aimed at raising attainment, for example the National Literacy Strategy, the National Numeracy Strategy and CASE. The Literacy and Numeracy Strategies are government initiatives and are widely known. The original CASE project at KS3 has been showing significant positive effects nationally for several years (Adey and Shayer 1993). CASE@KS1 is in its infancy but, as reported in Chapter 2, is already showing a positive effect on pupils' cognitive development.

As a member of the research team investigating pupils' cognitive gain as a result of CASE@KS1, I am interested in examining pupils' understanding of what helps them learn. How do pupils construct the pedagogy promoted during CASE? Do pupils transfer any learning strategies from CASE to other areas of the curriculum? The aim of this investigation is to enable teachers to provide more effective learning opportunities for pupils and so raise attainment. The limited amount of research to date informed by Year 1 pupils could lead to the supposition that researchers doubt that pupils of this age can offer insights into their learning, but it is my belief that it is essential to listen to the lived experience of pupils and use this information to inform teachers so as to improve the learning possibilities.

## Personal construct theory

Kelly's Personal Construct Theory (1995) incorporates the idea that thinking and feeling are not two separate processes, but that the whole human experience is one living, inter-connected process. Kelly believes that what individuals know and learn is not something separate from themselves. In his own words, 'This is a theory about how the human process flows, how it strives in new directions as well as in old, and how it may dare for the first time to reach into the depths of newly perceived dimensions of human life.' The ability to take control of life and do something with it is inherent in humans and for Kelly this belief converts philosophy into a 'living psychology'. As Salmon (1988) says, 'It is our personal construct systems which allow us to read our lives. Constructs are essentially interwoven within a personal system of meaning.' A construct is built up by observing recurrent themes and their differences and then placing unique interpretations on them. This is not simply a verbal label. Construing is anticipating and experiencing. A central notion of this theory is that the human person is a scientist. Constructs are not chaotic, but are organized into a system. A person develops hypotheses, tests them out, revises them and develops theories to make sense of their world. By enabling pupils to explore their constructs, insights can be gained into how they understand their world. Barnes and Todd (1978) state that 'Each of us can learn only by making sense of what happens to us through actively constructing a world for ourselves.'

CASE lessons aim, amongst other things, to encourage pupils to become more conscious of their cognitive processes. It is believed that by becoming increasingly aware of the process of learning, they in turn may take more control over their learning. Does this, then, alter their constructs of what helps them learn?

## Adult understanding of pupil learning

Listening to pupils as they work through CASE activities reveals something of their reasoning processes. Pupils can be heard describing their ideas, explaining their reasons and asking questions in the social space. As an adult observer of many Year 1 lessons trying to understand pupils' learning, several questions have emerged. What sense, if any, do they later make of this process? How do they understand any learning that is taking place? How are they construing learning? Are they becoming more conscious of what helps them to learn?

Learning has been described as 'a change in construing which takes place within the learner' (Thomas and Harri-Augstein 1985). The authors go on to say that learning involves simultaneous changes in the perception of thinking and feeling which then alters behaviour. If these changes are valued by adults, there follows a perceived increase in competence. It could be argued that attainment could be raised further if teachers understand what brings about these changes: understanding, therefore, how pupils are construing their learning.

## Investigating pupil constructs

Mueller (1996) has shown that children's interior perceptions of self and self in relation to others, as revealed through imaginative play, are related to their state of mental health. One form of assessment used in the study of pre-school children was the 'Teddy Bear's Picnic'. This is a semi-structured task using teddy bears in nine story scenarios, designed to elicit information about the internal world of pre-school children. It is based on the hypothesis that children reveal aspects of their interior world through imaginative play. It aims to uncover a child's personal constructs which are believed to be guiding behaviour and allows the child's own perceptions of self and others to be examined. This technique gave a unique understanding of each child which could then be the subject for qualitative analysis. It is believed that a highly negative set of constructs characterizes an emotionally troubled child. If this is brought to light, it enables the child to receive the professional help required to address the difficulties. Teachers' understanding allows them to perceive the child as neither naughty nor ill-disciplined, but as emotionally in need of support. This, in turn, can alter the way the teacher generally behaves towards the child to an approach characterized by compassion rather than annoyance.

Another common technique for eliciting constructs is the repertory grid. Here constructs are perceived as bi-polar, and the individual is asked to name ways in which people, events or situations lie on a scale between these poles. Examples of such bipolar constructs are 'naughty–good', 'talkative–quiet' and 'generous–selfish'. Ways in which people and situations are the same or are different are explored, both similarities and differences are given equal importance. Ravenette (1975) has developed forms of grid techniques particularly helpful for pupils from about the age of 8. He recommends the use of photographs and pictorial representations of situations. With younger pupils and those with limited language it has been possible to use pictures of facial expressions to elicit constructs.

The elicitation of constructs using a repertory grid technique involves interviewing children individually. It has long been agreed that it is difficult to interview young pupils for the purpose of finding out how they construct learning. Piaget (1976) invites interviewers not to talk too much and not to be suggestive. He advises that a good interviewer must know how to observe and let the child talk freely and at the same time be alert for anything definitive which proved or disproved the working hypothesis. Rich (1972) suggests that the task of the interviewer is to exploit those factors which increase communication and minimize those which block it. He also warns, 'What is common is the way a child can be led, simply by the form of the question put by an adult, to make false statements.' Giving a pupil some measure of control over the interview may encourage more open communication.

For the present purpose of examining 5- and 6-year-olds' constructs of learning, I chose to adapt the repertory grid idea to be administered by individual interview. Thus, it was necessary to design an interview schedule which allowed pupils to talk freely but remain focused on the matters under consideration, to explore how they understand what takes place during lessons without being led, and to be the central focus, while maintaining a measure of control.

## The sample

Over the academic year of the main CASE@KS1 study, I regularly observed six classes during their numeracy lessons. The numeracy hour had recently been introduced and all six teachers were using the National Numeracy Strategy as the basis of their lessons. Of these six classes, four also receive CASE lessons. The remaining two non-CASE classes were identified as part of the control group of the main project (see Chapter 2).

Four groups of pupils within the four CASE classes were also regularly observed during the CASE lessons. Each teacher was asked to choose a typical group representative of her class to be the focus group. All CASE groups included a range of ability. The pupils to be interviewed from the control classes were chosen by the teachers. For each group they were each asked to choose three girls and three boys with a mixed range of ability. One pupil in each group was identified as speaking English as an additional language (EAL).

The following pseudonyms will be used:

- Cherry School, Groups A and B (CASE school);
- Willow School, Groups C and D (CASE school); and
- Alder School, Groups E and F (Control school).

## The interviews

Interviews were conducted with each individual pupil after a CASE or numeracy lesson. CASE pupils had two interviews. Interviews took the form of conversations with a view to eliciting pupils' constructs of how learning takes place during a numeracy lesson and during a CASE lesson. Groups A and C were interviewed first about numeracy and a week later about CASE. Groups B and D were interviewed first about CASE and a week later about numeracy. These conversations took place in March, when pupils already knew me as someone familiar in the class, observing and taking notes, with whom they had had three previous individual conversations, and who had carried out quantitative assessments of them with regard to conservation, motivation and self-concept.

The interview began by pupils talking about the lesson just observed. Each CASE pupil then named the pupils in their group. As the names were given, they were written on cards by me and placed on the table according to pupil position around the table during the lesson. The non-CASE pupils were shown the names of the focus pupils. It was ensured that each pupil knew who the others were. Each pupil was asked to think about the lesson just completed and to consider what helped her to learn during that lesson or any numeracy/CASE lesson. When a pupil suggested an activity, the word was written on a small card. The pupil was asked if all the pupils in this group do that activity in the same way. This was to enable the pupil to produce bi-polar constructs, for example 'I explain, but he doesn't give reasons.' All other questions were prompted by constructs produced by the pupil being interviewed and phrased in a tentative manner to leave the pupil free to elaborate or change direction as desired, for example 'Mmm I wonder what that means. . . .'

## Threats to validity

### *Do these pupils understand what is being asked of them?*

The pupils in Cherry and Willow Schools had been working in their CASE group on a weekly basis for 7 months when these interviews took place, so both the CASE group and the context were familiar to each of them. In numeracy they work with different pupils, but a portion of each lesson is spent discussing with at least one peer and usually more. The concepts of 'same' and 'different' were familiar to each pupil as by this stage of the year considerable time had been spent in classification activities during CASE lessons. Each pupil appeared to understand this concept without explanation.

The chosen pupils in Alder School were not identified as a group. In class, pupils sit in what is described by the teachers as 'ability groups'. The reality, as observed, was that numeracy sessions began with the whole class sitting on the carpet. At the end of the lesson input, pupils sat at tables of six, where they worked individually completing work sheets. Observed numeracy lessons did not include discussion or any activity in which pupils had to communicate directly with their peers. To verify pupil understanding of 'same' and 'different', the teachers were asked if classification activities had been pursued. Each teacher said that pupils learnt to sort and classify in the Reception class so they would have a good understanding of those concepts. Indeed, the pupils did seem to understand same and different as each one was able to give several bi-polar constructs.

Alder School teachers were also asked whether pupils had experience of discussing their work and identifying what helped them to learn. Teachers seemed less clear about this. One said that pupils liked to see the ticks on their work because then they knew they had it right. The other teacher said that in the busy schedule of a day there was not really time for discussion. She also thought that pupils were too young to know what helped them to learn.

The content of each interview was largely dictated by the pupil. Had any pupil not understood initially what was being asked, the interview would not have got underway as they would not have had anything to say. In fact, this did not happen at all. However, it could be argued that Alder School pupils did not understand what was being asked of them with regard to what helped them learn. Although when asked they each gave constructs, they were largely unable to explain why these actions helped learning. They may simply have been repeating words frequently used by their teachers. Also, having little or no experience of discussing with peers may have made it too difficult for them to know whether other pupils acted in a similar or different way from themselves.

### Should pupils be asked to comment on their peers?

It could be argued that it is unethical to ask pupils to discuss their peers behind their back. However, the explanation preceding the interview clearly indicated that the point of interest was what helped and hindered everyone to learn. This focus was maintained and, even though comments about others were made, they were given as statements of fact not as criticisms. For example, 'I give reasons but Temi doesn't'. The pupils were also aware that the behaviours had been witnessed by the researcher, so they were not being encouraged to share anything that had not already been seen and heard. During their personal interview full attention was being given to their unique understanding of events.

### What weight can be attached to children's answers?

It may be the case that when pupils are asked in an interview what they do during CASE/numeracy lessons that helps them learn, they simply repeat what they frequently hear teachers encouraging. They may be conscious that their teachers want them to use these behaviours and a natural response could be to reproduce them when asked by another significant adult. One of the hazards cited in interviewing young children is that pupils say what they think the interviewer wants them to say (Rich 1972), but it would seem difficult for pupils to explain their reasoning, as has been noted, if they were merely repeating words frequently heard without their having taken on a personalized meaning. One pupil gave several constructs which, although similar, she construed clearly as different, that is play, order, sort, feel objects. These activities are not mentioned by any of the other 22 pupils.

## Results

Pupils' constructs were collated for analysis, original words being retained as far as possible. Where words were clearly understood to have the same meaning, they were classified together, for example 'explain', 'tell someone what

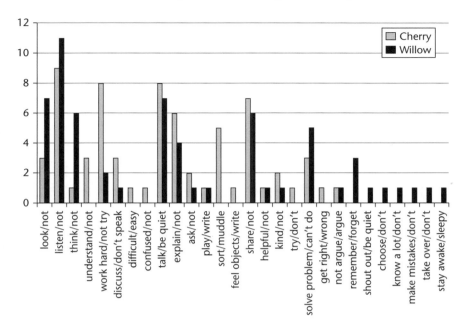

**Figure 4.1** Constructs of what helps learning in a CASE lesson (maximum numbers possible: Cherry 11, Willow 12)

your idea means' and 'give a reason' were all classified as 'explain'. 'Solve a problem', 'work a hard thing' and 'sort a problem' were all classified as 'solve a problem'.

The constructs were collated first by group and then by school. Figures 4.1 and 4.2 show the frequency of constructs relating to a CASE lesson and to a numeracy lesson respectively. In identifying the constructs, the first word given is the construct named by pupils as helping them to learn, namely listen, talk, get right and so on. The word after the slash is the opposite pole of their construct, namely don't listen, keep quiet, don't try and so on. On average, the pupils identified as speaking English as an additional language produced one less construct than the others, but required no extra instruction.

It is evident that the number of pupils interviewed is very small (35) for statistical analysis but the following section gives some examples of reasons given by pupils as to why these constructs are important in learning.

### What helps learning in CASE?

*Cherry School*
Listening, working hard, talking and sharing were the most frequently cited constructs. All the pupils in Cherry School gave an explanation as to why these activities are important in the process of learning. Some of the reasons given were:

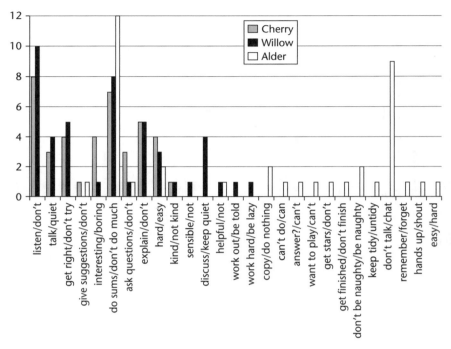

**Figure 4.2** Constructs of what helps learning in a numeracy lesson (maximum numbers possible: Willow and Alder 12, Cherry 11)

'If you work hard you learn new things and that's interesting, it makes it not boring.'
'When you talk you can get help from each other and get ideas from your friends how to solve the problem.'
'We share things like the toys and ideas and that way all the group can learn because you all do the problem when you share.'

A few constructs such as 'be kind', 'be helpful' and 'not argue' appear to be more concerned with behaviour than learning, but the pupils explained them as being important in learning. For example:

'If you're kind everybody can get a chance to solve the problem then all your friends can learn because they can all fix it.'
'When you help everybody in your group you can say ideas they don't know and then we all learn them, but if you don't help you just keep your own ideas and they might be wrong and you don't learn and your friends don't either.'

*Willow School*
Eleven out of twelve pupils mentioned listening as important in learning. They gave various explanations:

'If you listen, you hear your friends' ideas and that gives you some and then you can help to solve the problem.'
'When you listen, you can hear people explain their reasons and that helps you to understand.'
'I help Karen to listen so she can understand because sometimes she wants to sleep and when she does she doesn't learn what is going on in the problem.'

Several of these explanations link to another construct mentioned five times in this school, namely 'solve a problem'. The pupils said that solving a problem was often hard at first, but during the lesson it became easier. When asked how this was so, they gave various reasons:

'When you try to solve a problem you can't do it by yourself because it's too hard. If you all try together you have lots of ideas and when you try those ideas it makes the problem easy and then you can do it.'
'Well in the beginning it's hard and you don't know what they're talking about, but then you listen and you sort things and then it just comes like right, ain't it?'

Six pupils in this school suggested the construct 'thinking'. When asked how thinking helped them to learn, they spoke about 'thinking making their brains work' and 'thinking helping them to have ideas to solve the problems'. Pupils in this school also mentioned constructs which seemed more related to behaviour than learning. However, the links were clear in explanations given:

'You have to stay awake so you don't sleep and not learn what is going on. I want to sleep sometimes because it's hard to think.'
'Sometimes Nemur takes over, then we don't get no chance to learn because he does everything.'

### What helps learning in numeracy?

*Cherry School*
The construct most frequently cited in Cherry school was 'listening'. Eight out of eleven pupils mentioned its importance. The main reasons given were:

'You hear new things.'
'Miss tells you things what you need to understand, she explains things.'
'Your friend might tell you something what they understand and then I understand it too.'

Seven pupils said that doing sums helped them learn, but no one could explain how doing sums helped. However, five pupils said that explaining was important. The element of sharing knowledge and understanding appeared to be a key factor in this construct: 'If you explain something you understand, you help someone else to understand too.' During numeracy lessons these pupils were observed frequently listening to their peers and giving explanations in small groups, with a partner and in the plenary time towards the end of a lesson.

*Willow School*

Ten out of twelve pupils in Willow School mentioned listening as a key factor in learning. They explained in various ways why listening to the teacher and their peers is important and how it helps them to learn. Eight pupils mentioned doing sums as being important. Several pupils gave reasons:

> 'You need to know how to count.'
> 'Doing sums gives you a chance to practise counting.'
> 'You need to know money for shopping.'
> 'So I can count my Pokemon cards.'

They seemed to have reasons for counting which were relevant and explicit. Pupils in this school were frequently observed using counting skills in activities and games where the context was based in everyday situations. Five pupils said that 'getting it right' was important in numeracy. Their explanations for how getting things right helped them learn were linked to 'trying'. The opposite pole of this construct was 'not trying', the implication being that 'if you try you will get it right'. Four pupils said that talking helped them, whereas if you kept quiet you did not learn as much. Five pupils said that explaining helped them and four also mentioned 'discuss'. This gave a substantial proportion of speaking activities cited as being helpful in the process of learning. Pupils were frequently observed during numeracy sharing ideas with partners, small groups and in whole-class sessions.

*Alder School*

Nine pupils in this school said that it was helpful *not* to talk, their reason being that talking disturbs everybody:

> 'That makes a noise.'
> 'It means you are chatting and causing trouble.'
> 'Miss gets cross because we annoy some people.'

Two said that hard work helped them learn. When asked why, they said:

> 'It makes you think. Easy work you can just do quickly and it's boring like doing worksheets all the time.'

One pupil said that answering questions helped him learn. This was explained as 'Then Miss knows I know', but he was unable to explain how this helped him. Another pupil said 'Remembering helps me because I won't forget.' She was unable to develop this thought further. All of the other constructs were given by only one or two pupils and related mostly to behaviour routines. There were no explanations as to how any of these behaviours helped the process of learning.

## What can be learnt from these interviews?

### Constructs provided by non-CASE pupils

Each pupil was able to provide several constructs which related to classroom behaviours. However, there is some doubt as to whether these pupils understood what was being asked of them in terms of what helped them to learn. Generally they were unable to explain how these behaviours helped in the process of learning. The large number of pupils who expressed the view that 'not talking' was important could offer a crucial insight. Vygotsky believes that pupils need to use language so as to integrate learning, making it explicit. How does the process of learning become integrated for each pupil if there is no opportunity to discuss in a safe environment how learning takes place? It remains unclear what these pupils understand about what helps them learn. Many of the constructs they did provide related to behaviours frequently expected of them, such as 'don't talk', 'put your hands up' and 'don't shout out'. Pupil understanding of these constructs seemed to relate to 'keeping Miss happy so she won't get cross'. Of course, these behaviours relate to good classroom management but, in themselves, do not make explicit how they help in the process of learning. Could it be that, if these behaviours become the focus of attention for teachers, they detract from pupils' possibilities in constructing actively helpful learning behaviours?

### Constructs provided by CASE pupils

Each pupil was able to provide several constructs relating to CASE and to numeracy lessons regarding what helped them to learn. Figure 4.1 indicates the most frequently cited constructs as listening, talking, sorting, explaining, sharing, solving a problem, looking, thinking and working hard. These are all behaviours actively promoted during the PD associated with CASE. Teachers frequently remind pupils of these behaviours during CASE lessons, as can be seen from lesson transcripts, for example:

Ms A: 'Let's listen to what Jack says to see if that gives us an idea and helps us to sort out our muddle.'

Ms D: 'Right, take a few minutes to think of your idea and then we'll take time to share them all and see how they help us. Remember to tell us why you think it so we can all try to understand what's going on here.'

In interviews, pupils were also able to talk about the constructs in a way that indicated their understanding of them as skills helping them to learn. This echoes Vygotsky's (1978) notion that pupils develop and integrate understanding of concepts as they integrate language they first hear in the social space. If it is true that pupils integrate concepts in this way, it may be assumed from the information drawn from these interviews that pupils are also integrating skills that facilitate learning. For example, pupils are able to give reasons why looking, listening, thinking, remembering, asking, sharing and explaining help them:

*Paige*: 'We [indicating certain members] all look carefully.'

*R*: 'I wonder why?'

*Paige*: 'Cos if you look you can see what clues there are and then you can know what way to solve the problem.'

*R*: 'I see. And what about these people [indicating the cards with other names].'

*Paige*: 'Well, they don't look much so they can't get clues then.'

It could be argued that the more effectively these learning skills and strategies are verbalized as pupils use them to do the tasks, the more effectively pupils will integrate them and consequently use them independently as they learn. It can be seen from Figure 4.2 that CASE pupils mentioned several similar activities as helping them to learn during numeracy. They seem to be independently transferring these learning strategies to another context. It could also be that teachers are promoting the same strategies during numeracy as they have found them helpful to pupils during CASE.

### What does the teacher emphasize?

In every CASE lesson concrete materials are used and, in many lessons, pupils are asked to order or classify in some way. On the whole, the materials are rather different from those usually used in class. It is surprising, therefore, that the materials are not the subject of more constructs. One explanation suggests that because pupils generally use CASE materials once, whereas activities such as listening, talking and thinking are being mentioned during every CASE lesson, pupil attention is being drawn away from materials and more towards learning strategies. This suggests that teachers are successfully making the process of learning more explicit and that pupils really are becoming more skilled in using learning strategies and more conscious of metacognitive processes. As Bruner (1996) argues, pupils who become more aware of how learning takes place can be helped to achieve full mastery. If this is so, it can be expected that pupil attainment will be raised and, therefore, CASE will be achieving its main objective.

### Talking or not talking?

Pupils in Cherry and Willow Schools said that 'talking helped them learn' and provided the following reasons:

'Talking helps me to get ideas from my friends because they share some.'
'It helps me when we talk because it gets easy then because people tell me things what I don't know and then I understand and tell others too.'

Pupils in Alder School said that it helped them *not* to talk. The reasons they gave were:

'It disturbs people when you talk.'
'Miss doesn't like a noise.'
'You waste time when you talk.'

It is clear that talking in these two situations is being perceived with completely opposing constructs. It would seem that pupils in CASE classes are being taught that talking can enhance learning. They are being encouraged to talk, explain and discuss with the purpose of verbalizing reasoning. In the non-CASE classes talking is seen as a distraction, an activity hampering learning.

In order to provide the best possible learning environment, teachers need to consider the value and place of verbalization in pupils' learning. Results would seem to indicate that pupils find talking a useful tool in the learning process. It could be that talking enables pupils to develop their thought processes and make learning more explicit.

### *Listening?*

The majority of pupils in Cherry and Willow Schools mentioned 'listening' as being helpful in learning and could give reasons. No pupil in Alder School mentioned this construct. If pupils are not explicitly helped to become aware of listening to one another in order to learn from one another are they losing a valuable opportunity for developing ideas and reasoning ability? One of the advantages of mixed-ability groups is that pupils are exposed to a greater variety of ideas. Explicit encouragement to listen to these ideas and use them as they work together to solve problems is an additional benefit to the learning process. Pupils' comments indicate that they do find sharing ideas useful, but the fact that pupils in Alder School do not mention listening implies that pupils need teachers to encourage listening in an explicit manner.

The PD associated with CASE devotes considerable time to helping teachers consider useful ways for developing metacognitive skills and encouraging pupils to express their reasoning processes. Evidence from these interviews suggests that pupils are more aware of behaviours helping them to learn and that this awareness is not simply confined to CASE lessons, but is transferred to numeracy lessons, and possibly to other areas of the curriculum also. Teachers report that pupils become more independent and use learning strategies more effectively in these classes than in Year 1 classes they had taught previously.

## Conclusions

The main purpose of this chapter is to examine Year 1 pupils' constructs of what helps them learn in numeracy and in CASE so as to inform teachers with a view to their providing a more effective learning environment. From the evidence gathered, it would seem that this method of eliciting information from Year 1 pupils yields constructs relating directly to learning. Eliciting pupils' constructs helps us to understand pupil learning and behaviour during numeracy and CASE lessons, as well as providing an opportunity to hear how pupils perceive learning taking place in these contexts and hearing aspects perceived by pupils as impacting on learning. It is my belief that this method yields insights into pupils' perceptions which, if taken into consideration, might lead to a more effective learning environment being provided for pupils.

During CASE lessons pupils are expected to express ideas, explanations and reasons, offer suggestions, agree and disagree with peers, ask questions and reflect on their learning processes. It seems that CASE pupils are able to express some important constructs derived from these processes and provide additional coherent explanations, and lesson transcripts confirm the origin of the constructs. Evidence suggests that pupils having had the experience of working in a CASE group for several months are more able to express how they construe the process of learning. It would appear that this particular type of learning environment enables pupils to make greater sense of their learning. The corollary is that pupils in turn will be more effective learners and, thus, attain more from their education.

# CREATING METACOGNITIVE EXPERIENCES FOR 5- AND 6-YEAR-OLD CHILDREN

## Shirley Larkin

### Theoretical background

Metacognition is a form of cognition, a second or higher level process. It involves both a knowledge of cognitive processing ('How am I thinking about this?') and a conscious control and monitoring of that processing ('Would it be better if I thought about this differently?'). A tension arises in the theory when metacognition is prescriptively described as an ability to abstract, to look down upon thought processes from a height or to go 'above and beyond' (Adey and Shayer 1994). This is the hypothetical, abstract thought-processing described by Piaget as 'reflected abstraction' (Piaget 1976); an aspect of formal operational thought. Developmentally formal operational thought occurs during adolescence, but may never be achieved even by adulthood. It involves being fully conscious of one's thoughts and able to verbalize them. Kuhn has made the connection between the development of metacognition and the development of an evaluative epistemology in which the individual recognizes that 'All opinions are not equal and knowing is understood as a process that entails judgement, evaluation and argument' (Kuhn 2000). Described in this way, metacognition involves a true reflection on thought. It can be ongoing with cognitive processing or a subsequent reflection on cognitive processing. Either way, it necessitates being able to hold in the mind different variables simultaneously – to think about how one is processing information whilst actually working on a task – and then to remember how one worked on a task in order to reflect upon it. The ability to hold different variables in the mind at different levels of abstraction develops with age.

However, the developing mind develops not in isolation, but within a social, cultural and linguistic environment. The need to explain and justify to others makes reflection on one's own thoughts and language necessary. In turn, becoming more metacognitive enables the learner to provide for herself the supporting and scaffolding role originally assigned to the adult or peer (Brown 1987; Moss 1990). The tension in the theoretical concept of metacognition arises from the description of metacognition as late developing, involving highly abstract thought-processing, when many researchers have described children as young as 4 years displaying metacognitive processing. Flavell's recent work shows that whilst age is a determining factor for degree of metacognitive knowledge, young children do have some knowledge of thought processes.

## Why is metacognition important for learning?

Metacognition involves self-regulation and reflection on learning. Becoming metacognitive necessitates an active involvement in the learning process. As Hartman says:

> Metacognition is especially important because it affects acquisition, comprehension, retention and application of what is learned, in addition to affecting learning efficiency, critical thinking and problem solving. Metacognitive awareness enables control or self-regulation over thinking and learning processes and products.
>
> (Hartman 1998: 1)

Empirical work by a number of researchers over the years has found positive correlation between metacognition and cognition. Swanson (1990) found that individuals with a high level of metacognitive processing outperformed those with lower metacognitive processing on problem-solving activities regardless of their overall general aptitude level. Research on reading shows that poor readers have poorer general metacognitive knowledge (Papetti et al. 1992). Lucangeli et al. (1994) trained students in metacognitive knowledge about memory and found that this increased performance not only on memory tasks but also in reading comprehension and problem-solving. Work with gifted children has also shown that they have a greater metacognitive attitude (Schwanenflugel et al. 1997). Other research has shown that people with higher metacognitive attitude are better at transferring skills and strategies from one domain to another (Cavanaugh and Borkowski 1980; Borkowski et al. 1983). Sternberg (1998) has noted that it is 'metacognition about strategies, rather than the strategies themselves, that appears to be essential'.

Metacognition cannot be seen as independent from other factors of the student, including ability, motivation and personality.

> A teacher's understanding of metacognition will probably be most useful if it is complemented by an understanding of these other aspects of students' functioning and of how they interact with metacognition.
>
> (Sternberg 1998: 128)

Whilst acknowledging the constructivist position that suggests repeated individual problem-solving can have as much impact on performance as collaborative problem-solving (Flavell and Wellman 1977; Kontos and Nicholas 1986;

Cornoldi 1998), I take the view that independence is difficult to define within an education setting and with this age group. Moreover, collaboration with peers and adults, resulting in practice in explaining one's thought processes and seeing things from another's point of view is important in encouraging metacognitive development.

## CASE and metacognition

The CASE@KS1 project as described in Chapter 2 seeks to aid the development of metacognition in 5- and 6-year-olds. It aims to sow the seeds of this level of cognitive processing. In order to do this, CASE lessons aim to provoke metacognitive experiences. Flavell described metacognitive experiences as more likely to occur in situations that 'stimulate a lot of careful, highly conscious thinking'; where the situation is novel and requires planning and evaluation; where decisions are weighty and risky; when the cognitive enterprise is in trouble; and when attention and memory are not distracted. Metacognitive experiences may be in the form of a feeling of being puzzled, or that you are still a long way from solving the problem, whilst others Flavell has described as 'items of metacognitive knowledge that have entered consciousness'. An example would be remembering a similar problem that you had successfully solved before. He goes on to describe metacognitive experiences as forming an overlapping set with metacognitive knowledge and having an important effect on both cognitive goals and strategies and metacognitive knowledge. Metacognitive experiences develop and revise the stored base of metacognitive knowledge and are important in its development (Flavell 1979). The CASE lessons, focused into 30-minute problem-solving tasks involving children collaborating with peers and their teacher, meet the requirements necessary for metacognitive experiences to occur.

The following examples of classroom observations show how metacognitive experiences can be provided and seek to untangle aspects of children being metacognitive from the complex interactions that make up a Year 1 classroom.

## Method

Observation of classroom data is only one aspect of a larger project concerned with the development of metacognition during the CASE intervention. In addition to the observations, pre- and post-intervention tests were carried out with 24 children from four of the experimental schools and with 18 children from three of the control schools. As children are grouped into six for the CASE project, seven groups were followed throughout the year. Classroom observations of CASE lessons were taken fortnightly and observations of non-CASE lessons in both the experimental and control schools were taken termly. The seven participating teachers were also interviewed at the beginning and end of the intervention year.

Observations of groups of children in classroom settings are obviously fraught with problems: the impact of the researcher on the participants and subsequent data; the level of background noise rendering some interactions inaudible; the frequent interruptions from other children, teachers and assistants; and the need of the teacher to be aware of the whole class whilst working with a group. The researcher sought as far as possible to be a non-participating observer, but felt obliged to respond when directly addressed by a child. As the year progressed however, the researcher found it easier to become part of the background. All observations were audio taped and field notes made. The tapes were then transcribed and a coding system developed.

## Coding

Initial readings of the transcribed observations showed that at this age (5–6 years) the majority of the interactions were between teacher and child/children. When the children interacted with each other they did so largely in terms of themselves, making statements beginning with 'I'. Questioning between children was also largely in the form of 'I' as in 'I don't understand what you are saying.' Based on these initial observations, a coding system was developed using two methods. First, the need to identify how metacognition is displayed in this age group led to a theory-based approach to code the student language and behaviour. The theory was derived from Flavell's description of the constituents of cognitive monitoring, being:

(1) metacognitive knowledge, which is further broken down into (a) person, (b) task and (c) strategy variables;
(2) metacognitive experiences;
(3) goals/tasks; and
(4) actions/strategies (Flavell 1979).

Flavell suggests that it is the interactions between these constituents that provide for monitoring of cognition. The categories obviously overlap, for instance a metacognitive strategy aimed at the metacognitive goal of assessing one's own knowledge may also lead to the cognitive goal of better understanding. Thus, it can be difficult to analyse these constituents as discreet entities theoretically. However, when coding actual data, subsequent actions can give clues to whether the verbalized report relates to a cognitive or metacognitive act. Since the observation data here is in the most part verbal (although field notes were made about non-verbal behaviours), it is very difficult to code for metacognitive experience as this is an internal state experienced by the subject and unless it is verbalized or displayed obviously in some other way it is difficult to detect. Even non-verbal clues, such as a look of puzzlement, may not refer to the internal state of the subject about the cognitive enterprise, but may be due to some other affective factor. With these limitations in mind a coding system (see Table 5.1) was devised, based on the theory, to code student language which could be described as metacognitive.

**Table 5.1** Coding of student behaviours for metacognition

*Metacognitive knowledge (1)*

| Code | Explanation | Example |
|------|-------------|---------|
| *Person variable (a)*: | | |
| SELF | Shows knowledge of self in relation to cognition and/or predicts from this | 'I know what to do' 'Oh I love hard work' 'I've got an idea in my head' |
| OTH | Refers to what others may think/desire | 'She doesn't know' 'He doesn't want to be last' |
| UNIV | Refers to universals of cognition | 'We've got to solve a problem' |
| *Task variable (b)*: | | |
| UND | Questions task information and/or seeks clarification | 'Something is missing' |
| PRED | Predicts success/failure | 'We'd be done in a minute' |
| RAT | Rating: refers to ease/difficulty of task | 'It's so hard my head might explode' |
| COMP | Compares with other tasks | 'This is like when we made stairs' |
| *Strategy variable (c)*: | | |
| EVA | Evaluates: indicates knowledge about what might be useful | 'We should build up the boxes' 'That's the quickest way to do it' |
| PLAN | Refers to planning how to do the task | 'We need to know which way to go round the table' 'We should talk about it together' |

*Metacognitive strategies/actions (4)*

| Code | Explanation | Example |
|------|-------------|---------|
| PAR | Paraphrases to confirm understanding | 'Did you mean . . .' |
| SQU | Asks questions of self | 'Is that right'* |
| CHE | Checks work | 'This one's good, this one's not'** |

*Notes:*
\* Asking questions of self is a difficult category for this age group. Often it is not verbalized, however subsequent behaviour can give a clue to where this has happened, such as in a sequencing activity involving putting story cards together:
    '*Case lesson observation School D 26 January 2000*
    128 Ab: [relates what is on each picture, but there is no real sequence so the pictures cannot be connected in any meaningful way. After a long pause during which time she looks at all the pictures, she moves putting on clothes picture to end of line]
    129 Ch: [moves putting on clothes picture to beginning of line] Cos she gets up in the morning and puts on her clothes.
We can assume that both children have asked themselves whether the sequence of pictures is correct. In Ab's case this is indicated by the 'thinking time' before she moves the pictures. In Ch's case it is indicated by his spontaneous explanation.
\*\* Checks work can be both a cognitive and a metacognitive strategy. Again this is often not verbalized but is shown in behaviour.

**Table 5.2** Coding of teacher behaviours which appear to influence metacognitive processing in students

| Code | Explanation | Example |
|------|-------------|---------|
| TS | Refers to self-learning strategies | 'What could you do if you've got problems?' |
| TK | Questions acquisition of knowledge | 'How do you know that?' |
| TI | Teacher prompts regarding information provided | 'We found the biggest, what else could we do?' |
| TE | Teacher aids explanations | 'X explained putting the biggest to smallest very well' |
| TQ | Teacher questions/comments on strategies | 'How are you putting them in order?' |
| TP | Teacher asks for predictions of success | 'Will this make it easier?' |
| TL | Teacher shows expectations of planning | 'How are we going to do this, what do we need to think about?' |
| TO | Teacher expects checking | 'Check what you are counting in' |
| TC | Teacher refers to own cognitive processes | 'I don't understand it either' |
| TT | Teacher refers to thinking | 'Let's put on our thinking caps' |
| TU | Teacher refers to universals of cognition | 'We are learning how to solve problems' |

In addition to trying to describe metacognition in this age group, it is necessary to code the interactions between the teacher and student to attempt a description of what it is in those interactions that leads to metacognitive processing. For this analysis a coding system (see Table 5.2) was derived directly from the data using a grounded theory approach to categorize the teacher behaviours.

The following examples are taken from the second half of the intervention year, so in the experimental schools (for example 1 and 2) the children have now had quite a lot of experience in working together on CASE activities.

### Example 1: CASE activity clowns School A

There are six children involved in this activity – four boys and two girls. The activity is about dressing a clown whilst following a rule about what he can wear. In this excerpt each child has a clown. In the centre of the table are sets of clothes such as hats, shoes and trousers in different colours. These children used this equipment some weeks earlier with a different rule for how the clowns could be dressed. The cognitive conflict in this task usually comes from choosing and swapping items of clothing, ensuring that the children work collaboratively so that all members of the group end up with a completed clown. However, in this lesson the teacher begins the task by expecting the children to think about what is required and how they might achieve this. This excerpt comes after a period of concrete preparation when the children have familiarized themselves with items of clothing, asking questions of each other and all choosing one item which has to be different from that chosen by anyone else in the group.

| | | |
|---|---|---|
| 34. | *T:* Today we're going to dress our clown and he's going to have | |
| 35. | a different colour for each bit of his clothing except for his | |
| 36. | gloves and his shoes. Before we start, can anyone think of | TT |
| 37. | any ideas of how we are going to organize this, how we are | TL |
| 38. | going to do it. Before we start, what might we need to think | TT |
| 39. | about? Ja what do you think we're going to have to think about? | |
| 40. | *Ja:* Taking turns round the table, first B takes his turn, then Y, then | |
| 41. | O, then J, then M, then me. | PLA |
| 42. | *T:* That's very organized. | |
| 43. | *B:* It won't be very easy though going round cos you might not know | EVA |
| 44. | who's after you and you will need the order. | |
| 45. | *O:* I think we should pick the same colour and do different clothings. | PLA/EVA |
| 46. | *T:* Oh! | |
| 47. | *O:* Cos then we will be able to pick all the colours really easily. | EVA |
| 48. | *T:* What does anyone think [teacher moves Y to another chair]? | |
| 49. | Now we've got two different ideas, we've got Ja and B's idea | |
| 50. | of all taking turns, what was the other idea M? | TQ |
| 51. | *M:* Er, do same colours, I think we should do the same colours | |
| 52. | because then it wouldn't be as tricky as it was before. | COMP/EVA |
| 53. | *J:* It would be really really easy, we'd be done in a minute. | PRED |
| 54. | *M:* Yes, we'd be done in a minute. | |
| 55. | *J:* And then we could just sit here. | |
| 56. | *Ja:* And wait five hours. | |
| 57. | *T:* Maybe we could do both ways? | TI |
| 58. | *O:* How can we do that? | UND |

59. *B*: Yeah, I know some could take same colours and
    some different                      EVA
60.     colours then it would work.                PRED

*Analysis*

In lines 36–39 the teacher frequently refers to thinking. She asks a particularly interesting question of Ja: 'What do you think we're going to have to think about?' This enables the child to shift his point of view from how he would do the task as an individual to how the task could be done as a group. He presents a strategy which is then evaluated by another child, B (line 43), who goes on to explain why the strategy may not work. The teacher does not question this, but allows a third child, O, to present and explain another strategy and to evaluate for himself how successful that might be. The teacher then facilitates the collaborative process by bringing in other children who have not yet spoken: 'What does anyone think'. She points out that there is more than one way of organizing this task (line 49). This gives child M the chance to express her thoughts, which she does by evaluating the strategy she prefers in the light of her past experience with the equipment. Lines 51–2: 'I think we should do the same colours because then it wouldn't be as tricky as it was before.' Towards the end of the activity (not shown in the excerpt above), this same child refers again to her past experience as she evaluates the success and failure of the strategies used.

188. *T*: Why do you think it helps [referring to the strategy they have used]?
189. *M*: Because we didn't have too much muddling, last time we had seven hundred per cent muddling.

In the example 1 excerpt M's evaluation is reaffirmed not by the teacher, but by another child, Ja (line 53). As the conversation begins to tail off, the teacher prompts by giving her own idea to use both strategies (line 57). Child O is puzzled by the suggestion, but does not sit in silence, he asks for clarification and this is given by child B who feels he understands and predicts success for his idea (line 60).

This excerpt continues with the children planning and discussing how they will attempt the task before starting it. The teacher occasionally reminds them of the rule 'not the same colours', but otherwise rarely intervenes. The children evaluate each other's ideas. They are expected to think for themselves, but also to think about how they can achieve the task as a group. Throughout this excerpt and in the rest of the lesson the teacher in combination with the activity is providing a metacognitive experience for the children. She does this not by continuous questioning, but by herself becoming part of the group. She allows the children to sort out their own ideas in a supportive atmosphere:

36/37. *T*: Can anyone think of any ideas?
48.    *T*: What does anyone think?

The teacher refers to thought processes in a naturalistic way. She indicates she is listening without judging.

46. *T*: Oh!

She adds her own idea for evaluation:

57. *T*: Maybe we can do both ways?

She allows the children time to think. Her focus in this excerpt is on planning, generating ideas, evaluating and explaining to others rather than on completion of the task. In a relatively short excerpt the quality of the interactions is high, the children are enthusiastic and committed to the task. They are engaged in metacognitive processing, reflecting on their own and others' ideas and evaluating their own understanding.

### Example 2: numeracy lesson School A

This example follows the guidelines of the numeracy hour with whole-class teaching on the carpet followed by children sitting in groups but working individually with worksheets and then a plenary session for the whole class at the end. Because of this format, short excerpts have been extracted from each part of the lesson.

*Excerpt 1: whole-class teaching*

| | | |
|---|---|---|
| 34. *T*: | Now I'm going to try and trick you, you have to use your | |
| 35. | brains and tell me what I'm counting in and how many I've | TT |
| 36. | counted [T counts silently by showing fingers firstly in 2s | |
| 37. | and counts up to 6]. | |
| 38. | [Children put up hands to answer.] | |
| 39. *T*: | [Does same counting in 10s.] | |
| 40. *D*: | Six. | |
| 41. *T*: | Is it six? Watch again. | |
| 42. *D*: | Three. | |
| 43. *T*: | What am I counting in? | |
| 44. *S*: | Tens. | |
| 45. *T*: | Right, why did D get it wrong? | TQ |
| 46. *S*: | He's not thinking. | OTH |
| 47. *L*: | He's not counting on. | EVA/OTH |
| 48. *S*: | He's not counting in 10s. | EVA/OTH |
| 49. *T*: | Yes, I was counting in 10s and so the answer was 30 not 3. | |

*Analysis*

In this excerpt the teacher begins by referring to thinking, and indicates the reason for using 'your brains' (line 35), is so that they do not get tricked. At line 45 she asks the children to take on another's point of view and to explain the lack of success. The answers are interesting. The first child, S, picks up on the importance of thinking – this must be D's reason for failure (line 46). Whereas the second child refers to a failure to use the correct strategy (line 47). The first child, S, then changes her own idea, it might be a lack of strategy rather than lack of thought that causes failure and she adds her own idea (line 48): 'He's not counting in 10s.' The teacher confirms that she agrees and explains why: 'I was counting in 10s.' The children are being asked to reflect on someone else's failure and to suggest alternative strategies that may be more successful. The children S and L have the metacognitive experience of feeling they know why child D failed.

*Excerpt 2*
As the teacher sets up the children to work in groups, she asks them to reflect on the task in hand.
49. *T*: Good. That's what I'm asking you to do this morning.
50.    Use what you know about counting in 2s, 5s, 10s. Check   TO
51.    what you are counting in.
52. *T*: [Explains worksheets, same as board questions.]
53. *T*: What is the first thing you have to do?
54. *S*: Put date and name.
55. *W*: Start work.
56. *K*: Don't know.
57. *T*: Check what you're counting in. I've got 2ps here. What   TO
58.    should I be counting in?
59. *A*: 2s.
60. *T*: [Repeats this with 10ps.] [Goes through first, for example on worksheet.]
61. *T*: [Asks K to explain to the class what they have to do first.]   TE
62. *K*: Put date and name, know what you're counting in and
63.    then put answer in the box.
64. *T*: What could you do if you've got problems?   TS
65. *P*: Ask teacher.   EVA
66. *N*: Use number squares.   EVA
67. *C*: Put hand up.   EVA
68. *Kr*: Use hand prints [on wall showing counting in 5s].   EVA
69. *T*: Any questions before we begin?

*Analysis*
In this excerpt the teacher begins by referring to stored knowledge and to checking (lines 50–1) and then seeks confirmation that the children have understood (line 53): 'What is the first thing you have to do?' She allows the three children, S, W and K, to have different ideas or to indicate lack of understanding without judgement (lines 54–6). At line 64 she is seeking self-learning strategies and whilst one child, P, refers to asking the teacher,

the other two provide self-learning strategies. At line 69 the children are given the chance to check their understanding of the task and seek clarification before they begin.

*Excerpt 3: towards the end of the lesson*
  93. *T*:  [Tells everyone to return to carpet.]
  94. *T*:  What did you find hard?
  95. *J*:  I tried [then tails off into silence].
  96. *D*:  I tried to work it out.
  97. *T*:  There were a lot of answers wrong because you
  98.       didn't check what you were counting in.          TO
  99. *Ch*: The first one was hard for me there were          RAT
  100.      too many pennies for me.                          SELF
  101. *T*:  Did you do it?
  102. *Ch*: The answer was 12.

*Analysis*
In this plenary session the teacher follows the numeracy-hour convention of asking children to reflect on the ease or difficulty of the task. She refers again to checking. This repetition from the beginning of the lesson indicates the importance this teacher places on checking for oneself. At lines 99–100 Ch's answer is interesting, as he reflects on his own performance and shows knowledge of his own cognition, indicating that he knows why he found it difficult: 'There were too many pennies for me.'

## Example 3: numeracy lesson in Control School X 19.6.00 9.30am–10.25am

This lesson has been chosen for comparison because it shows more attempts by the teacher to facilitate metacognition than do the other control school observations. However, I will argue later that there are qualitative differences between this lesson and the other two examples above. Again three excerpts have been chosen because of the format of the lesson.

*Excerpt 1*
  1. *T*:  Now get your thinking thumbs ready. [Children stick up
           a thumb.]                                          TT
  2.       I want you to put up your thinking thumb if you can
           tell me
  3.       what is 2 more than this [T shows a card with 4 on it].
  4.       Children put up their thumbs. Teacher chooses a child
           in each case.]
  5. *Ja*: 5.
  6. *T*:  What did you do Ja?                                TQ
  7. *X*:  She added one.
  8. *T*:  What is one more than [holds card with 1 on it]?
  9. *D*:  One more than one is 2.

10. *T*:  Two more than [card with 5 on it]?
11. *Do*:  5.
12. *T*:  [Repeats question.]
13. *Do*:  7.
14. *T*:  10 more than [card with 6 on it]?
15. *M*:  16.
16. *X*:  That's easy.                                                    RAT
17. *T*:  How did you do it?                                              TQ
18. *M*:  I added it in my head.
19. *T*:  10 more than [card with 17 on it]?

*Analysis*

In this first excerpt of whole-class teaching the teacher refers to thinking in terms of 'thinking thumbs', she does not refer to thinking as an abstract term or give reasons for thinking. At line 16 child X refers to finding the sum easy, although it was not his question to answer. The teacher does not question his assumption that the sums are easy, but asks the child who got the sum correct for the strategy used (line 17): 'How did you do it?' When the child responds with her strategy, 'I added it in my head', the teacher passes on without comment. The lesson proceeds with the children calculating more sums.

*Excerpt 2*

This takes place on the carpet a little while later and has been chosen because of the frequency of more metacognitive type questioning here than in other parts of the lesson. The children are asked to join three paper coins on the board and total them.

43. *T*:  We are sitting beautifully this morning.
44.       [M joins up 20, 20 and 10.]
45.       [Class shout out 50p.]
46. *T*:  How did M add up his coins?                                     TQ
47. *Lo*:  He added up 20, 20 and 10.
48. *T*:  Can you do it any other way or was that the quickest
          way?                                                           TQ
49. *Lo*:  That's the quickest way, then you don't need to go 10,
          20, 30, 40, 50.                                               EVA
50. *T*:  Why did M choose 20 first?                                     TQ
51. *Lo*:  Because it's the biggest coin first.                          EVA
52. *T*:  Yes, and that's a good way to add coins, the biggest first
          then the smallest.                                            TE
53. *Lo*:  I know . . . [he is ignored and his sentence tails off].      SELF
54. *La*:  [Joins up 1p, 2p 1p] 4p.
55. *T*:  How did you add it up?                                         TQ
56. *La*:  2 plus 1 plus 1.

*Analysis*

At line 46 the teacher asks for a child to explain from another's point of view and picks up the answer with a question designed to evaluate the strategy (line 48): 'Can you do it any other way or was that the quickest way?' By asking this double question, the teacher in effect gives the answer and the child, Lo, repeats this (line 49). At line 52 the teacher herself evaluates the strategy, when Lo wishes to add his own idea 'I know' (line 53) he is ignored and the teacher continues with the task.

Following the excerpt, the children go to their groups and have to draw around coins and then join up three, putting the total into a grid at the bottom of their worksheets. They are supposed to work in pairs, but in reality this means that they take turns at doing the task, drawing the coins, joining them up and totalling them. The teacher occasionally visits each table and asks individuals how they made a total. The children respond with '20 + 20 + 10', and so on.

This third excerpt is from the plenary session when the teacher asks individuals from each table to explain what they have done.

*Excerpt 3*

| | | | |
|---|---|---|---|
| 147. | *T*: | What is the smallest you have made? | |
| 148. | *Th*: | Smallest, 4p. | |
| 149. | *T*: | How did you make it? | TQ |
| 150. | *Th*: | 1, 2 and 1. | |
| 151. | *T*: | Did anyone make anything smaller? | |
| 152. | *Lo*: | 3p. 1, 1 and 1. | |
| 153. | *T*: | What about the group over here, what was your largest amount? | |
| 154. | *To*: | £2.05. | |
| 155. | *El*: | £2.05. | |
| 156. | *To*: | £3.00. | |
| 157. | *Ma*: | £1 and £1 and 5p. | |
| 158. | *T*: | Yes, you had the pound coins over here, didn't you? | |
| 159. | | [L and J are still drawing their grid during this time and continuing to do the work.] | |
| 160. | *T*: | El, how did you make your largest amount? | TQ |
| 161. | | [El has trouble describing how she did it.] | |
| 162. | | [L and J have made a very good grid working collaboratively.] | |
| 163. | *T*: | We will have to finish there for now. | |
| 164. | | [Ends 10.25am] | |

*Analysis*

Whilst this session of a numeracy-hour lesson is where we would expect to find the metacognitive reflection taking place, it is obvious from this transcript that this does not always happen. Whilst the teacher does ask 'How' at line 149, referring to a strategy, the child responds 'mechanically' (line 150) with '1, 2 and 1.' Whilst this format of child doing the sum and the teacher asking how it was done, has been repeated throughout the lesson, the teacher does not go any further and accepts a simplistic answer, thus a possible metacognitive experience, where the child would have to really reflect on their thinking, is lost.

## Discussion

From the three examples of classroom activities shown above it is clear that the CASE lesson (Example 1 clowns) and to a lesser extent the CASE school numeracy lesson (Example 2) include more metacognitive activity and activity of a qualitatively different kind than does the control school numeracy lesson (Example 3). In the CASE lesson the teacher engages the children in planning and evaluating strategies, and in thinking about thinking. She asks the metacognitive question 'What do you think we're going to have to think about?' She is providing the important role of posing the questions that students will eventually need to ask of themselves when confronted with a problem to solve. The CASE activity provides the framework for this type of questioning; the emphasis is on communication, collaborative working and the process of problem solving rather than the final outcome. Example 2 of a CASE teacher in a numeracy lesson also shows examples of facilitation of metacognition. Here the teacher refers to thinking; she asks the children to reflect on the task and to generate self-learning strategies. She engages the children in thinking about the problems they may encounter and strategies for dealing with them and concludes with the children's reflection on their thoughts regarding the difficulty of the task. In both examples references to metacognitive processing run throughout the lesson. They are not tagged on at the end as a period of reflection. It can be very difficult for children of this age (5–6 years) to reflect retrospectively.

The third example from a control school class follows the conventions of the numeracy hour. The example was chosen because it displayed more attempts at facilitating metacognition than other control school observations. Certainly the teacher speaks of thinking, but here it is reduced to 'thinking thumbs'. She asks students to evaluate strategies, but does not continue the process in any depth, although the children are responding in a 'thinking way'. Her concern is with successful calculation of number rather than the process of problem solving. This is not to disparage the teacher, rather the context within which she is working puts metacognitive processing to the end of the lesson as a means of reflecting on what has been learnt. This is difficult for the children not only in terms of memory capacity, but also affectively: young children tire quickly after an hour of cognitive activity especially when the playground beckons. The teacher too often runs out of time and it is very difficult to achieve any meaningful reflection in the last few minutes when distractions abound.

An important aspect of the CASE intervention is the teachers' ability to model a language of learning. Without a shared communication which responds to the children's attempts to explain their thinking and which encourages them to explore their thinking within the group, any metacognitive development will be left within the individual and may have a negative effect. Nuthall has suggested that the learning process is 'deeply embedded in, or [is], in fact part of the sociocultural processes and structures of the classroom' (Nuthall 1999: 244). How children view school and learning will impact upon their ability to adapt to a more metacognitive classroom. Some teachers have found that introducing metacognitive experiences into the classroom can be met with hostility as preconceptions of teaching and learning are challenged. Providing metacognitive experiences then, has to also challenge the dominant ideas of the nature of learning. Teachers, teacher trainers and wider society need to become more metacognitive, reflecting and questioning ourselves on the best ways to promote metacognitive development in children.

The CASE@KS1 project working with young children has the means to redefine learning and to create metacognitive experiences from an early age. This chapter has given one method of describing the interactions which facilitate metacognition. It provides evidence even in these short extracts of metacognitive awareness in children of 5 and 6 years old. If self-regulated learning is a goal of education, then providing metacognitive experiences to aid the development of metacognitive processing seems to be a good way to achieve this. In creating metacognitive experiences for young children, the seeds of this future development are sown.

## 6 PUPILS' COMMUNICATION AND PERCEPTIONS OF GROUP WORK IN COGNITIVE INTERVENTION ACTIVITIES

## Kevin Wall

### Introduction

This chapter focuses on work that has used the context of the CASE@KS1 Project to explore a little-researched aspect of English primary school classroom practice, namely the gestural and verbal actions and interactions among 5- to 6-year-olds and their teachers during group work. A series of reviews over the last three decades (Blurton-Jones 1973; Woolfolk and Brooks 1983; McNeil 1995) has identified the need to move away from laboratory-based investigations of children and teacher's gestural behaviours, which have tended to focus on interactions between pairs of individuals during a range of learning tasks, towards a more realistic examination of interactions among children and their teachers in ordinary classrooms. The approach described in this chapter uses novel, non-video based, methods to explore the nature of these interactions.

The chapter is organized in four sections. The first seeks to define verbal and gestural communication in terms of social skills. The second looks, qualitatively, at the gestural and verbal aspects of the study informed by the use of two examples. The third section looks at pupil comments about group work, and is followed by a concluding section which draws from our wider study to comment on the results and to suggest possible implications for teachers' classroom practice.

### Communication and social skills

When children and adults interact with each other in a classroom context, various interpersonal modes can be seen in action. The most obvious is the verbal mode which involves the exchange of words between participants with an assumption of shared meanings. In a classroom context the majority of these words are already known and understood by the teacher whereas they are *being learnt* and understood by the pupils. A second mode is that afforded by the exchange of gestures, be they facial expressions, postural changes, hand gestures or variation in the pattern of words in speech through the use of emphasis, pause and intonation. While speech uses the auditory channel, gesture uses predominantly the visual channel, so 'communication' can be seen as the sum of these two modes of signalling as they interact one with the other.

There is an evident structuring of verbal interactions between people in the sense that turns at speaking are taken and opportunities for intervention are offered, or blocked. This structuring occurs as speakers actually interact; it is in a real sense 'talk in interaction' as suggested by Schegloff (1991). These skills seem to develop with experience and maturity. Different contexts seem to offer different opportunities for patterns of action, so that interactions face-to-face might be different from those on the telephone, but they retain many common aspects. These have been theorized by Grice (1975), for example, in terms of the 'co-operative principle' which implies that there are mutually accepted rules of conversation. They may, however, also differ depending on the environment in which they occur. Those in a person's home involving a friend are more obviously 'conversational' than those in a doctor's surgery or in a classroom, reflecting their different intentions. Purpose as well as context then, may also affect the way any interaction occurs and develops.

For 5- to 6-year-olds, gesture may arguably take on greater significance than amongst adults as they are still developing the breadth of vocabulary needed to express what they want to say and, at the same time, the gestural elements of speech – intonation, pause and so on – that allow full communication. The primary classroom constitutes an institutional setting in the sense that rules of action, both explicit and implicit, exist which are used to structure and permission particular forms of interaction (the 'educational ground rules' suggested by Edwards and Mercer 1987). We do not usually put our hands up to gain permission to speak at home, but we might do so in a debate, public meeting or classroom if we are in the role of student. These 'ground rules' are imposed by those organizing the institution to allow it to achieve its institutional objectives – in this instance, raising a hand to speak allowing interaction with a large number of pupils so that what is being said can be heard.

When children are grouped for a particular activity, the potential for interaction is presumably greater, particularly if they are working on a task that *requires* interpersonal communication in the form of questioning or listening to one another (see, for example, Johnson and Johnson 1979, 1994). One might also anticipate that the nature of both verbal and gestural actions might change when a teacher not only joins the group of pupils in question, but also takes an active part in the group's activities. If the teacher is leading the group (perhaps by explaining the tasks or 'refereeing' a discussion), those interactions might well be different again. In such a context the capacity of individual children to participate in the group's activity could relate to their current social communication skills as well as their underlying cognitive development. From a pedagogic point of view, one might ask about the way children and teachers engage socially in such contexts and whether there are particular behaviours, manifested gesturally by children that may be of use to teachers as they work with groups of children. Such patterns of behaviour might alert teachers to particular learning needs on the part of the children, or alternatively, particular behaviours evinced by the teacher in a group context, which may compromise the group and thus the pupils' ability to work and learn effectively.

Multimodal approaches to human communication involve a number of assumptions. One is that others exist externally to ourselves in a concrete reality and act independently of us but must also be interacted *with* if their intentions and purposes are to be understood. This understanding develops over time and is apparent in children's very early development. It also implies that the external 'other' is conscious and can understand what we mean through our various communication signals; that is, that there is some common understanding that allows meanings to be accessed and, in the context of those perceived meanings, actions to be taken. Again, these meanings develop over time from the shared understanding between primary carer and very young baby (see, for example, the review by Argyle 1991) to those of the classroom teacher and primary pupil as evidenced when the pupil puts their hand up to give a response or initiate an intervention. It is likely that this may vary between individuals as they develop at different rates. In a teacher-led group, for example, the teacher might have a significant role in the organizing of social interaction, both as a personal model for the children involved and as a moderator of the behaviours of other group members as they interact with each other; the teacher's response to a particular act providing a marker of approval or disapproval for that behaviour being adopted by others in the group. Within a typical CASE activity the teacher serves as an organizer, monitor, analyser, approver and editor of the group's interactions as she moves the group through its task. The CASE activities seek to develop analytical and interactive skills (listening, asking pertinent questions and so on) that could allow the teacher's role to diminish in this respect over time as the pupils concerned become more competent.

How might this implicit emphasis on communicative aspects relate to social communication skills? There is very little in the literature relating to this issue that focuses on groups of 5- to 6-year-olds, but Hargie et al. (1994: 2–4), using previous work based on adults, have discussed the notion of social skills as involving six separate but interacting components:

1 Their goal relatedness, which at some level is directed towards the achievement of a particular purpose.

2 The interrelatedness of behaviours organized in a synchronized way to achieve the goal in question.

3 The matching of interactional processes and strategies to the environment in which the interaction takes place.

4 That social skills are based on definable 'units' of behaviour which, when organized into particular patterns or sequences, can lead to a particular end.

5 That such social skills are learned. One form of learning is through an imitative modelling of actions which have been experienced or have been seen enacted by others which are then imported into the individual's own repertoire of behaviours. Bandura (1986) has suggested that such processes underlie all learnt behaviours. The 'models' in question are those around a person. Their observed behaviours act as models, particularly where the other person praises a particular action. This implies that feedback on behavioural performance is crucial if behaviour is to be established successfully. This is apparent in the pedagogic practice of praising approved actions.

6 The last strand to the social skill concept is that the behaviours displayed are in some sense under the control of the individual. One might suggest that performing appropriate social actions in a particular classroom relies on knowing, through learning, what *is* appropriate in that classroom. This in turn implies the need for an induction into locally accepted communicative practices. What then are the gestural and verbal actions that constitute the 'educational ground rules' for intra-group actions between teacher and pupils in this context and what are their implications for teacher pedagogy?

## Sample and methods

My overall study has involved 72 pupils and 6 teachers drawn from 4 schools and 6 classes participating in the CASE project proper, described in Chapter 2. The approach adopted has meant that groups of children with and without their teacher as a group member were compared. CASE intervention schools provided the teacher-led groups, while the non-CASE schools provided the teacher-less groups. Within each class, two groups of up to six pupils were observed over a 6-month period on up to four occasions each.

The study took place in two phases: a one-term pilot phase followed by two terms of observations using a range of techniques. Lessons observed in the non-CASE schools all followed a similar pattern in that they involved a teacher introduction, a discussion of aspects of the task, exchanges of questions and recapping of what was to be done and why and then a group activity task of between 8 and 15 minutes, during which time the teacher circulated around the various groups. This was followed by a debriefing activity in which re-capitulation of the activities and their results took place and their meanings reviewed. In contrast, the CASE activities, which typically took between 20 and 40 minutes, superficially exhibited the same structure but *within* the specific activities and employed the CASE approach. These took place in the group as they were sitting around a table rather than to the whole class on the carpet (as in the non-CASE schools). In addition to their classroom teacher, all of whom were female, all the classes in the study had a range of other adults present in the classroom on a routine support basis, focusing on language, special needs, ICT and reading support. The teacher and pupil interviews indicated that the author quickly came to be viewed as another adult who was helping in the classroom. All observations and interviews were tape recorded. Additional background information was recorded in structured field notes and post-lesson audio-taped comments.

Following the start of the lesson, participant observation of the group activity took place using a range of observation techniques. The first involved the structured observation of gestural actions focusing on facial gestures, expression, posture and movement across an observer-memorized array of 40 specific behaviours, themselves based on those observed during the pilot phase. To simplify the observation procedure a particular gestural and postural position was used as a default; only departures from it were recorded, so, for example, a neutral facial expression was used as the default, meaning that only smiles or frowns were recorded in that dimension of the observation protocol.

An audio-taped warning fed via an earpiece to the observer at 20-second intervals prompted each observation cycle. Each person in the group was surveyed in turn through the 20-second period and the observations subvocalized and recorded onto a second audio tape, via an ear-mounted microphone. A third audio tape simultaneously recorded the verbal interactions within the group during the same period. The different recording sources were time synchronized through the use of fixed, start/stop signals and consistent recording and playback speeds. The other pupils in the class continued with their assigned work. Thus the observations were as naturalistic as possible, although they only represent a structured sampling of the participants' total actions.

A second approach was aimed at validating my interpretation of participant's facial gestures and involved participants doing three very short activities. The first asked participants to produce expressions on their own faces relating to particular affective states, initiated by key words such as happy, sad and so on. The second involved examining a series of publicly available, multi-ethnic, black and white photographs of children at or near to the participants' own ages, each picture showing a particular facial expression. The choice of photographs and their interpretation as exhibiting particular types of expression were characterized by reference to work on facial gestures (particularly that of Ekman and O'Sullivan (1991: 163–99) and by using a pilot group of children as additional gestural referees. Teachers completed the same activities. Comments from a sample of 30 teachers of various sexes and ethnicities further supported the teacher interpretations. Pupil and teacher interpretations were consistent with those of the observer and the existing literature. The third activity involved both groups of participants being asked if they could say what the expression shown in a photograph might indicate about what the person was thinking or feeling. All the instruments involved were kept as short as possible to minimize concentration issues. These picture activities served to corroborate that:

1 the expressions the observer was identifying on the participants' faces were ones that had some meaning for them;
2 the participants were capable, physically, of making the expressions themselves;
3 the expressions were part of their repertoire even if individuals did not produce them during observations;
4 participants could recognize similar expressions in others and could infer a mutually comprehensible meaning; and
5 there was consistency of identification and attribution of meaning to particular expressions between observer and observed.

The audio tapes of the gestural observations were transcribed using a visual code and represented diagrammatically as a sequence of 'frames' over time, each frame representing a 'bird's-eye' view of the group as it was working. This captured the spatial arrangement of the pupils in their group whilst allowing the focus of particular actions to be recorded and displayed. They were then scored to allow analysis at three levels: first, who interacted with whom and the nature of the interaction; second, the frequency of particular actions and whether it changed as observations were subsequently repeated later in the year; and third, whether there were sequences of interactions that represented stable patterns of behaviour that transcended particular tasks. These latter two levels will be referred to only briefly in this chapter.

## Results and analysis

Frequency figures for particular categories of interaction were expressed as a percentage of an individual's total sampled actions throughout the task. To help analyse the spatial relationships between participants and their pattern of interactions, a form of block diagram was used like that shown in Figure 6.1. The blocks for each participant could also be arranged in a group to support the analysis of the spatial and proximity aspects of their actions.

The recordings of verbal behaviours were transcribed using the methods of conversation analysis (Sacks et al. 1974; Sacks 1995; Hutchby and Wooffitt 1998) and the two transcriptions, gestural and verbal, then combined using a common timeline for detailed analysis. Limitations of space allow me to give an illustrative account of only two observations arising from the gestural action data: one from a CASE group and the other from a non-CASE group. In reviewing the results, three issues need to be borne in mind: first that the teacher needed to give explanatory information about the 'rules of the game' being played (many of the pupils were only just beginning to

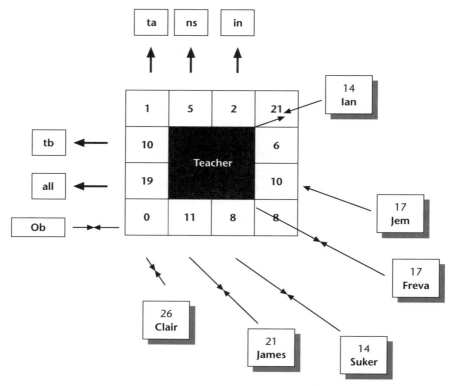

**Figure 6.1** Block diagram showing teacher's pattern of interactions and their relationship to the relative position of pupils during the activity
*Notes:*
Abbreviations:
   **all** an action initiated by an individual and directed at the whole group;
   **ob** an action of any type initiated by an individual towards the observer;
   **ta** an action in which the individual turned away from the task, excluding a turn towards the observer;
   **tb** an action initiated by an individual and involving task materials;
   **in** an action initiated by an individual which disrupted the group's activity;
   **ns** an action initiated by an individual but not apparently aimed at any specific individual.
All figures show a particular category of interaction as a rounded-up percentage of an individual's total interactions.
Pupil boxes show position relative to teacher and each other and the percentage of their actions directed at the teacher.

read); second, the nature of the task itself and the extent to which it required participants to offer views in a structured way ('one turn after another') or in an unstructured way ('make a contribution when you want to'); and, third, the need for participants to work with particular combinations of partners at specific stages of the task. CASE teacher interviews revealed these as features to be considered in the planning of their interpretation of the activities. These aspects were barely alluded to by the non-CASE teachers. These organizational aspects may also structure the types of participation in which the children could engage. The teacher interviews suggest that whilst they considered the verbal aspects very carefully, they gave little conscious regard to their gestural behaviours or the impact that these might have on the group.

Direct questioning by the teacher, within the group, may have cut across the usual turn-taking structure of interactions by *requiring* a contribution, possibly out of the perceived turn or when a particular participant was not anticipating answering at that time. These *within* context aspects might also be associated with *between* tasks aspects, arising from pupil-perceived differences in the organization of successive tasks and the extent to which they learnt from previous experience about how to work in each task context.

Two examples will inform the general discussion that follows. The first was a CASE task (Activity 15, Adey et al. 2001) based around the classification of animals. The second was a teacher-produced task on a similar theme relating to the differences between living and non-living things. Table 6.1 shows the percentage of an individual's total sampled actions directed at another particular individual for the CASE group in question, and Table 6.2 shows the actions directed at other targets, expressed in the same terms, also for the

**Table 6.1**   Matrix of interactions between individuals as a rounded-up percentage of their total sampled interactions (CASE activity)

|  | Participant | | | | | | |
|---|---|---|---|---|---|---|---|
|  | *Teacher* | *Ian* | *Jem* | *Freya* | *Suker* | *James 1* | *Claire* |
| Teacher | 0 | 21 | 6 | 10 | 8 | 8 | 11 |
| Ian | 14 | 0 | 3 | 3 | 4 | 1 | 3 |
| Jem | 17 | 7 | 0 | 7 | 7 | 6 | 2 |
| Freya | 17 | 3 | 3 | 0 | 6 | 7 | 2 |
| Suker | 14 | 4 | 0 | 5 | 0 | 4 | 3 |
| James 1 | 21 | 3 | 2 | 3 | 7 | 0 | 9 |
| Claire | 26 | 3 | 5 | 4 | 3 | 5 | 0 |
| Observer | 0 | 0 | 0 | 0 | 0 | 0 | 0 |

*Notes*: For the percentage of the teacher's total actions, initiated by the teacher and directed at Ian, start at 'Teacher' in the left-hand column and travel across the matrix to the column headed 'Ian'. To find out how much of Ian's interactions he directed at the teacher, identify 'Ian' in the left-hand column and repeat the same process. This gives the percentage of Ian's total actions initiated by Ian and directed towards the teacher.

**Table 6.2** Individual's other interactions by category as a percentage of their total interactions (CASE activity)

| Participant | Category of interaction | | | | | |
|---|---|---|---|---|---|---|
| | all | ob | ta | tb | in | ns |
| Teacher | 19 | 0 | 1 | 10 | 2 | 5 |
| Ian | 5 | 7 | 4 | 35 | 4 | 17 |
| Jem | 2 | 3 | 5 | 33 | 1 | 10 |
| Freya | 3 | 2 | 2 | 37 | 2 | 17 |
| Suker | 6 | 3 | 7 | 35 | 4 | 19 |
| James 1 | 6 | 0 | 5 | 40 | 1 | 13 |
| Claire | 3 | 1 | 2 | 31 | 1 | 16 |

*Notes*: Categories represented by the columns are:
**all** an action initiated by an individual and directed at the whole group;
**ob** an action of any type initiated by an individual towards the observer;
**ta** an action in which the individual turned away from the task, excluding a turn towards the observer;
**tb** an action initiated by an individual and involving task materials;
**in** an action initiated by an individual which disrupted the group's activity;
**ns** an action initiated by an individual but not apparently aimed at any specific individual.

**Table 6.3** Matrix of interactions between individuals as a rounded-up percentage of their total interactions (non-CASE activity)

| | Participant | | | | | | |
|---|---|---|---|---|---|---|---|
| | Teacher | Frank | Anna | Ami | Karela | Michael | James 2 |
| Teacher | 0 | 20 | 0 | 0 | 0 | 0 | 40 |
| Frank | 2 | 0 | 7 | 4 | 4 | 4 | 7 |
| Anna | 0 | 8 | 0 | 9 | 15 | 15 | 12 |
| Ami | 16 | 16 | 3 | 0 | 5 | 5 | 8 |
| Karela | 2 | 9 | 12 | 13 | 0 | 13 | 15 |
| Michael | 3 | 0 | 4 | 6 | 0 | 0 | 16 |
| James 2 | 5 | 6 | 6 | 8 | 14 | 17 | 0 |
| Observer | 0 | 80 | 0 | 0 | 20 | 0 | 0 |

*Notes*: For the percentage of Frank's total actions, initiated by Frank and directed at Anna, start at 'Frank' in the left-hand column and travel across the matrix to the column headed 'Anna'. To find out how much of Anna's interactions she directed at Frank, identify 'Anna' in the left-hand column and repeat the same process. This gives the percentage of Anna's total actions initiated by Anna and directed towards Frank.

CASE group. Tables 6.3 and 6.4, respectively, show the same target focus for individuals' actions but relating to the non-CASE group.

The diagrams in Figures 6.2 and 6.3 show the spatial arrangement of each group of participants in the CASE and non-CASE examples respectively. As

**Table 6.4** Individuals' other interactions by category as a percentage of their total interactions (non-CASE activity)

| Participant | Category of interaction | | | | | |
|---|---|---|---|---|---|---|
| | all | ob | ta | tb | in | ns |
| Teacher | 0 | 20 | 0 | 0 | 20 | 0 |
| Frank | 0 | 20 | 4 | 38 | 0 | 8 |
| Anna | 0 | 0 | 0 | 39 | 0 | 3 |
| Ami | 0 | 0 | 0 | 46 | 0 | 2 |
| Karela | 0 | 3 | 0 | 30 | 0 | 3 |
| Michael | 0 | 7 | 3 | 57 | 0 | 4 |
| James 2 | 0 | 0 | 0 | 42 | 3 | 2 |

*Notes:* Categories represented by the columns are:
**all** an action initiated by an individual and directed at the whole group;
**ob** an action of any type initiated by an individual towards the observer;
**ta** an action in which the individual turned away from the task, excluding a turn towards the observer;
**tb** an action initiated by an individual and involving task materials;
**in** an action initiated by an individual which disrupted the group's activity;
**ns** an action initiated by an individual but not apparently aimed at any specific individual.

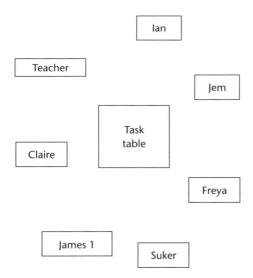

**Figure 6.2** Spatial arrangement of participants around the CASE task table

the general discussion proceeds, I will relate the points made to the two examples referred to above (where interactions figures are given in Tables 6.1 and 6.3). The examples also serve to highlight difficulties arising from this approach and the interpretation of results.

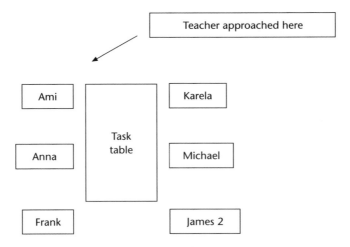

**Figure 6.3** Spatial arrangement of participants around the non-CASE task table

In the activities examined so far teacher gestures are not uniformly distributed amongst pupils in the group – this may be affected by where the pupil sits relative to the teacher and her visual field or, as in the case of Frank in the CASE example or James 2 in the non-CASE example, the teacher's expectation of difficult behaviour (which did not materialize in either instance). On the whole, teachers tended to interact most with those sitting nearest them (Ian and Claire), or those sitting directly opposite them by line of sight (Freya). In the non-CASE setting, the point at which the teacher joined the group for checking purposes fulfilled a similar role spatially with an emphasis on actions directed at those opposite the teacher in the line of sight (Frank and James 2).

## Discussion

Teachers primarily used speech to communicate with children in their groups, but pupils did this much less, perhaps reflecting a different emphasis in mode of communication or the difference in verbal competency, although one has to recall that much of the teacher speech was information-giving or organizational whereas pupils had to do less of this, spending more time responding to rather than initiating speech. Nonetheless, pupil gestures to teachers were between two and five times those from teacher to pupil without a clear spatial relationship in terms of proximity to the teacher (compare Claire to Jem, for example). In the non-CASE groups, the teacher being only periodically present, the actions were, not surprisingly, mainly focused on other group members, although often the pupil nearest the point at which the teacher joined the group would gesture very actively, even if little conversation then ensued (Ami for instance). Most of the actions directed towards the teacher in the non-CASE groups took place when the teacher was away from the table and may well have reflected pupil monitoring or checking of the teacher's position in the room.

Teachers use gesture in their instructions and interventions as a support for speech, while many of the pupils (although not all) appear to use gesture to take the place of speech as their words literally 'failed' them. This was most apparent in the CASE groups when pupil explanations were directed at the teacher or towards other pupils. Often an action between teacher and pupil or pupil and another pupil (particularly in the non-CASE observations) would be monitored by actions arising from other participants and directed at the teacher or pupil in question. This could distort the interpretation of the interaction frequencies by apparently inflating the attention directed at a particular individual. This can be studied further by using the third level of analysis mentioned earlier which focused on sequences of interaction rather than simple frequencies. Taken together, the teacher-directed pattern of interactions in the CASE activities involved less pupil-initiated inter-pupil action overall, but what was there was more evenly distributed between pupils than in the non-CASE groups where a pupil's actions seemed to be mostly directed at two other pupils, partly depending on where they were sitting around the table. Thus, those at the corners of a table tended to act mostly with those directly opposite them or nearest them as they turned towards the rest of the table (for example, Frank with James and Anna), although this in turn was influenced by who was friends with whom in that particular activity (Karela and Ami were close friends for example, but Karela was also friends with James 2, whereas Ami was not) and who was notionally working with whom (so, for example, James was working with Michael, but was also friends with Karela).

To summarize this aspect, in both types of group one can say at present that four factors apparently relate to pupil gesture targets (who interacts with whom). The first is the teacher, if present, who is prioritized. The remaining three are not clearly prioritized at present but are: second, proximity and position opposite; third, partner status (if working in a pair); and fourth, by whether or not the target person is a current friend. Thus, one might say that the distribution of pupils around the table may affect pupil-pupil and teacher-pupil interaction. In both types of group, pupil gestures directed to all group members (as opposed to just spoken or gestured without a target) are generally rare (see Tables 6.2 and 6.3 for the current examples), but in the CASE context are more frequent and also more likely if the group is stable over successive observations. Generally, in CASE activities gesturing across corners is more common than when pupils sit side by side or in a line, but this is associated with the partnering pattern in the specific activity. In both types of group, across-table gestures are less noticeable than those across corners or in a line. If the teacher is absent, these interactions are affected by the distribution and allocation of resources around the table. Gender inter-actions are not revealed as necessarily prioritized in the data so far.

In the non-CASE groups a key pupil(s) may have a role in structuring interactions either through friendships or through dominance in conversation or control of access to resources (such as glue and scissors), as for example James 2 and Michael in the non-CASE group. In both types of group there is a substantial degree of physical interaction with the materials being used in the task (the 'tb' categories in Tables 6.2 and 6.4), but in the non-CASE groups this also included gaining access to materials which, as presented here, artificially inflates the incidence of these actions. This requires careful interpretation, although generally there was more task-related materials interaction in the CASE groups. What is interesting is the extent that pupils turned away from the task (category 'ta' in Tables 6.2 and 6.4), in effect being distracted from what they were doing. In the CASE groups this was mainly due to interruptions from outside the group, related to other pupils seeking the teacher's assistance. This seldom happened in the non-CASE groups, where the teacher was actively working with all the groups in rotation. Both groups were subject to the arrival of pupils from other classes seeking materials on behalf of their teachers or the unscheduled arrival of visitors. Interruptions by group members within the group were much more noticeable in the CASE groups, but were associated with task-orientated comments among these groups and making an active contribution outside the current turn-taking process, perhaps reflecting their relative inexperience at recognizing turn-permissioning devices in this context.

The last of the action categories ('ns' in Tables 6.2 and 6.4) is also interesting because it reflects actions made by participants but not directed at individuals or materials. These are in a sense additional actions that may inform communication in some way. These were much richer and more extensive in the CASE groups, perhaps reflecting the more active and more cognitively challenging communication going on in those groups. In the other groups self-directed actions such as nose rubbing and face tapping were more apparent.

The second and third levels of analysis mentioned earlier give further detail suggesting that particular behaviours are more common than others; that these relate in, as yet, unclear ways to the phase of a task and the nature of the task itself; and that pupils and their teachers show sequences of behaviours that seem to perform particular communicative tasks and which are stable across time and across context.

Some general factors that seem to relate to how the participants interacted with each other appear to be the nature of the task, the organization of the task and patterns of pupil partnering; the spatial arrangement of pupils around the task table; and the distribution of materials within the task.

From a methodological point of view, interactions with the observer need to be considered. References to the observer in the first of the four observations in a sequence were usually at their highest and then declined subsequently, but particular individuals had particular patterns of referencing which in some instances, such as Frank in the non-CASE example, involved consistently high referencing. Discussion with the teacher helped to interpret these further, as in the case of Frank which involved issues particular to his family circumstances. This emphasizes the need to take these factors into account when interpreting such results. Readers should bear in mind that the children's school environment was almost exclusively female. A male researcher, even as 'another adult' in the classroom had novelty value and was commented on by both pupils and teachers in their interviews. This clearly raises questions about possible gender-biasing effects in the observations, but these may have been unavoidable in the single-observer context of the study.

## Pupil perceptions of group work

Another observational technique used in this part of the overall study was one aimed at eliciting pupils' perceptions of what went on in groups. Subsequent to a group's task being completed, each pupil was interviewed separately in a quiet part of the classroom or in an adjacent area outside the classroom. Each audio-taped individual interview consisted of a number of activities. The first, in preparation for a picture-story task about group work, invited pupils to give names to a cartoon group so that they might use them in their accounts of the story task. This also served to identify any particular friends the children might have (which emerged during the pupils' accounts of why they had chosen specific names) and whether or not these friends were part of the group that had just been observed. This indirect approach to identifying possible friendship links was used to obviate the possibility of problematizing a lack of friends for particular pupils.

In the picture-story task that followed, the participants were asked to examine a series of five three-frame cartoon stories showing a group of children around a table with their teacher. The cartoon story depicted three phases of a group's task: the beginning, middle and end of the task. Pupils were told that the children in the pictures had been asked to sort out a muddled-up collection of coloured pencils by their teacher who had asked them to pair pencils of the same colour and to arrange them in a row. All children had experienced this activity or its equivalent in their own classrooms as confirmed by their teacher at some time prior to the observation. Thus, they all had concrete experience of the activity to draw upon in understanding what was happening in the task.

The first picture story showed a group that had sorted the pencils into pairs by the middle of the story and then lined them up at the end of the story, thus completing the task. The second story had the same starting picture and ending picture, but the middle picture showed only a partial pairing of coloured pencils suggesting that half-way through the story only part of the task had been completed. Nonetheless, by the end of the story the remainder of the task had been completed. The third story showed the same beginning and middle picture as the last story, but also included the middle picture (only a partial sorting of the coloured pencils into pairs) as the end point of the story, intimating that the group had only partially sorted the pictures and had not completed the task. The fourth story showed the same first and last pictures as were used in the first story, but had a middle picture showing that some pencils had fallen onto the floor (children had to specify in their account how they might have got there) and that the remaining pencils remained unmatched. However, by showing the pencils sorted and lined up in the last picture, it was implied that the group had overcome the missing pencils and successfully completed the task. The fifth story had the middle picture of the fourth story, showing pencils on the floor, in the final picture position, suggesting that the group had not progressed beyond the missing pencils and thus not completed the task.

The stories thus represented a series of tasks with different outcomes apparently affected by what went on in the group as seen in the pictures. By offering explanations, pupils could weave their own account of how the events in the pictures might have happened and how the children in the group might have acted to bring about the events depicted. This served to structure the children's responses and permissioned possible critical comments about the fictional actions of others rather than the actual actions of their friends. The semi-structured interview format also allowed a degree of consistency between different pupils' accounts of the same story and their own subsequent accounts of the same story in later observations.

The interviews were all taped for transcription and analysis. The picture story tapes were transcribed and analysed for content. Members of both the CASE and non-CASE groups made comments that suggested some clear understandings of what could contribute to positive or negative task performance in the picture story groups, and hence by implication in their own groups. The types of comments that have been identified at present are given in Table 6.5.

The following features emerge from this analysis.

1 The non-CASE group make fewer comments on thinking and discussion-type behaviours compared to the CASE groups where comments relating to thinking, sharing, listening and working together are more prominent.
2 Both types of group felt that they should not be selfish and keep things to themselves, perhaps reflecting their concerns about being friends and not wanting people to feel sad.
3 In the context of thinking, 'thinking about things together' was viewed positively and received greater comment in the CASE groups, but 'working on your own' was not necessarily negative for these groups. This may reflect an awareness that there are times when one or the other approach is more useful, perhaps representing a strategic approach.
4 Many of the actions commented on are communicative and suggest that the activities were perceived in terms of a social, rather than task or work perspective.
5 Pupil perceptions of friends, the making and breaking of friendships, and whom they did or did not want to work with were also prominent in both groups.

**Table 6.5**  Indicative list of comment types made by pupil participants arising from the picture story observations

| Behaviour comments | |
| --- | --- |
| *Positive* | *Negative* |
| Sharing with each other* | Keeping things to yourself* |
| Listening to each other* | Not listening but shouting* |
| Helping each other | Messing about |
| Talking about things together* | Just doing your own talking* |
| Not fighting | Fighting |
| Not being selfish | Keeping things |
| Working together* | Doing everything yourself* |
| Thinking about things together* | Working on your own |
| Taking turns* | Interrupting people, barging and shouting* |
| Not snatching | Snatching and grabbing |
| Passing things to each other | Taking things* |
| Keeping the table tidy | Dropping things on the floor |
| Listening to the teacher | Not listening to the teacher |

*Note*: *Behaviours referred to more commonly in the CASE groups.

6 Turn-taking is commented upon more in the CASE groups than in the non-CASE groups, perhaps reflecting the emphasis placed by the teacher in each group on this form of action. Equally 'taking things' was viewed negatively in the groups, where again the teacher commented on the need to share and work together in a way that did not occur in the non-CASE groups.

## Comments and implications for teachers' practice

The observations analysed here reinforce those reported by Grady Venvillein Chapter 3, which showed that children in the CASE groups exhibited a number of verbal-orientated behaviours (such as explaining, highlighting discrepancies, adopting new ideas, demonstrating thinking and working collaboratively and asking questions) which were less evident in the non-CASE groups. In the non-CASE groups the majority of interactions were procedurally related in the sense that they were associated with requests for the use of resources and for help, addressed to other members of the group. Much comparison of pieces of work was evident and comparative exchanges of this type were common. Side conversations relating to off-task issues such as boyfriends and girlfriends were common in the non-CASE groups, also reflecting a strong socializing priority in these groups and a relative lack of work focus.

All the non-CASE tasks analysed so far, suggest that teacher-nominated pupil-partner pairings broke down over time and were, in some instances, reconstituted to patterns of the pupils' own making. However, in the CASE activities, the teacher 'policed' the pairing structure and organization of the task which remained consistent throughout the tasks. In the CASE activities, the pupils' physical experience of the materials being used were introduced *through* the activity and were used to *develop* the activity conceptually, as opposed to those in the non-CASE activities where they were presented simply as materials to be used without any linkage to the tasks' development. It may well be that the CASE approach of developing the analysis of a problem, through the materials being used in this way, is an approach more supportive of task engagement.

This chapter has offered a glimpse of work in progress relating to the nature of interactions in pupil groups. What are the issues currently emerging from the larger study? These may be summarized in the following way. There is some evidence of more turn-taking, listening and supportive mutual interactions in the CASE groups over successive observations compared to the non-CASE groups. Interruption and permissioning is evident, usually through glances, pointing and forward leaning. Most intervention is through pointing at materials in the non-CASE groups and by glances at people in the CASE groups. Repair of interruptions so that interaction could continue seems to be through smiles and hand gestures, with touching evident in the observations early in each observation sequence. This was particularly apparent in the CASE groups. Actions could be deflected from a particular course by glances in the CASE groups, whereas handling of materials appears to play the same role in the non-CASE groups. Pupils mirrored teacher actions in their interactions with other pupils in the CASE groups but pupils mirrored other pupil actions less evidently in the non-CASE groups. Support for a particular action was garnered by glances in both groups, but was more apparent in the CASE groups where co-operative and collaborative exchanges were more noticeable. It is worth reflecting that the greater emphasis on physical interaction gestures with materials in the non-CASE groups rather than the non-physical gestures in the CASE groups may reflect the greater verbal interaction in these latter groups.

In more general terms, gesture and speech in both types of groups appear to be co-ordinated and it can be argued that as well as being used to both support language use in this age group gesture may also support the development of understanding. Among the younger members of the group, gesture may precede speech or substitute for it, whilst for older children gesture and speech may co-occur. Being aware of this may help teachers to recognize children's contributions to the group in both modalities. This also means that some pupils can gesture an explanation without being able to explain it in words, so teachers sensitive to pupil use of gesture may be better able to estimate the true capacities of all of their pupils. This is consistent with what has been noticed during the observation of children carrying out Piagetian conservation tasks in which both pupil spoken accounts *and* gestures were considered. These suggest that in addition to those who could conserve (both verbal and gestural responses showed an understanding of conservation) and those who could not (neither verbal nor gestural responses reflected conservation) a third, transitional group existed which could not conserve verbally (their spoken accounts did not indicate conservation) but which did show evidence of understanding conservation through their gestures (Breckinbridge-Church and Goldin-Meadow 1986; Goldin-Meadow et al. 1992; Alibali and Goldin-Meadow 1993). Pupils may also be able to exchange conceptual or task-related information through the interpretation of other pupils' gestural behaviours (Kelly and Breckinbridge-Church 1997).

It may be that persistent non-recognition of a pupil's contribution, albeit gesturally communicated, might lead to lowered pupil self-esteem and reduced motivation. Gesture rather than speech can signal a pupil's desire to intervene and contribute. If a teacher is present, she becomes the focus of communication in the group, implying that the teacher's use of speech *and* gesture needs to be carefully considered if it is to act as a positive model for the children around her. Further, it suggests that teacher use of gesture could support pupils who are less verbally confident. Patterns of interaction differ during different phases of an activity and in different types of activity and it may well be important to structure activities so that gestural responses can be recognized as valid contributions to the group's work. Teachers in the context of CASE activities seem to have a positive effect on the development of pupil communicative skills as compared to when they are absent from a group. In addition, there are particular sequences of gestures that may indicate a desire to intervene or prevent the intervention of others in a group that are used by pupils instead of, or adjacent to verbal interruptions. These may reveal pupil understanding and confidence in a particular phase of a task. Finally, it emerges that teacher use of gesture may profoundly influence pupil participation and action in a group, as may that of children in the group.

This chapter has introduced some issues relating to the nature, extent and use of both gesture and verbal modes of communication amongst 5- to 6-year-olds working in groups, with and without a teacher. The CASE approach has offered a group-based context in which to explore these issues. It has been suggested, firstly, that although focused on cognitive development, the CASE activities may also be developing communicative skills as evidenced in pupil use of gesture; and, secondly, that when linked to the verbal interactions taking place between group members, a rich and revealing view of how such groups work may be made available to us. Most importantly, it has identified a need for teachers to consider the nature and impact of their gestural actions when working with pupils in this context. Given that the teachers involved had had little initial or continuing training in these areas, a need to develop this aspect of teachers' professional practice is clearly signalled.

# 7 COGNITIVE ACCELERATION IN MATHEMATICS EDUCATION IN YEARS 5 AND 6: PROBLEMS AND CHALLENGES

## Mundher Adhami

### Introduction

This chapter reports on a cognitive intervention project focused on the mathematics learning for children in Years 5 and 6, and on related PD programmes. The 3-year project was part of the large-scale Leverhulme Numeracy Programme at King's College London (1997–2001).

Behind this work lies successful achievement in two previous intervention projects at the early secondary level: CASE and CAME. Both have reported large-scale effects both on children's cognitive development and school achievement in science, maths and English (see Chapter 1). Application of the same intervention methodology in Years 5 and 6 in primary school faced the following two problems.

1 The success of the secondary interventions may have been due to their immediately following a major brain-growth spurt at age 11, where it could be argued that with the occurrence of new inter-neuronal growth through the creating of new synapses the children's brains were in a favourable state of flux. Would the ages 9 to 11 be as favourable to cognitive development? This is essentially an empirical question, to be tested by gathering pre- and post-test research data.

2 Secondary CAME and CASE work through specialist maths and science teachers, and where they have been most effective they depend on the department members to collaborate in the description and development of the new teaching skills required. With primary schools we have generalist teachers and no subject 'departments', and so they need two sources of input for the development of intervention teaching skills: one concerned with further insight into the *maths*, and the other related to the *class-management* skills. Thus, the style of PD may need to be different for primary teachers from that used in secondary CAME.

**Table 7.1** Year 5 and Year 6 CAME research plan

|  | Year 1 | Year 2 | Year 3 |
|---|---|---|---|
| *Research team* <br> Working in two 'lab' schools | Year 5 lessons development and trials | Year 6 lessons development and trials | Refining guidance material |
| *Main study teachers* <br> Working in eight schools |  | TM lessons in Year 5 classes | TM lessons in Year 6 classes <br> Post-tests |
|  |  | Pre-tests | KS2 tests |

### Research plan

The challenge was to work with a single LEA (Croydon) towards a PD model which, if the intervention proved successful, could be utilized in the promotion of CAME methods in primary school throughout the LEA, and then nationally.

The applied research toward this end was to trial the primary CAME on an initial sample of seven schools as a pilot project, and profit from the feedback received from the experience of the PD programme.

To prepare for this the research team worked for the first year in only four classes in two 'laboratory' schools. These were mainstream LEA schools and classes with an average intake of children. The work here was to generate the new thinking maths (TM) lessons which would be needed the subsequent year for the teachers in the seven main study schools to begin the intervention with their Year 5 pupils. Then in the second year the research team would generate the Year 6 TM lessons in the laboratory schools in preparation for the last year of the project when the eight main study schools would use them with their pupils as they moved up to Year 6.

Table 7.1 shows how the research team worked 1 year ahead of the main-study teachers to generate and trial lessons. In the first 2 years the research team worked in regular rounds of planning, trials and reflection, leading to the write-up of guidance. Observation of lesson trials had a cognitive challenge perspective, looking to match the reasoning steps in each activity to the range of ability in the age group. In the third year the research team refined the lessons and guidance for publication[1] through reflection on the experience of PD with the main study teachers. The aim was to communicate to teachers ways of organizing whole-class and small-group work in each activity to ensure engagement of children across the ability range in work appropriate to them.

As a result of the differences between the primary and secondary maths teaching mentioned above, a different kind of research team was set up from that of secondary CASE and CAME. From the outset, the plan was for a team to consist of four primary teachers (from the 'lab' schools), the LEA maths adviser, and the three King's staff (two mathematicians and one psychologist). The four teachers, named as teacher-researchers (TRs), were intended by the adviser to collaborate with her in the delivery of PD to the teachers in the seven main study schools when they were ready, with limited assistance from the King's staff. Given the fact that they began as generalist teachers, it was expected that this would make them particularly understanding of the difficulties other generalist teachers would face in the PD process.

Such a research team required reconciliation of members' diverse perceptions and agenda. King's staff with the assistance of the LEA maths adviser needed to share the intervention theory they were hoping to apply with the four TRs. They had to learn to develop a collaborative role with practitioners on the ground, as distinguished from their 'headquarters' CASE and CAME teams, with whom they had taken for granted a common jargon. From the TRs' perspective, the initial maths and psychology jargon of the King's team seemed daunting and repulsive. Their experience with children across several learning situations gave them the strength to stand up to the King's staff when necessary. However they did need to learn more about their own and children's maths learning problems during the project. The experiences of the TRs over the 3-year cycle was the subject of research by a King's PhD student, Jeremy Hodgen, who gives a detailed description of the evolution of two of them in Chapter 8.

The main-study teachers started using the TM lessons in the second year of the project, as shown in Table 7.1. Once each half-term, guided by the adviser and the TRs, they would work through two new TM lessons in a 'simulation' mode, reflect on their classroom experiences in earlier ones, and discuss how the intervention approach fitted in with the rest of their teaching. Some of the lessons by main-study teachers were observed or supported by the members of the research team and this aided subsequent team and PD discussions. The plan was for each teacher and class to experience 12 TM lessons in Year 5, and similar number in the following year when they were in Year 6. Pre- and post-tests to measure gains in main-study and control classes were conducted at the start of their Year 5 and end of their Year 6 respectively, the latter coinciding with KS2 tests.

## The intervention model

As discussed elsewhere (see Chapters 1 and 11), all the interventions featured in this book draw both from Piagetian and Vygotksian theory. As with the secondary CAME project, the Piagetian aspect was handled by using the empirical evidence gained from the Concepts in Secondary Maths and Science Programme (CSMS)[2] and Graded Assessment in Mathematics Education (GAIM)[3] projects. Five core and four subsidiary strands of mathematical activity were described at every Piagetian level from 'early concrete', 2A, to 'mature formal', 3B. The subsidiary strands are seen largely as contexts for applying the reasoning in the core strands.

Table 7.2 shows in outline how maths curriculum descriptors in these strands were matched with Piagetian cognitive demand levels. This table was used in lieu of a taxonomy like that for science (Shayer and Adey 1981) and the Arts (see Chapter 9). But in order to plan a TM lesson, finer detail is required with special emphasis on the concrete operations levels relevant to work in the primary classes. Figure 7.1 shows the analysis of the 'multiplicative relations' strand, using descriptors from the National Curriculum (NC) – within the ellipses – and GAIM. This strand underlies several TM lessons, including the two on fractions discussed in Chapter 8. An intermediate level 2A/2B is included in the Piagetian scale on the left of Figure 7.1, while GAIM levels are placed on the right. GAIM levels are subdivisions of the NC levels, and are empirically designed to reflect an average yearly progress, a level of detail convenient to this study. Each TM lesson is planned to cover three or four Piagetian sub-levels allowing appropriate challenge to children in mainstream mixed-ability classes. For the upper primary classes this is from the early concrete operations (2A) to concrete generalization (2B*), with due adjustments for early Year 5 and late Year 6 lessons. This range has a wide overlap with secondary CAME lessons, so nine of those were adapted to this project. Altogether, 34 lessons were considered for development, and 24 finalized for publication. Table 7.3 shows how the lessons are distributed across the attainment targets and in the strands.

Designing a TM lesson, however, is not a direct coverage of a portion of a curriculum strand. Each teaching activity may have a mixture of strands. The design task is to structure the activity into a sequence of reasoning steps so that different children can achieve in a valid way, at different levels (shown on the right of the figure). The diagram of the reasoning steps in the pegboard symmetry lesson (Figure 7.2) illustrates this Piagetian structuring. Reasoning at the bottom of the figure relates to the co-ordinate grid and axes, and their reflection in a visible line on the pegboard actually used at the start of the lesson. The tabulating of co-ordinate pairs then leads to generalization on number patterns, and then to general number and even algebra. Hence the structure of the task helps children integrate maths involving different strands within a rising level of cognitive demand.

Thus, the Piagetian or cognitive aspect of an activity concerns the match between reasoning levels implicit in the mathematics and the characteristics of pupils of the given age on the other. A TM lesson is designed so that for each pupil the challenge is aimed ahead, but not too far, of his or her present cognitive level. This raises the question: given the cognitive aim of the lesson, what form of social interaction will best serve to achieve it?

Our answer to this question comes from Vygotsky's theory of the ZPD. Our belief is that cognitive development occurs through *mediation*: the learner, possessing a partial strategy, sees or hears in someone in her current social world the complete strategy applied to just that situation on which she is working. She instantly assimilates this, completing her mental structures for that concept. This implies that the best mediators may be a child's fellows, because they are closer to her both in thinking and also in personal style.

**Table 7.2** Piagetian reasoning levels in strands of mathematics activity

| Piagetian level | 2A Early concrete operations | 2B Mature concrete operations | 2B* Concrete generalizations | 3A Early formal operations | 3B Mature formal operations |
|---|---|---|---|---|---|
| **Core strands** | | | | | |
| Number properties | Add and subtract whole numbers, count in 2, 5, 10 | Place value in numbers (including decimals) | Number multiplication, negative numbers | Generalized number, estimation in calculations | Irrational numbers, convergence, error bounds |
| Multiplicative relations | Halving and doubling, concrete '1 to many' | Simple fractions, notion of %ages | %age as fraction, equivalent fractions, concrete scaling | %, fractions and decimals as operators, proportions | Analytical proportions, inverse proportions |
| Expressions and equations | Comparison words, equal sign as equivalence | Word expression of a number relation | Symbolizing relations, solving linear equation | Solving inequalities and simultaneous equations | Algebraic manipulations and graphical methods |
| Functions | 1-1 mapping and its descriptions | Two step 'function machine' | Linear functions, mapping on Cartesian co-ordinates | Tangent as ratio, non-linear graphs | Function variables' effects on graphs, area under graph |
| Geometric relations | Differences between shapes (line, angle) | Area and perimeter of rectangular shapes | General area, circle ratios, four quad co-ordinates | 3-D co-ordinates, Pythagoras, trig ratio | Trig function, circle geometry |
| **Subsidiary strands** | | | | | |
| Shapes | Simple regular shapes | Relationship between sets of shapes | Symmetry, angles in parallel and intersecting lines | Locus, reflections in axes, 2-D relations and measures | Congruent triangles, 3-D relations and measures |
| Orientations (space) | Four directions of movements | Location in 2-D co-ordinates | Routes' networks, 4-quadrant plotting | Bearings, vector notations | Relative movements, addition of vectors |
| Probability | Always, never, sometimes | Likelihood scale | Probability as fractions or %, adding to 1 | Probability as a relative frequency, P calculations | Conditional probability, any combination |
| Data representation and correlation | Concrete tally tables | Stem and leaf, pie charts, mode and median | Comparing averages, frequency chart, scattergram | Box and whiskers, cumulative frequency, semi-quantitative correlation | Describing dispersion, judging representations |

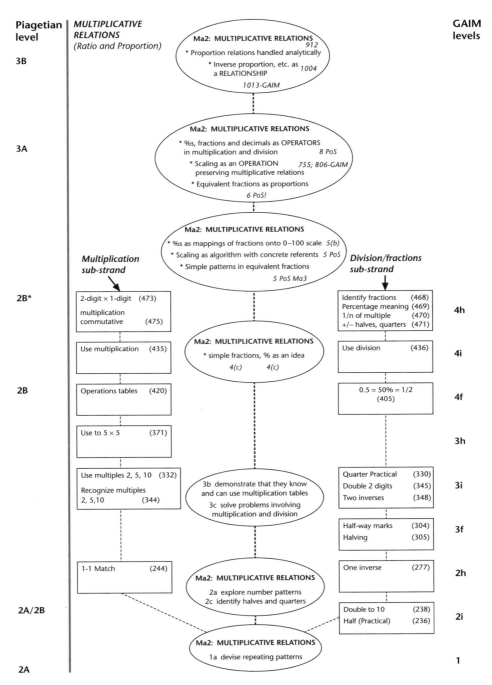

**Figure 7.1** Detail of the multiplicative relations strand from Table 7.2

**Table 7.3** Overview of primary CAME lessons in terms of curriculum links and strand

|  | *Curriculum links* | *Strands* |
|---|---|---|
| *Year 5* | | |
| Sports league | Multiplication, combinations, systematic | Number relations/algebra |
| Digit detective | Inverse operation, place value | Number properties |
| Largest rectangle | Area, perimeter, properties of rectangles | Shape, geometric relations |
| Share an apple | Fractions | Number properties |
| Scaffolding | Number patterns, ratio, algebra | Number relations/algebra |
| Comparing texts | Mode, range, sampling, representing data | Data representation |
| Picturing numbers | Mental calculation, vertical number line | Number properties |
| Cups and saucers | Circles (pre-II), ratio | Shape, number relations |
| Mini clubs | Calculating, systematic within constraints | Number properties |
| Tessellating triangles | Translation, rotation, reflection, angles | Shape, geometric relations |
| Design a desk | Three dimensions, averages | Data representation |
| Roofs | Number in spatial context, algebra | Number relations/algebra |
| *Year 6* | | |
| Half-time scores | Systematic grouping, algebra | Number relations/algebra |
| Good enough to eat | Types of number | Number properties |
| Robots | Angle, position, direction | Orientation, geometric relation |
| Caterpillars | Number patterns, systematic listing | Number properties |
| Gardens | Two-step word rules, graphs, algebra | Number relations/algebra |
| 'Who dunnit?' | Measures, ratio, averages | Data, number relations |
| Pegboard symmetry | Co-ordinates, reflection, general number | Shape/general number |
| Halving and 'thirding' | Fractions, ratio | Number properties |
| One-way tracks | Branched reasoning, networks | Shape, orientation |
| Bean-bag pick up | Number in spatial context, algebra | Number relations/algebra |
| Pigs | Probability, data, inverse relationship | Data and probability |
| Pencils and rulers | Calculation, simultaneous linear relations | Number relations |

The teacher may desperately wish to model the solution for the child, but is usually too far beyond where the child presently is to be able to interact, unless he relies on the child's own ideas and simultaneously with her peers. He needs to manage the children's interactions so it is they who construct the solution(s) within the task.

To allow the teacher to integrate both Piagetian and Vygotskyan sources of theory in the context of children's maths learning, the classroom activity has to be designed specifically for this purpose. To that end we used a variant of the standard CASE and CAME lesson model of the three phases of *concrete preparation, construction* and *reflection* to structure lessons in two rounds, or cycles labelled 'episodes'. The first episode is intended to motivate and engage all the children at their current levels of work, to handle misconceptions, then to lead to common understanding of the further challenges posed

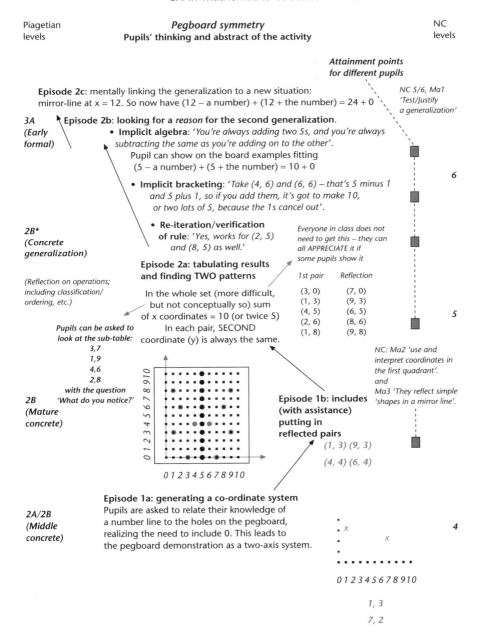

**Figure 7.2**  Reasoning steps in one activity in relation to Piagetian and NC levels

**Whole class preparation (about 5–10 mins)** 1
- *We are going to do some thinking work with co-ordinates.*
- Reminder of the convention of labelling axes and co-ordinates (along the path and up the ladder).
- *Put a green peg in (1, 3). Check with others on the table. Now put a blue peg in (7, 2).*
- *What mistakes could people have made?* (Mixing up *x*s and *y*s, forgetting to count 0.)
- *What things must we remember?* (Along the path and up the ladder.)
- Repeat with other colours in other positions.
- Draw some coloured pegs on the board grid and get children to record co-ordinates.
- *Place pegs in (5, 1) (5, 7) (5, 9) (5, 4). What do you notice?* (They are in a line.)

**Paired work (5–10 mins)** 2
- *Place a variety of coloured pegs anywhere on your board to the left of your mirror line, record their co-ordinates.*
- *Reflect the pegs in the mirror line and record the co-ordinates after reflection* (keep reflected pegs the same colour to avoid confusion).
- *What do you notice about the numbers before and after reflection?*
- After a few minutes, model a recording system on the board.
- Colour     Old Peg     New Peg
- Green      (1, 3)      (9, 3)

**Class sharing (about 10 mins)** 3
- Orchestrate the feedback
- Individuals draw their 'before' and 'after' co-ordinates on the pegboard OHT and record their co-ordinates on the class recording system.
- *What if an original co-ordinate was (4, 7)? What is the reflected co-ordinate?*
- *What do you notice about the pairs of numbers?* (*Y* co-ordinate stays the same, *x* co-ordinates add up to 10.)

**Paired work (10–15 mins)** 4
- Ask pupils to explore their ideas further and formulate answers to '*What did you notice about the numbers with mirror line at $x = 5$?' How would you express what you know as a sum on the page?* $(5 - 1 + 5 + 1 = 10; 5 - 3 + 5 + 3 = 10$, etc.)
- *What is happening here?* $5 -$ (a number) $+ 5 +$ (the number) $= 10 + 0$
- *How is this 10 connected with $x = 5$?* (Double.)

**Class sharing (10–15 mins)** 5
- Discuss results from the paired work: looking for a general rule in words or symbols.
- If time permits follow with a 'mental' task (without the pegboard): *What would happen if the mirror/vertical line was at $x = 12$? Without doing it, think about what would happen if we put a peg in at (10, 3), what is the reflection? What about (1, 5)? How would you express what you know as a sum? How does this relate to the case when the mirror line was at $x = 5$?*
- $12 -$ (a number) $+ 12 +$ (the number) $= ?$

**Figure 7.3**   Guidance for managing the pegboard symmetry activity in the classroom

in the second episode. The latter is normally more open and leads to handling higher order concepts or reasoning patterns. This can be seen in the reasoning steps diagram for the pegboard reflection Figure 7.2. Tabulating results and finding patterns is arrived at collectively at the end of the first episode, with the second focusing on the question 'Why does that happen?', which is open. The second episode allows the handling of general number and implicit bracketing, and can potentially lead to algebraic symbolization and manipulation. This allows some children to progress further in their thinking, while the others, perhaps, store some partially achieved strategies in their ZPDs.

In order to manage the activity in the classroom the generalist teacher needs more than the outline diagram of the lesson. For this the teacher-researchers suggested a convenient form of lesson-crib. Each of the steps is expanded in terms of suggested actions, coupled (in italics) with a sample of typical questions they might use. Figure 7.3 shows this part of guidance for the pegboard symmetry lesson which, together with some practical reminders about resources, vocabulary and links with the NC (not included here), comprises a two-page A3 spread useable by the teacher in the classroom.

Teachers in the main study found the guidance exemplified in Figure 7.3 useful, especially valuing the sequence of key questions. But they also realized that the main job of teaching resides in a different type of question, one that can be termed *tactical*. Given the general lesson strategy, how are they to relate to particular pupils' responses, involving negotiation of meaning, handling of misconceptions and attention to minute and idiosyncratic steps of reasoning? A sequence of key questions is only half the story, and the teachers needed more support. A partial solution was to include in the guidance typical expected outcomes from children-handling key questions, and ways of responding to them.

But effective questioning – that is, responsive mediation of children's learning – is an advanced professional skill not possible to transmit by 'telling' in guidance notes. Teachers also need to learn by mediation by reflecting on practice in collaboration with more capable colleagues. Hence the importance of the project's 2-year PD programme for main-study teachers. True, it proved impossible to ensure that the same teachers conducted the lessons with the same classes in Year 5 and Year 6 as envisaged, because so many teachers were moving schools or leaving. Nevertheless, even teachers who attended only part of the PD programme did benefit from it, something I discuss later.

## Pre- and post-test research results

### 'Laboratory' schools results: 1997–9

In the first year of the project we worked with the teachers of two Year 5 classes in two schools to generate and test new TM activities, and this work

**Table 7.4**   PRT I summary data for laboratory schools

| | Means | | CSMS percentiles | | %le | Effect-size |
|---|---|---|---|---|---|---|
| School | Pre-test 97 | Post-test 99 | Pre-test 97 | Post-test 99 | Gain | (SDs) |
| L1 | 4.69* | 5.76 | 46.5 | 63.6 | 17.1 | 0.83σ |
| L2 | 4.78 | 5.54 | 46.4 | 55.0 | 8.6 | 0.42σ |

Note: *The test means are on a Piagetian scale, where 2A/2B = 4 to 5, 2B = 5 to 6 and 2B* = 6 to 7.

carried on the next year with the same children (now in Year 6). Each of the classes in these schools were given in the winter term 1997 a pre-test of PRT I: spatial relations, one of the Piagetian tests used in the CSMS survey of cognitive development for which we possessed national age norms. This test asks children to draw their answers to four questions. The first two involve jam-jars imagined half-full of water, at different inclinations, and similar questions about a jar with a plumb-line suspended from the middle of its lid. In the next they are asked to draw a house on the side of a hill, and then to draw three or more trees on the other side of the hill. In the last they are asked to imagine they are standing in the middle of an avenue looking into the distance, and to draw the trees both near and afar. Through their drawings the children show the number of variables they are able to hold in mind at a time. This minimizes problems to do with second language in relation to cognition. In June 1999 the classes were given the same test to see whether there was any evidence of cognitive change in the children. Table 7.4 summarizes the data for these schools.

The percentiles shown in Table 7.4 are population norms derived from the CSMS survey of 14,000 children between the ages of 10 and 16 (Shayer et al. 1976).

### Pre- and post-tests in the main study: 1998–2000

In September 1998 the teachers in the seven main study schools began the intervention with their Year 5 classes. Unfortunately, it was not possible for any of these teachers to move up with their class to Year 6 in 1999–2000, but in several cases they did continue to teach the Year 6 TM lessons to the Year 6 teacher's class. In other cases the Year 6 teachers attended new PD sessions in 1999/2000.

*Testing schedule*
The research design involved the use of three control schools, giving 6 classes (N ≈ 180) for comparison with the 11 classes in the main study that would be receiving the TM intervention. As with the laboratory schools previously, all classes were given PRT I: Spatial Relations as a pre-test in September 1998 in anticipation of using the same test as the post-test in June 2000. This was

to gain a general measure of the children's cognitive ability by which to assess any gains during the 2-year period over and above what would be expected as the children mature. The control classes were all tested by Michael Shayer, and the main study classes were tested by their class teacher. These tests would then enable the cognitive gains achieved by the main-study classes to be compared with the control classes, with due allowance made for differences in initial abilities of the children in each class. They would also allow the year 2000 KS2 results of the classes to be compared, again in relation to the different initial abilities of the children in control and main-study classes.

*Results*

Table 7.5 gives the PRT I pre- and post-test data for all classes. The overall comparison between experimental and control classes is certainly statistically significant, with a mean effect-size of 0.26 standard deviations. The effect-sizes were computed by subtracting the mean control school change

**Table 7.5**  Changes in CSMS %les for control and experimental classes over 20 months

| Classes | Effect-size (SDs) | p | Pre-%le | Post-%le | Change |
|---|---|---|---|---|---|
| *Controls* | | | | | |
| C1A | −0.17 | ns | 65.3 | 61.9 | −3.4 |
| C1B | −0.15 | ns | 71.1 | 68.1 | −3 |
| C2A | 0.06 | ns | 60.4 | 61.6 | 1.2 |
| C2B | −0.05 | ns | 59.7 | 58.7 | −1 |
| C3A | 0.18 | ns | 61.2 | 64.8 | 3.6 |
| C3B | −0.02 | ns | 63.0 | 62.6 | −0.4 |
| **Mean** | **−0.02** | | **63.45** | **62.94** | **−0.51** |
| *Experimentals* | | | | | |
| M1 | 0.47 | <.01 | 59.2 | 68.4 | 9.2 |
| M2A | 0.56 | <.01 | 57.6 | 68.5 | 10.9 |
| M2B | 0.18 | ns | 63 | 66.2 | 3.2 |
| M2C | 0.21 | ns | 57.2 | 61 | 3.8 |
| M3A | 0.08 | ns | 56.4 | 57.6 | 1.2 |
| M3B | 0.48 | <.01 | 50.5 | 59.8 | 9.3 |
| M3C | −0.14 | ns | 59.3 | 56.0 | −3.3 |
| M4 | 0.18 | ns | 52.6 | 52.9 | 0.3 |
| M5 | 0.04 | ns | 66.4 | 69.5 | 3.1 |
| M6A | 0.16 | ns | 58.5 | 61.3 | 2.8 |
| M6B | 0.36 | <.05 | 55.0 | 61.8 | 6.8 |
| **Mean** | **0.23** | | **57.79** | **62.09** | **4.30** |
| **E-C** | **0.26σ** | | | | **4.81** |

Overall t-test. E-C, t = 2.7, p = 0.0082

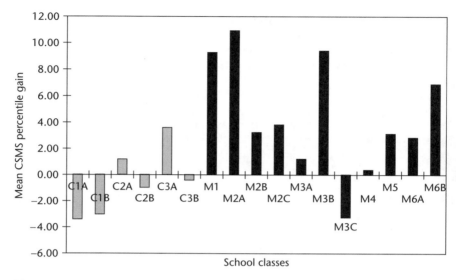

**Figure 7.4** Pre-post gains on PRT I

from the pre- to post-test of each school, and dividing this difference by the standard deviation of the whole sample at pre-test (± 20.53 per cent).

The pre- and post-test gains of control school classes and main-study school classes are shown in Figure 7.4. Four of the main-study classes have shown substantial gains and, with one exception, their general trend is positive compared with the control-school classes.

### Comparison between main study and control classes at KS2

Figure 7.5 gives the mean KS2 levels in mathematics for all the schools, plotted in relation to the pre-test mean percentile on PRT 1: Spatial Relations. There is clearly a problem in comparing control with main-study schools in this study. Eight of the main-study classes have mean pre-test levels on PRT I lower than that of the lowest of the control school classes, and hence their pupils are less able than the control schools' pupils and may be at a competence disadvantage in mathematics before they enter Year 5. However, bearing in mind the position of classes C2A and C3A on the graph (compare also C2B with C2A), no meaningful statistical tests can be made on the data. All that can be said is that two of the control classes have KS2 results which are out of the frame of the other schools. The regression line sums the data of the other four control classes, and in comparison with that (as with the earlier data on pre- and post-test results on PRT I shown in Figure 7.1), all the main-study classes lie above the line. Hence there is *some* evidence of a general enhancement of their pupils' mathematics.

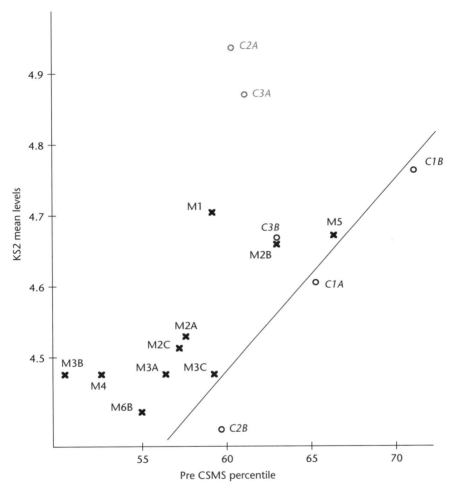

**Figure 7.5**   Mean Key Stage 2 Levels for control and main study classes

A possible explanation for this anomaly is the fact that the CAME intervention occurred at the same time as the introduction of the numeracy hour in Croydon. It may be that the teachers of classes C2A and C3A drew special benefit from this, as their numeracy consultant was also one of our teacher-researchers.

A valid comparison can be made between the size of effects in these Years 5–6 main-study schools, and the corresponding Years 7–8 main-study schools in the original CAME II research. The classroom intervention and tutorial input in the two programmes were of a similar nature and magnitude. The effect sizes for the 68 classes in CAME II[4] were only slightly higher, at about 0.37 SD at post-test, compared with 0.27 SD for the primary school main study. The proportion of classes having high and low effects is about the same in both data-sets.

## PD programme

In Phase 1 of the project the teacher-researchers were involved in two roles. The first was collaborating with the King's team in the creation and trialling of new TM lessons, and the second was preparing to deliver PD to the main-study teachers in Phase 2.

### *PD of teacher-researchers*

By the end of the first year of Phase 1, the teacher-researchers had experienced enough of the underlying CAME intervention theory and practice to have at least a working model of the PD to offer to the new teachers in the first year of Phase 2. However, it was certainly not the case that the King's team began Phase 1 having a model of the PD to offer the teacher-researchers. As described earlier, the King's team needed to share with the adviser and teacher-researchers what they had learnt from secondary CAME practice, and then they all needed to pool their different professional experiences in the process of constructing and describing the teaching skills which would later form the basis of the PD offered in Phase 2. As argued by Jeremy Hodgen in Chapter 8 such an experience is markedly different from anything that could be described as a PD programme.

The research team was relatively stable compared with the main-study teachers. The maths adviser and three of the original four TRs remained involved throughout the 3 years, although two of the TRs became LEA numeracy consultants in the second year. A colleague who left in the first year to start a family was replaced later by two new colleagues from the main study. This continuity helped a team ethos of vigorous and productive interactions to emerge. That ethos also needed the King's researchers to acknowledge their limited experience in teaching at the primary level, and their willingness for their theoretical knowledge to be challenged by the intuitions and theories-in-actions of the practitioners. Thus, PD was taking place with *all* members of the team.

The team worked in cycles structured around lesson trials. In the first year alone there were 20 whole-team whole-day sessions, plus numerous paired and small-group work in the 'lab' schools. The shared observation of pupils' responses and ideas in trial TM lessons was crucial to the emergence of a common language over the 2 years of Phase 1.

### *Roles in TM lesson development*
Some potential TM lessons were suggested by the King's researchers either by adapting existing secondary CAME activities or by locating GAIM investigations which looked promising. Some were suggested by the TRs based on their

experience of mathematics contexts which their pupils found difficult. Often the team expressed more doubts than praise when the lesson plans were first mooted, but almost invariably children's responses at the first classroom trial revealed richer possibilities than the mind experiments beforehand.

In fortnightly meetings the research team argued in detail from records of the classroom trials to a final form of the lesson. The specific roles of the members of the King's team were to analyse the maths and reasoning in sessions before and after trials, and they also had to clarify for themselves and to the TRs exactly what was involved in the design of cognitive intervention lessons, something that had largely been implicit in their own practice so far.

*Distinctions in pedagogy*

At the same time as we clarified the mathematics reasoning in each lesson, we looked at the possible differences in emphasis in classroom interactions. One important distinction that was established was between the conduct of TM lessons and open-ended problem-solving lessons. Although the latter may help with pupil motivation, the disadvantage is that children often tackle only a perception of the problem that is well within their current competence. Inspection of Figure 7.2 shows that children's attention is constrained all the time by the context to move upwards in thinking level – it is held within a kind of magic bottle where there is no diversion sideways allowed. The teacher's art is to keep a gentle pressure on for the whole lesson so that each child is moved ahead from their present level.

Related to this is the skill of being willing to learn with the pupils all the complexities of the mathematics understanding involved in each TM activity, first by promoting small-group discussion, and then by conducting whole-class discussions so that the whole class actually listens to what each group has constructed. If the teacher *listens*, without anxiously reaching to provide 'the correct answer', then by probing with the right questions children's misconceptions at all levels will be revealed for all to comment on, and hence the confusion between natural and maths language can be resolved (the Vygotskian aspect). Likewise, the teacher's listening-with-respect to each pupil models to the children respect for each other's contributions, so in the end they come to value the process.

The TRs' insights on the reasoning in lessons, and on pedagogical orientations, underpinned their PD work with teachers in the main-study. The demand on the TRs to support others in an approach of which they have only recent experience was an added impetus to make sense of this experience, and to find ways for its communication.

## PD in the main study

The planned 12 half-day sessions for this group (one each half-term) were to introduce the TM lessons and ensure their delivery in experimental classes over 2 years. Using these sessions to develop a model for PD was a by-product which will be discussed later.

The group suffered from substantial turnover with teachers moving schools, switching classes within the school or leaving teaching. No experimental class had the same class teacher in Years 5 and 6, although some Year 6 lessons were delivered by the class teacher of the previous year. The attendance in PD sessions fluctuated, as did the delivery of lessons. At project completion, teachers reported that an average of 17 of the 24 TM lessons were taught to experimental classes – about 70 per cent. The uneven delivery and change of teachers meant loss of some experimental classes, including those in the two 'lab' schools whose earlier classes in the first round of testing showed promising results. Undoubtedly, this unevenness in lesson delivery and attendance at the PD sessions contributed to unevenness in pupils' results.

One main plank of the PD programme was what we termed 'TM lesson simulation'. The adviser and TRs would deliver a TM lesson to the teachers as if to a class of pupils. The teachers sat in groups of three or four round a table (usually with one member of the research team) and were asked to work in small groups or as a whole class in different phases of the activity. Teachers were comfortable with this as they immediately found the experience revealing about the mathematics involved and about their pupils' difficulties. By experiencing for themselves beforehand the processes and hidden pitfalls their pupils would encounter, they could store possible strategies to use later with their own classes. By listening to and seeing the queries and solutions of the other groups, they could see how their pupils could benefit from whole-class discussion. In effect, they gained much mathematical understanding by looking at formal curriculum areas from a flexible conceptual and reasoning angle, rather than just as memorized procedural knowledge.

A second aspect of the PD sessions was reflection on classroom practice. These were also conducted in TM lesson mode, that is teachers first talking in small groups, consulting any notes they had written, on the scenes of the last TM lesson they had taught. General discussion then follows, preceded by each group summarizing their highlights, on what ideas the children came up with, and how the discussions went. Issues raised included when best to raise the level of challenge, how to close or open a discussion, when to use misconceptions or avoid them, and how to ensure inclusion and promote orderly talking and listening. Teachers gradually realized that the times for episodes suggested in the guidance can vary widely, and that resources and worksheets can be changed or not used at all, providing the teacher follows the essential agenda of the lesson.

At the time of the Leverhulme project the National Numeracy Strategy (NNS) was being introduced in Croydon. So in some sessions there was discussion on how TM might relate to the NNS. In fact, the three-phase model of the numeracy hour was found to overlap considerably with the 3-act TM model for each cycle of a TM lesson. Two of the teacher-researchers were appointed to provide PD for the NNS within the LEA, and found it possible to suggest infusing its lessons with the TM spirit rather than the reverse.

The chief change in PD was in the in-school tutorial support. The initial plan was for King's researchers to continue classroom work with the TRs and for the TRs in turn to act as visiting tutors to the main-study teachers. The aim was to coach individual teachers by first observing and/or sharing the teaching of TM lessons followed by discussion. However, when such tutor visits were made there was usually no time for discussions after the lesson in the busy school day, and often teachers had other priorities. The TRs found this very frustrating.

One reason for the uneven attendance at the half-day PD sessions was that they were timetabled at the teachers' centre from 1.30pm until 5pm. Already the bulk of the effort for the day would have been expended, and there could be last-minute emergencies at the school to attend to. Also those teachers with children of their own to collect from their schools might need to leave early.

For the last three of the PD sessions a new model was adopted, whereby both the PD session and tutor input were carried out on the same day. The PD session with main-study teachers was conducted in the morning, from 9.30am until lunch. Then the large group split into three or four smaller groups, each going to one class in the afternoon, and each included members of the research team to act as peer tutors. Here teachers team taught one of the lessons just simulated. A 'post-mortem' session immediately followed by the same small group. The emphasis in this model shifted towards group peer-tutoring and looking at potentials and constraints, and away from personal coaching and power relationships.

This model of PD created a positive momentum at the final phase of the project, something evident in the last formal session. Headteachers and LEA personnel were invited and the main-study teachers made presentations on the features they found most useful for themselves and their classes. Teachers' comments and the posters with pupils' positive feedback showed that many of the features of the approach discussed had been assimilated.

## Conclusion

First, the data on pupils' gains show the potential of the TM approach in Years 5 and 6 for raising general ability. The effect-size is slightly smaller than that for lower secondary school, but is still significant. These data suggest that the timing of the population brain-growth spurt at around age 11 does not prevent the intervention from affecting both cognitive development and also mathematics learning. Thus, although there is no doubt that all children do undergo a brain-growth spurt at this point, their brain cells may still be capable of responding to stimulus before it.

Second, the value of the approach to the generalist teachers is in developing mathematical knowledge and in pedagogy. However, the PD cannot be to give them a 2-day intensive course and then tell them to go off and do it. It has to be organized over a period of at least a year, so that by reflecting with other teachers on actual classroom practice teachers' professional skills can evolve gradually. The model of PD cycles developed at the close of the project has been adapted for King's programme of dissemination,[5] with the materials published by BEAM, a national publishing and PD organization specializing in primary mathematics.

Third, the question may be asked 'To what extent might the model of applicable research used in this project be of general value, or was its application specific to the needs of this particular project?' Variants of this model were arrived at quite independently by those concerned with the CASE@KS1 project reported in Chapter 3, and with the Wigan Arts project featured in Chapter 6. The project developed the intervention activities by a headquarters model similar to the one used in the original CASE project, but worked closely through teacher-tutors when it came to providing the PD for their main-study test. The Wigan Arts team generated all their 'thinking Arts' lessons from teacher members of the team. The common link between all these projects was that they were concerned with developing complex teaching skills all of which were theory-based. Since the praxis requires internalization of the theory, practising teachers are essential members of the team, both in the construction of thinking lessons and later in the PD of other teachers. But the teams also need the theory – hence the university-based members of the team. Perhaps the key is that there is a subtle connection between the processes of learning for cognitive development by the children in class and the process of developing the teaching skills by the teachers that promote children's development. Both need to evolve over time in a comparable way. Possibly this style of applicable research is limited to the creation of comparable skills.

The counter-argument is that if PD for teaching is delivered in the form of instructing teachers by telling them what to do, then it follows that their style of teaching will be to tell pupils what it is that they are to learn.

## Notes

1 To be published by BEAM.
2 Funded by the Social Science Research Council (1974–9). This was a joint team of three scientists and three mathematicians under the direction of Geoffrey Mathews. The maths team carried out the representative survey of 14,000 children between the ages of 10 and 16 on 12 aspects of mathematics, published as Hart (1981).
3 A 6-year project (1983–9) based at Kings College London, directed by Margaret Brown, with funding by Nuffield Foundation, Inner London Education Authority, King's College London and the University of London Examination Board. The GAIM GCSE Grades A–G syllabus, co-ordinated by the author, continued in modified forms until 1994. It was based on moderated teacher assessment of candidates' portfolio of coursework on a set of open tasks and fulfilment of topic criteria, about 30 per level. The 15 GAIM levels cover empirically identified achievements in topics from the lowest to the highest in the secondary school, with each level corresponding to an average of 1-year progress of the median pupil. GAIM levels are used in CAME

research as subdivision of NC levels, especially for levels 2–4. The full set of GAIM materials was published 1992 by Thomas Nelson and Sons (ISBN 017 4202415), including 40 investigations, 40 practical problems, topic criteria, topic tasks, level self-assessment sheets in the pupils' language, cross-referencing and teachers' guides.

4 Shayer et al. (1999).

5 CAME PD programmes are run by the Centre for the Advancement of Thinking (CAT) at King's College, London School of Education. Contact: CAT@kcl.ac.uk, tel: 0207 848 3134; fax 0207 948 3182. A network of tutors and teachers organize local PD programmes.

# 8 PRIMARY TEACHERS AND COGNITIVE ACCELERATION IN MATHEMATICS EDUCATION: TRANSFORMING TEACHERS' MATHEMATICAL KNOWLEDGE THROUGH REFLECTION

## Jeremy Hodgen

## Introduction

The knowledge that teachers need in order to teach mathematics is very different from the knowledge that adults need in order to do mathematics. Clearly, teachers need to know not only the basic ideas in the school mathematics curriculum, but also the ways in which children understand mathematics, and teaching strategies that enable children to learn mathematical ideas and concepts. There is a growing body of research demonstrating that the *way* in which teachers know mathematics is as important as *what* they know. (See the Appendix to this chapter for a more detailed discussion.) Put simply, the problem of teachers' mathematical knowledge is less about teachers learning to do more mathematics and more about transforming their existing mathematical knowledge. Teachers need to make connections between mathematical ideas, to see problems from multiple perspectives and to understand the nature of mathematical argument.

It is commonplace for commentators to point to the importance of reflection in changing teachers' professional knowledge. (See the Appendix to this chapter for a more detailed discussion.) Many mathematics teacher education programmes, therefore, have formally allocated time for reflection within PD activities. However, enabling teachers to reflect is not a simple task. There is no guaranteed way of ensuring that reflection moves beyond discussion focused simply on organization and resources. Whilst there is considerable evidence that teachers need time to reflect, the provision of time in itself is not sufficient. Teachers do not reflect deeply simply because they are told to.

They reflect because they choose to and because they perceive a need to. Even where a teacher feels such a need, the activity of reflection itself is difficult. It involves a stepping outside of one's immediate situation in order to examine one's own thinking.

Reflection becomes even more problematic in the area of primary mathematics. Much of the kind of mathematical knowledge that I have outlined above is less tangible than, say, the learning of a new algorithm for multiplication. Moreover, primary teachers in the UK are generalists, and as generalists some teachers may be more interested in other subjects. Developing one's mathematical knowledge is in itself not straightforward. To do this alongside similar changes in other NC subjects is even more difficult.

The issue that I address in this chapter is how to enable teachers to reflect deeply on their mathematical knowledge. Using Alexandra and Ursula,[1] two teachers involved as teacher-researchers in the primary CAME project, as a case study, I will discuss ways in which these obstacles to deep reflection may be overcome. By looking at their role in the development of two TM lessons, I discuss how both an imperative to reflect and an opportunity to step outside their practice as a teacher of mathematics may be created.

## The primary CAME project

The research reported on is set within the primary CAME project, as described in Chapter 7 (see also Table 7.1 for a timeline of the project). A group of teachers were followed over a period of 3 years as they participated with a group of academic researchers in the process of lesson development and wider dissemination. (See the Appendix to this chapter for a brief outline of the research methodology.) Teachers and researchers collaborated on teaching lessons and writing lesson materials.

From its inception, the project research team consisted of four researchers, four teacher-researchers (see Chapter 7) and the LEA mathematics adviser. In Phase 1, during the school year 1997/8, the research team met fortnightly to assess the feasibility of the approach and to develop TM lessons specifically for primary children. Initially, two of the academic researchers, Mundher Adhami and Michael Shayer, slightly adapted four of the secondary CAME activities, and the teachers taught these themselves to serve as material for discussion at the fortnightly research meetings. Thereafter, the teacher-researchers began to suggest contexts for the generation of new primary TM lessons.

During Phase 2 of the project, over the school years 1998/9 and 1999/2000, a further group of teachers from seven more schools joined the project to begin implementing the TM lessons more widely.[2] The primary CAME PD for the Phase 2 teachers was a 2-year programme consisting of twice-termly central seminars and a package of teaching materials. In Phase 2, the Phase 1 teachers acted as tutors to the new cohort of teachers as well as continuing to develop lessons, leading central PD sessions and visiting teachers in their classrooms to observe, team-teach and reflect with them on TM lessons.

**Table 8.1** A timeline of the key events in the development of the lessons

| Date | Activity |
| --- | --- |
| January 1998 | First trials of the initial fractions lesson |
| | First research team reflection discussions |
| | Alexandra's diagrammatic solution to Whisky and Water |
| | Reflection discussion about children's errors, strategies and misconceptions in the area of ratio and proportion |
| April 1998 | Trials of revised Share an Apple and Halving and Thirding lessons |
| May 1998 | Second reflection discussion at research team meeting about children's errors, strategies and misconceptions in the area of ratio and proportion |
| October 1998 | Lesson simulation of Share an Apple to Phase 2 teachers |
| | Phase 2 share an apple lessons taught |
| January 1999 | Informal reflection discussion with Alexandra about the Whisky and Water problem following tutor visit to Phase 2 school |
| August 1999 | Alexandra and Ursula's joint academic paper written |
| | Preparation for Alexandra and Ursula's presentation at an academic conference |
| February 2000 | Lesson simulation of Halving and Thirding to Phase 2 teachers |
| | Phase 2 Halving and Thirding lessons taught |

### Fractions and the Whisky and Water problem

In December 1997, the research team identified fractions as a potential topic for TM lessons. Alexandra and Ursula subsequently developed and trialled a potential fractions lesson with Ursula's Year 6 class in January 1998.

The lesson development process was typical of many of the primary CAME lessons. There was a brief period of intense collaborative activity when the lesson was team-taught four times. During this period, the teaching experiences were formally discussed as part of the agenda at three research team meetings. This initial period was followed by a longer and less intense period of re-drafting and further trials. (See Table 8.1, for a timeline of the lesson development.)

This initial fractions lesson focused first on different diagrammatic representations of fractions, then it moved on to explore the multiplication of fractions. The lesson concluded with the children tackling and discussing the following Whisky and Water problem.

> I have two glasses. One glass contains whisky, whilst the other contains water. If you pour half of the whisky into the water, mix it up, then pour half of that quantity back into the original whisky glass, which glass now has more whisky?[3]

Following a research-team discussion, a second trialling of the lesson placed a greater emphasis on the construction of a variety of forms representing fractions. A further reflection session followed at which the team decided to split the initial lesson into two more focused lessons: a Year 5 lesson, entitled 'Share an Apple'; and a Year 6 lesson, entitled 'Halving and Thirding'. These two revised lessons were then trialled in April 1998.

In Share an Apple the focus is on representations and comparisons of fractions. So, for example, children are asked to consider various ways of representing and comparing the magnitude of simple fractions of everyday

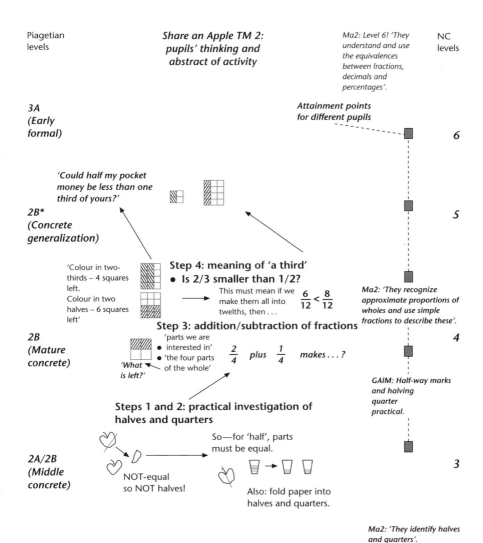

**Figure 8.1** Agenda of TM lesson Share an Apple

objects. (See Figure 8.1.) In Halving and Thirding the focus is on developing and connecting different representations for the multiplication of fractions. Halving and Thirding concludes with the children tackling and discussing the original Whisky and Water problem in the context of mixing different coloured paints. (See Figure 8.2.)

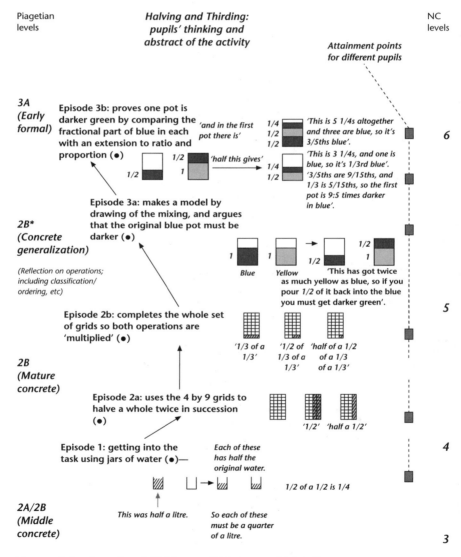

**Figure 8.2** Agenda of TM lesson Halving and Thirding

## Reflection and the transformation of mathematical knowledge

In this section I will illustrate the role of reflection in transforming mathematical knowledge for teaching using three examples. In the first, I will explore Alexandra and Ursula's collaborative reflection in relation to their perspectives on children's understanding of mathematics. In the second, I will examine Ursula's developing understanding of mathematical discourse and argument. In the final example, I will look at how Alexandra made a connection between her 'everyday' mathematics and formal mathematics. The focus of attention will shift from developing multiple perspectives on children's learning, through understanding of the nature of authority within mathematics, to making connections between 'everyday' and formal mathematics. I use this somewhat artificial split for the purposes of presentation and I do not mean to suggest these are wholly separate aspects to mathematical knowledge.

### *Developing multiple perspectives on children's mathematics*

In developing these TM lessons, Alexandra and Ursula were using their own intuitions based on knowing at first hand the source of some of the children's learning difficulties. However, this knowledge was limited in several respects. For example, they underestimated the difficulties that children would have discussing and comparing simple diagrammatic representations of fractions. In March 1999, in an interview, Ursula recognized this:

> Take that where we started with fractions and we started with assuming, kind of assuming that Year 6 kids would understand the full notation of fractions but actually what it's turned into is a Year 5 lesson on half an apple and what do you mean by half.

Nevertheless, their reactions to the university researchers' initial attempts to introduce a more explicitly research base had not been not positive. In January 1998, the university researchers led a discussion about children's errors, strategies and misconceptions in the area of fractions (for example, see Johnson 1989). This discussion included difficulties children have with fractional notation, with the various meanings of fractions and with diagrammatic representations of fractions. A further discussion in May 1998 was focused on Mundher Adhami's mathematical background notes to the children's mathematics in both lessons, which were essentially a write-up of the January 1998 discussion.

In March 1998, Ursula commented that the January discussion was 'way beyond' her needs:

> I mean the input we've had into fractions so far has been an argument about, I don't know, some mathematical term or whatever between the

[academic researchers] that hasn't been helpful to Alexandra and I in developing the lesson at all. One-off chats with Mundher [Adhami] have, because they've been about developing the first part of the Year 5 lesson. But then what we've had actually at, at the meetings has not been helpful, because it's too high powered and it's not related to the task necessarily from my eyes. It's way beyond it.

A year later she still remembered the discussion as a 'nightmare'. In May 1998, Alexandra commented that she felt this explicit research base was unnecessary: 'These background notes, unless you've got somebody who's particularly interested in the sort of mathematical side of it, this is too complex.'

Yet, 18 months later, in August 1999, writing a paper to present their lesson development work to an academic conference, Alexandra and Ursula took a rather different position in relation to the mathematical background:

The finalized Year 5 lesson, Share an Apple (see attached background notes [the same notes Alexandra had earlier described as 'too complex'] for clarification) . . . is largely based on the refinements made at this stage, although part of the work done at this stage (the operating on fractions within the context of bars of chocolate) has now been moved to the Year 6 lesson. The agenda can be summarized as: meaning of fractions; notation; adding simple fractions; comparing size of fractions . . . [Halving and Thirding] naturally follows within the spiral curriculum of the CAME lessons. Like Share an Apple, it deals with exploring the distinction between the part-whole relationship expressed in a fraction, and the ratio relationships between the parts that make up the whole.

Here Alexandra and Ursula referred explicitly to the agenda of the mathematical discussions that they had previously described as 'too high powered'. Moreover, they referred to the mathematical background notes as a clarification. Throughout this joint paper, Alexandra and Ursula demonstrate significantly more sophisticated and explicit understandings of children's difficulties.

Whilst recognizing that writing a paper for a wider audience encourages a far more considered analysis than off-the-cuff remarks at a relatively informal meeting, the changes in their mathematical knowledge are nevertheless significant. Indeed, the imperative for a considered analysis was a critical factor in enabling significant changes in their mathematical knowledge for teaching. The writing of this joint paper was certainly not the only event in Alexandra and Ursula's PD. The 'nightmarish' research-team discussions were a key factor in providing them with the mathematical language in which to frame their reflections.[4] However, these discussions in themselves did not produce transformations in the teachers' mathematical knowledge. The act of writing and collaborative reflection, and the necessity to assume new identities as tutors over and above their identities as teachers, were, I contend, critical factors in enabling the two teachers to explore their own thinking as teachers. Moreover, it is noteworthy that Alexandra and Ursula catalysed each other's reflective activity rather than being led by others.

### Developing an understanding of authority in mathematics

I now turn to consider Ursula and the validity of mathematical knowledge. Her first reflections on teaching the fractions lesson in January 1998 were dominated by feelings of excitement. Presenting the lesson to the research team for the first time, she described the children's reaction to the Whisky and Water problem as follows.

> They were really noisy. I had stand-up arguments between children about the maths, shouting at each other. If anyone had come in, they'd have thought it was chaos, but I loved it.

Schools and classrooms are generally characterized by order and control. It is significant, therefore, that Ursula used what in other circumstances might be interpreted as the negative descriptions of 'chaos' and children 'shouting at each other' to emphasize the excitement and enthusiasm that both she and the children felt in the lesson. This excitement is framed in language which appears to challenge the teacher's control of the mathematics classroom. This highlights, I suggest, an intuitive feeling that authority in mathematics rests not with the teacher but through mathematical discussion.

In August 1999, in the joint paper described above, Ursula (together with Alexandra) described the children's reaction to TM lessons in rather more mathematical terms:

> One of the outstanding features of TM lessons . . . is the enthusiasm with which classes tend to greet them . . . For several children these lessons have changed the way in which they view maths, engendering a far more positive attitude to the subject than previously held . . . In many ways this excitement reflects not just the content and structure of the lessons but, equally importantly, the fact that one important feature is the dialogue that is central to this way of teaching and learning, not just between teacher and pupil but also between pupil and pupil. The lessons are about all members of the class, including the teacher, exploring mathematical ideas and challenges together in a climate in which everyone's views are valued.

I note the contrast with Ursula's initial reflections about children's excitement. In this later writing, she was certainly celebrating the children's excitement. However, this excitement was related explicitly to changes in children's attitudes to the discipline of mathematics, to the importance of mathematical dialogue and to the climate of the mathematics classroom. They went on to describe the children's reactions to the Whisky and Water problem during the first lesson trial:

There followed a brief silence and then uproar. Many of the children made intuitive guesses, but the result was that of an equal split between the whisky glass, the water glass and them both holding the same amount of liquid. Very quickly the pupils attempted to explain their answer and the majority of them instinctively began to draw their various glasses. Some children used colour, others used fractions, a few used ratio.

Again the contrast with Ursula's initial reflections described above is striking. The sense of excitement remains. However, it is now placed in much more explicitly mathematical terms. The earlier 'chaos' and 'stand up arguments' have been replaced with the 'uproar' of 'intuitive guesses' and 'pupils attempt[ing] to explain their answer' using a range of different approaches to tackle the problem. The change in Ursula's mathematical knowledge is a significant one. Her initial intuitive and implicit feeling about teacher authority in mathematics has been replaced with an explicit understanding of the importance of mathematical argument and discourse in judging the validity of ideas. Again, I contend that the opportunity presented by the academic writing exercise was critical in enabling Ursula to step outside her identity as a teacher of children.

### Connecting 'everyday' and formal mathematics

I now turn to consider Alexandra's 'informal' solution to the Whisky and Water problem and how reflection enabled her to build connections between her everyday mathematical knowledge and formal school mathematics.

In January 1998, when the Whisky and Water problem was presented to the research team, each of the academic researchers attempted to solve the problem using an arithmetical/algebraic solution. (See, for example, Figure 8.3.)

| | Contents of glass A | Contents of glass B |
|---|---|---|
| To begin with all the whisky is in glass A and all the water is in glass B | All whisky (X) | All water (Y) |
| Pour half whisky in glass A into glass B | $\frac{1}{2}X$ | $Y + \frac{1}{2}X$ |
| Pour half of the whisky and water mixture back into glass A | $\frac{1}{2}X + \frac{1}{2}(Y + \frac{1}{2}X)$ | $\frac{1}{2}(Y + \frac{1}{2}X)$ |
| Each glass contains an equal quantity of water. Glass A contains more whisky ($\frac{3}{4}$ of the total) | $= \frac{3}{4}X + \frac{1}{2}Y$ | $= \frac{1}{2}Y + \frac{1}{4}X$ |

**Figure 8.3** An example of an arithmetic/algebraic solution of the Whisky and Water problem

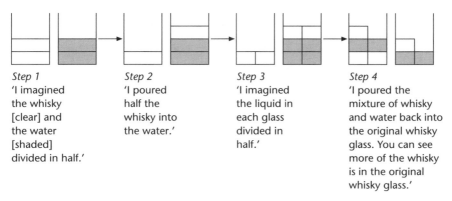

Step 1
'I imagined
the whisky
[clear] and
the water
[shaded]
divided in half.'

Step 2
'I poured
half the
whisky into
the water.'

Step 3
'I imagined
the liquid in
each glass
divided in
half.'

Step 4
'I poured the
mixture of whisky
and water back into
the original whisky
glass. You can see
more of the whisky
is in the original
whisky glass.'

**Figure 8.4** Alexandra's diagrammatic solution of the Whisky and Water problem

On the other hand, Alexandra had previously solved the problem using diagrams. (See Figure 8.4.)

When pressed to share her solution, Alexandra protested that 'It's not scientific.' Her belief was that her solution, although perfectly appropriate for everyday problem-solving and despite producing a convincing solution, was not truly mathematical, because it used diagrams. She believed in short that her solution could not form the basis of a truly mathematical argument. Alexandra's belief that her pictorial solution was not mathematical was shared by other teachers. At the lesson simulation of Halving and Thirding, in February 2000, having solved the problem using a method similar to Alexandra's, a group of Phase 2 teachers spent a considerable amount of time looking for 'a mathematical way of proving this'. In the subsequent reflection session a month later, the same group of teachers returned to the topic discussing whether a child's verbal explanation of a diagrammatic solution was mathematical. All these teachers accepted the diagrammatic method as a solution to the problem, but they found it hard to accept that this method was mathematically valid.

In fact, Alexandra's diagrammatic solution is both mathematically elegant and rigorous. In her solution she 'imagined' that, although the liquids are mixed completely, she could still separate out the whisky and water in each glass in order to solve the problem. This is exactly the same reasoning step that is needed for an arithmetic/algebraic solution. Moreover, the diagrammatic solution is much more efficient than an arithmetic/algebraic solution in generating answers to a variety of related questions regarding the problem. For example, the ratio of whisky to water in each class, and hence the strength of the two mixtures, can simply be visually read off the final diagram. In contrast, the arithmetic/algebraic solution requires further manipulation to answer this question. Alexandra's solution was indeed judged a mathematically better solution by the teachers and, significantly for Alexandra, by the King's researchers.

Alexandra was both pleased and excited at the positive reaction to her solution, exclaiming 'Oh, yes!' Although this pleasure and excitement did not in itself result in a fundamental shift in her mathematical thinking, the academic researchers' judgement did provide the basis for a further reflection. It was a year later, in January 1999, when reflecting on this discussion, that Alexandra appeared to experience a sudden mathematical insight about the mathematical validity of diagrams.

This unplanned and informal discussion took place following a tutoring visit to a Phase 2 teacher. Alexandra had taught another TM lesson, Pegboard Reflection, which, like the two fractions lessons, explored connections between numerical and diagrammatic representations. After the lesson, she had had a long discussion with a Phase 2 teacher about the children's misconceptions that they had observed. Alexandra and I had then returned to her own school to discuss the visit.[5] Alexandra commented on experiences of school mathematics:

> *Alexandra*: 'Thinking about that it was something no-one really made clear to me at school. You know that something like quadratic equations have a spatial meaning. No-one made the connections between the spatial and the number system.'
> *Jeremy*: 'A bit like Whisky and Water.'
> *Alexandra*: 'Yes, like at school we just did fractions using fraction notation, you know using the procedure to multiply and add fractions. No-one ever made it clear that diagrams were just as mathematical.'

When prompted to make a connection with the Whisky and Water problem, she linked her diagrammatic solution very explicitly to the standard algebraic/arithmetic procedures for the multiplication of fractions. Her insight appeared very significant to me at the time, as I noted:

> Alexandra talked about her school experience of quadratic equations, etc. and how no-one had made the connection for her between the spatial and the number systems. It felt like ideas slotting into place there and then for her . . . This felt like an 'ah-ah' moment, where this suddenly occurred to Alexandra.

It is worth noting that in a similar way to Ursula in the last example, Alexandra's notion of authority in mathematics education appears to have shifted. In contrast to her earlier pleasure at her diagrammatic solution being judged acceptable by 'experts', here she appeared to be understanding mathematical validity of diagrammatic solutions for herself. A later reflection in March 1999 emphasizes the shift in her mathematical knowledge:

> I would say now, Jeremy, it's using one preferred learning style to achieve an outcome and it's partly about that, isn't it . . . I'm going off at a tangent now, but do you remember when we were talking about number lines and I was explaining my convoluted number line that I had in my head. It never occurred, I know this sounds really stupid and pathetic,

but . . . I'd never thought about the fact that you'd have a number line in your head or [another teacher] wouldn't be able to visualize a number line in her head and . . . those shared experiences or lack of experiences depending on your particular learning style. It's made . . . me think more . . . about . . . the intellectual processes that kids go through to get somewhere.

In particular here, she was reflecting on the advantages of multiple perspectives on mathematical problems in terms of children's preferred learning styles, thus making a further connection between her knowledge as a doer of mathematics and her knowledge as a teacher of mathematics.

It is important to note that Alexandra's 'new' mathematical knowledge is in a sense relatively small. She has not learnt to use diagrammatic solutions – she could do these previously. Moreover, during the development of lessons, she demonstrated on many occasions an arithmetical proficiency that would suggest she would have been able to successfully perform the arithmetic/ algebraic solution used by the academic researchers. Nevertheless, in terms of her mathematical knowledge for teaching, the shift in her thinking is highly significant. Knowledge about how mathematical ideas are judged valid is crucial to the teaching of mathematics. Indeed, without such an understanding of the validity of diagrams in mathematical argument, it is difficult to see how a teacher could promote such an understanding for children and enable children to make similar connections between everyday and formal school mathematics.

In addition, the context for this shift in Alexandra's thinking is significant. In her role as a tutor, she had been forced to be communicative articulately with the Phase 2 teacher requiring her to think about her thinking. Whilst this discussion was not focused on the Whisky and Water problem, it appears to have prepared the ground for her insight about the validity of mathematical diagrams. In this case, the discussion about children's understandings appears to have created a need to resolve issues within her own learning of mathematics. As a tutor, she was able to step outside and reflect on her identity as a learner and doer of mathematics.

## Discussion

In this chapter, using the case study of two teachers involved in the primary CAME project, I have argued that teachers' initial reflections about teaching did not in themselves promote significant change in mathematical knowledge for teaching. However, these two teachers' initial reflections did appear to provide the necessary basis for further and more significant reflection. For the teachers discussed here, a critical factor in overcoming obstacles to change were situations in which the teachers not only felt the need to reflect deeply but had the opportunity reflect on their experiences as teachers and lesson developers from the outsider's role of teacher educator or academic.

Moreover, these were situations in which the teachers perceived *for themselves* the need to reflect. The teachers were themselves catalysts in their own learning.

The transformation of these two teachers' intuitive, implicit and everyday knowledge into explicitly mathematical understandings was considerable. It should be noted, however, that their PD opportunities within primary CAME were very different from those available to most primary teachers. The Phase 1 programme was a deliberately intensive approach: central research-team meetings were fortnightly over the first year; TM lessons were trialled on a sometimes weekly basis; and collaboration on lessons with other research-team members through team-teaching and observation was fortnightly. They have built up prolonged and significant relationships within the research team. This intensive programme was both a consequence of and necessary to their roles as lesson developers and tutors. These teacher educative and curriculum development roles themselves gave these teachers an imperative to reflect and enabled them to step outside their experience as primary teachers of mathematics and thus reflect on earlier reflections from an outside perspective. Moreover, the programme provided them with many and various opportunities in which to reflect. I contend that experiences like this are crucial to promoting fundamental changes in primary teachers' mathematical knowledge for teaching. Yet, to replicate such intense experiences for the majority of primary teachers would be an extremely difficult (if not impossible) task. The problem, then, is how to provide opportunities that provide teachers with an imperative to reflect and that enable teachers to step outside their immediate situation as a teacher. The experience of teachers from Japan suggests that the collaborative perfection of lessons may provide such an opportunity (Stigler and Stevenson 1991). In China the better maths achievement of primary school children is argued (Ma 1999) to be in part due to their teachers having been taught themselves at school in a reflective way, and in part because enough of teachers' school time is formally allocated to collaborative discussion of their pedagogy.

In its current work with teachers (see Chapter 8 for a discussion of these developments), the primary CAME project is aiming to provide structured opportunities for teachers to collaborate on teaching. It is to be hoped that these collaborative experiences will provide teachers with opportunities for repeated deep and substantial reflection.

## Appendix: research literature and methodology

### *Mathematical knowledge for teaching*

In a comparative study of Chinese and US elementary teachers, Ma (1999) found that Chinese children's better performance in international mathematical tests could be explained by the Chinese teachers' better mathematical knowledge. More of the Chinese teachers in Ma's study could successfully do more of the school mathematics curriculum. More significantly, however, the

Chinese teachers had a very much greater knowledge of different models, examples, explanations and mathematical arguments that they would use when teaching young children. Whilst many of the Chinese teachers had what Ma termed a 'profound understanding of fundamental mathematics', none of the US teachers had such a deep and broad understanding of elementary mathematics. This was despite the US teachers almost uniformly studying mathematics to a higher academic level.

Ma argues that substantive mathematical knowledge for teaching, or profound understanding of fundamental mathematics, consists of four inter-related elements: *connectedness* between simple and more fundamental ideas; consideration of *multiple perspectives* and approaches to mathematical ideas; knowledge about the *basic ideas* underlying the mathematical curriculum; and knowledge of the entire elementary, or primary, mathematical curriculum and its *longitudinal coherence*. Moreover, it includes knowledge about what Yackel and Cobb (1996) refer to as 'sociomathematical norms', that is the ways in which mathematicians do mathematics and how mathematical knowledge is validated.

In the area of ratio and proportion, a profound understanding of fundamental mathematics includes an understanding of the ways in which many children fail to understand fractions and decimals as equivalent. Such knowledge goes beyond knowing how fractions may be converted to decimals and vice-versa to the knowledge that both are different forms of expressing rational numbers. It also includes an understanding of the different ways in which rational numbers may be represented, numerically and diagrammatically.

These themes are borne out by other research. In a study of primary mathematics in the UK, Askew et al. (1997) found that teachers who understood and taught mathematics as a connected discipline were significantly more effective than teachers who did not.

### Reflection

There are many reviews of mathematics teacher education, which highlight the importance of reflection in teacher learning and argue that teachers need time to reflect in formal teacher education programmes (for example Clarke 1994; Grouws and Schultz 1996). Wood and Turner-Vorbeck argue that reflection is central to teacher education. Mathematics teacher learning, they argue, 'involves interpretative constructions and reconstructions in thinking through processes of reflection on the activity of self and others' (1999: 174). Schön (1983) distinguishes between forms of reflection: reflection-in-action, or reflection during the practice of teaching; and reflection-on-action, or overt review and analysis of teaching after teaching has occurred.

Whilst the provision of time is a necessary condition for reflection, it is not a sufficient one. Clarke warns that reflection is an active process not a passive one. It is dependent on teachers perceiving a 'need to become articulate, to be communicative, or to use thoughts as objects of systematic attention with their colleagues' (1994: 44). Teachers do not reflect simply because they have been told to do so. Cooney and Shealey point to the difficulties inherent in actually stepping outside oneself:

> A precondition for the act of reflection is the ability of the person to decenter and view his or her actions as a function of the context in which he or she is acting. Schön's (1983) reflective practitioner, a notion that enjoys so much credence in the field of education, cannot exist unless the individual is willing to step out of himself or herself and view his or her actions from a relativistic perspective.
>
> (1996: 100)

Yet, many argue, like Wood and Turner-Vorbeck (1999), that it is this difficult, challenging and complex process of decentring that is most likely to result in significant transformations of a teacher's knowledge.

### Methodology

The research reported here is based on a 3-year longitudinal study into the professional change of six teachers. I conducted the fieldwork between November 1997 and January 2001. Data collection was qualitative, using participant observation techniques. I analysed this data through initial open coding and subsequent progressive focusing (Miles and Huberman 1984). Throughout the study, I have discussed my ongoing analysis with the teachers. This explicit process of negotiation has been directed at ensuring the teacher influence on the development of my ideas and to subject my ideas to the rigour of scrutiny by the participants. Together with the other sources of data, this provided a significant degree of triangulation.

### Notes

1 I use pseudonyms for all the teachers and schools involved in the project. I refer to the academic researchers by real names.
2 In this chapter, I refer to the Phase 1 teachers as teachers, teacher-researchers or Phase 1 teachers, whilst I refer to the second group of teachers as Phase 2 teachers.
3 Note this is different to the well-known symmetrical problem in which a quantity of whisky is poured into the water and the same quantity of the resulting mixture poured back into the whisky. This revised problem is a considerable simplification accessible to a greater range of abilities than the original due to its potential for visualization. It is much more open to a wholly diagrammatic solution and produces a more concrete set of end results.
4 Significantly, I later observed Alexandra and Ursula lead discussions with primary teachers using this more explicit knowledge of children's learning difficulties. At the lesson simulation of Halving and Thirding in February 2000, Alexandra used their joint paper together with the academics' mathematical background notes as the basis of a presentation on children's difficulties with fractions. In June 2000, Ursula led a considerably more challenging discussion on the mathematical meanings of ratio and proportion at a National Numeracy Strategy training session. Hence, whilst

their initial reactions to these ideas were negative, they did later come to appreciate the value of what was at the time a very challenging and mathematically difficult discussion.

5 This informal discussion was not designed as a PD activity for Alexandra. Instead, it was conducted as part of my research into her own and the Phase 2 teachers' professional change.

# 9  CREATING A CA PROGRAMME IN THE ARTS: THE WIGAN LEA ARTS PROJECT

## Kenneth Gouge and Carolyn Yates

### What makes a CA programme?

The term CA has been used in the context of a series of projects originating from King's College London from the early 1980s. It describes the process of promoting the cognitive development of pupils in normal school settings. The underlying theory is both Piagetian and Vygotskian.

All CA programmes are based on the same guiding principles and are aimed at moving children through the stages of cognitive development first described by Piaget and Inhelder (Gallagher and Reid 1981) as pre-operational, concrete operational and formal operational, at a faster rate than is usual for 'normal' development. The Wigan Arts, Reasoning and Thinking Skills (ARTS) project, funded by Wigan LEA and the North West Arts Board, is no exception. Its particular aim is to accelerate adolescent development from concrete to formal operational levels through the medium of drama, music and the visual arts. The project takes a subject- or domain-specific approach to developing thinking skills (McGuinness 1999).

The ARTS project has produced 30 'thinking Arts' lessons in music, visual arts and drama, for use by Arts teachers with pupils in Years 7 and 8. Our working hypothesis is that by promoting reflection within cognitively demanding Arts activities, children will be induced into processing more chunks of information in their involvement in each of the Arts, with, over time, an effect on their general cognitive performance.

The lessons build in the following guiding principles for the design of CA programmes.

1 **Cognitive conflict** Piaget outlined a model of cognitive development as a process of equilibration that occurs when the learner's existing mental structures are challenged by cognitive demands which they cannot quite meet. Vygotsky describes a ZPD for individuals. It is that zone where the

learner is working just beyond the limit of their capability alone. Vygotsky says 'instruction is good only when it proceeds ahead of development, when it awakens and rouses to life those functions that are in the process of maturing or in the [ZPD]' 1978: 82). The transition of a teacher from a position of ensuring pupils are 'comfortable' with what they are trying to learn, to one where the teacher deliberately pushes pupils into their 'discomfort' zone, is not easy.

2 **Social construction** Vygotsky describes the construction of knowledge as a social process. He emphasized the importance of a 'mediator' in the process of learning, someone who encourages the learner to 'talk his or her thoughts out loud' so that both the speaker and listeners can interact to modify each other's ideas. Obviously, where the group consists of a teacher and pupils, the teacher plays a leading role in helping the pupils to construct new meaning. But more influential in children's development is their interaction with peers. Pupils working together construct knowledge as they question each other about meanings and argue over possible explanations. Teachers using CA techniques are expected to become adept at classroom management skills, maximizing the opportunities for pupils to work and talk together as 'peer coaches'. Vygotsky hypothesized that half-formed or potential problem-solving strategies turn into complete or successful skills either by chance, by spontaneous effort on the part of the learner or by the mediation of more able peers or older people (such as parents or teachers). The process of mediation involves either 'framing' the problem, that is helping the learner redefine it, or demonstrating how to do specific examples related to the problem so that the learner can 'mirror' the actions of the 'expert'. This is what Bruner calls 'scaffolding'.

The teacher has to ensure that the 'mix' of pupils interacting is at an optimum to promote discussion. The whole-class interaction is especially important, with the teacher ensuring that there is both collaborative learning within each small group and between each group to weave the whole class into a community of learning. This attempts to activate the ZPD for as many individual pupils as possible.

3 **Preparation and bridging** A community of learners needs to have a clear and shared agenda before it can be given challenging tasks to accelerate development. In this preparatory stage, the key words associated with concepts identified as being a focus for development within the lesson are introduced. The development of a shared language between teacher and pupils is critical to the success of the development of thinking in the lesson. Pupils also need to be given the opportunity to create links and transfer their newly constructed knowledge to their own 'outside' world. This is called 'bridging'.

4 **Metacognition** Piaget talks of 'reflective abstraction' as a feature of late adolescent formal thought. He means the ability to think about one's own thinking, to reflect on the abstractions of one's own thought. CA teachers give their pupils space and time to explore ideas amongst themselves, to offer justifications, to question others' arguments in a constructive way

and to feel safe to take risks with ideas. The Arts as a discipline have a reputation for developing this supportive environment.

5 **Reasoning patterns** These are the focus for each CA lesson. They provide the 'thinking agenda'. Pupils are not taught concepts directly, they are provoked to employ particular modes or 'patterns' of thinking which are based on Piaget's descriptions of formal operational thought. Existing CA programmes arising from CAME and CASE (Adey et al. 1995; Adhami et al. 1998; Adey et al. 2001) list the particular reasoning patterns they are designed to promote in children's thinking. Identifying these for music, drama and the visual Arts was a major part of the research and development phase of the ARTS project.

As well as writing and trialling the lessons to ensure they incorporate the principles detailed here, the ARTS team has developed and piloted in-service training for teachers to help them understand both the underlying theory of the programme and develop the special CA teaching skills required by the programme.

## Why use the Arts as a vehicle for CA?

The NFER report *Arts in their view: A study of youth participation in the Arts* (Harland et al. 1995) found that a large percentage of adolescents felt, amongst other things, that participation in the Arts gave them a sense of achievement, helped overcome shyness, and that they acquired useful techniques and skills. Policy-makers perceive the Arts as motivating for adolescents and beneficial to the nation as a whole. The Craft Council stated in 1998:

> There are few areas in life where the nation's priority for education, health and employment and industry are not dependent on the development and application of creative, practical skills.
> (National Advisory Committee on Creative and Cultural Education, 1999: 27)

> The National Advisory Committee on Creativity and Cultural Education also recognizes the Arts as a natural vehicle for promoting thinking skills, defining creativity as a mode of learning which encompass 'thoughtful playfulness' through experimenting, exploring, developing, critically evaluating and testing and a conscious attempt to challenge assumptions and preconceptions of self, expressed as the 'active effort to unlearning order to learn afresh'. Active engagement in creative learning encourages 'self-monitoring, reflection upon their own performance and progress, and thinking about their own thinking – metacognition' . . .
> (National Advisory Committee on Creative and Cultural Education, 1999: 92)

The report by the Calouste Gulbenkian Foundation (1982) describes the Arts curriculum in terms of learning in the Arts and learning through the Arts. Learning in the Arts is about developing personal artistic skills, and includes the development of a range of interpersonal skills. This model has been used to design good Arts curricula (Wigan Education Authority 1989), but it fails to provide much insight into developing higher levels of thought in young people who are usually categorized as not naturally 'gifted' or 'artistic'. These pupils enjoy their Arts experiences at school, but reach a plateau at quite an early age, not significantly progressing either in their own artistic skills or in a deeper awareness of aesthetics and critical reflection on artists' work. They do, however, continue to develop interpersonal communication skills and this is well documented.

Within the Arts subjects, formal operational thought in adolescence is characterized by the development of judgement, both of their own creative actions and those of others. Clearly, the Arts are also about creativity. We believe that creativity is not a special faculty with which some young people are endowed and some are not. It is a type of thinking that can be developed, provided we have a sound model of at least some of the component parts that contribute to it. Creativity requires mental discipline, previous experience and a firm grounding in knowledge. Few pupils reach this stage by the age of 16. Most pupils reach the concrete generalization level, where they can make simple assumptions and deductions to offer imaginative explanations. Formal operational thought can begin to develop at about the age of 12, but barely 20 per cent at present show this by the age of 14 (Shayer et al. 1976). Children who have reached this stage can reason about hypothetical events that are not necessarily in accord with their direct experience. The formal thinking of adolescents and adults tends to be self-consciously deductive, rational and systematic. Adolescents typically begin to examine their own thinking and evaluate it while searching for inconsistencies and fallacies in their own beliefs and values concerning themselves, society and nature (Peel 1971).

There is a broad consensus that the Arts are a rich vehicle for the development of young people's thinking, but the thinking strategies developed through the Arts are at an implicit level. A major aim of the ARTS project is to provide a model of how critical thinking can contribute to the development of what Michael Shayer calls 'intelligence-in-action'. It is recognized that the Arts should promote rigour and high-level thinking and that there are dangers in assuming the Arts are all about 'fun':

> There is such a thing as creative work and creative thinking and getting children to produce it is a matter of the highest educational importance. We do not, however, share the view of some past advocates of the Arts, that this amounts to a need to encourage 'free expression', that any response is acceptable from pupils because it is their response.
>
> (National Advisory Committee on Creative and Cultural Education, 1999: 29)

> Creative work has to stand on the shoulders of previous work and understanding in the discipline in question. In all of them we have to do the hard work of learning the grammar and syntax as part of our attempts to make advances or improvements within them. This is no less true of the Arts than of the sciences.
>
> (Calouste Gulbenkian Foundation, 1982: 33)

The members of the ARTS research and development team believe that we have made a significant contribution to the creation of a 'grammar and syntax' of children's cognitive development through the Arts and that this is encapsulated in the three 'taxonomies' described in this chapter. These provide a consistent structure for designing a programme of intervention lessons, taking into account both the intrinsic rigour of music, drama and the visual arts and the cognitive development of the adolescent. Teachers recognize many pupils' weaknesses as artists and critics, but rarely know how to help them overcome these other than by providing more and more opportunities to create or act as critics, without any systematic attempt at accelerating their cognitive development in these domains. The ARTS taxonomies are an attempt to deconstruct the neglected aspects of critical thinking which practising artists use intuitively, and which they usually have difficulty in articulating. They do not provide a description of learning in and through the Arts in its totality.

## The project outcomes

There is some justified criticism that many existing thinking-skills programmes are difficult to use, require specialist and expensive training programmes and are de-motivating for pupils. Kite states that 'In general, little guidance is given to teachers as to how they can translate the teaching of thinking into their classroom practice and there is a dearth of instructional material to help children gain the thinking skills they will need in their lives' (2001). From the outset, the ARTS team wanted to overcome these criticisms and create a package of materials that would be easy to use and motivating. At the same time we wanted to challenge teachers to restructure their attitudes and behaviour as mediators of cognitive development. The model created had to relate to teachers' subject expertise, be easy to use in the initial stages and, through the positive response of pupils and noticeable improvements in the quality of their thinking, draw teachers into experimenting and improving their pedagogic skills.

An initial research and development phase was undertaken between September 1999 and May 2001. The ARTS team is composed of experts in Arts education and identified 'good practitioner' teachers. This team had two tasks: to develop a taxonomy of reasoning patterns appropriate to each subject and describing cognitive development stages, and to write the intervention lessons. All members of the team taught the draft lessons themselves as well as supervizing their use by teachers in five pilot schools. Using video film of the lessons and feedback from the pilot schools, the lessons were redrafted. There are 30 lessons in the final programme. The response from pilot teachers has been very favourable. All Wigan LEA Arts teachers are now offered training in using the ARTS project materials. By February 2002 it is expected that the curriculum materials will be in use in the majority of Wigan LEA secondary schools.[1] Cognitive gains will be measured using Arts-specific tests and the Science Reasoning Tasks (Shayer and Adey 1981).

By June 2002 a full evaluation will take place, including looking for measurable cognitive gains in the first pilot schools' pupils.

## Constructing taxonomies for the Arts

Like Shayer and Adey (1981), the ARTS team sought guidance from the Piagetian model to begin constructing a taxonomy for identifying the level of cognitive development and the level of complexity of the curriculum in music, drama and the visual Arts. A review of a number of existing taxonomies and cognitive level descriptions (Bloom and Krathnohl 1956; Kohlberg 1966; Biggs and Collis 1982; Fusco 1983) was undertaken and, along with an analysis of the stepwise descriptions of competence from the NC in music, drama and visual arts, a single taxonomy for all three subjects was drafted. This was used to draft some preliminary lessons. There was then an iterative process between constructing the taxonomy and piloting the draft lessons under observation. This led to better descriptions of the characteristic behaviours of children in each of the Arts at concrete, concrete transitional and formal operational levels.

It became clear that whilst there are commonalities in the types of reasoning developed through each Arts subject, there were unique descriptors of how these were expressed. Three separate but overlapping taxonomies emerged.

In turn, the refining of the taxonomies and the clarification of the nature of each reasoning pattern led to further redrafting of each lesson. Detailed teacher's notes were written for each intervention lesson, describing how to mediate, intervene and initiate cognitive conflict, construction and meta-cognition through a questioning approach. A framework for questioning was constructed to assist teachers during their training to become more precise mediators and interventionists (Pout 2001).

The teaching sequence for the lesson package is determined by:

1 the difficulty of the reasoning pattern, in other words how accessible it is at concrete levels, determined by the ARTS taxonomies;
2 a school's own Arts subjects' timetable and model; and
3 the relative difficulty of each lesson, indicated by the pilot teachers' professional judgement.

In their final form, each of the three ARTS taxonomies has the following two dimensions.

1 The level of cognitive demand: We have chosen just three levels: concrete, concrete transitional and formal operational thinking to correspond with the expected cognitive development in KS3 pupils.
2 Six Arts-specific reasoning patterns: These are based mainly on Piaget's theories and Fusco's literature taxonomy (1983). With the exception of one, narrative seriation, which is only described in the context of drama, they are considered by us to be generic to the Arts.

The three taxonomies are shown in tables 9.1, 9.2 and 9.3.

**Table 9.1** Taxonomy for the visual arts

| Piagetian level | Symbolic representation | Frames of reference | Critical reflection | Intention, causality and experimentation | Classification |
|---|---|---|---|---|---|
| *Concrete* | Use signs and symbols in own work<br>Recognize common visual symbols, such as peace<br>Draw/create natural representations<br>Use stereotypes as a shorthand way to communicate ideas<br>Use basic understanding of scale, perspective and proportion to create an artwork | Recognize and describe aspects of a genre, content of work<br>Accept and offer alternative accounts of their own work and the work of others | Reflect on the artistic intentions of self and others<br>Respond to artworks using descriptive language based on experience and/or evidence | Link cause and effect<br>Make assumptions about an artwork based on direct experience or evidence<br>Create a simple hypothesis about causes or intentions | Sort and group artistic ideas and styles, such as Impressionists and Cubists<br>Put artists into a series or sequence using given criteria, such as date, technique or style<br>Recognize similarities and differences in artworks using two variables, such as media and time<br>Recognize the usefulness of classification systems to communicate about art |
| *Concrete transitional* | Use a range of symbols and icons to create meaning<br>Develop personal symbolic language for example use pictograms to describe a personal experience<br>Interpret hidden/implicit messages in an artwork by 'reading' symbolic meaning, such as heart motif<br>Understand and refer to universal explanations for symbols, for example a dove for peace<br>Change ratios and perspective to carry meaning in own artwork | Recognize and describe similarities and differences between artistic styles<br>Construct alternative interpretations of artworks<br>Recognize the importance of context to the interpretation of artworks<br>Recognize and interpret abstract forms<br>Recognize how style affects meaning | Refine own work in the light of feedback<br>Identify and reflect on the use of artistic techniques to create meaning, for example the use of multiple viewpoints to express time and space<br>Explain own work to others giving a logical sequence for decisions made, such as analysis and synthesis through sketchbook work<br>Justify opinions and actions in creating own art | Make and apply rules, such as systems painting based upon an artists self-imposed restrictions on the use of media<br>Find and test solutions to artistic problems<br>Make conscious changes to an artwork in order to achieve a desired effect<br>Explore a number of different approaches in the creation of an artwork<br>Identify an artist's explicit purpose | Re-classify an artwork in the light of new evidence/ experience and explain reasons for new classification<br>Compare and contrast artworks using reasoned arguments based on more than two variables |

| | | | | | |
|---|---|---|---|---|---|
| *Formal operational* | Recognize and speculate on intentions for the use of symbols in the work of others<br>Create and use coherent symbolic systems, for example from given information, speculate on the meaning of artworks from other cultures<br>Use in a complex way, ratio, proportion, scale and perspective to convey meaning | Make explicit implicit meaning<br>Select the appropriate style in their own work in order to achieve the desired effect<br>Experiment systematically with style and media in order to explore their impact on meaning, such as representing a 2-D object in 3-D | Understand and evaluate the artistic intentions of self and others using justified argument and counter argument<br>Use deductive reasoning to piece together to form a evidence judgement about an artist's intention, for example utilize standpoints such as form, content, process as a mood to develop discussion and pursue personal study through sketchbook<br>Make clear and justifiable connections between their own work and the work of others<br>Offer and justify multiple interpretations when viewing artworks | Create a reasoned hypothesis about an artwork<br>Make the invisible visible, for example making concrete things that only exist in the imagination – Surrealism<br>Experiment with artistic rules and conventions in order to achieve a particular response, for example Magritte and altered scale<br>Deduce an artist's implicit purposes<br>Experiment with a wide variety of media and styles in order to communicate meaning | Recognize that an artwork consists of multi-variables and be able to categorize and re-categorize aspects of a work using three or more variables, such as form, content, process and mood<br>Make rich comparisons between two or more artworks simultaneously<br>Create and justify own system for classifying artworks to judge and evaluate its impact<br>Recognize that all classification systems are purposeful and driven by social constructs such as style and convention, which can be re-defined or created |

**Table 9.2** Taxonomy for music

| Piagetian level | Symbolic representation | Frames of reference | Critical reflection | Intention, causality and experimentation | Classification |
|---|---|---|---|---|---|
| *Concrete* | Create naturalistic representations, such as drum roll for thunder<br><br>Use simple accepted conventions to create and/or interpret music, such as rhythmic patterns | Recognize basic features of a piece of music, such as rhythm<br><br>Accept and offer alternative accounts of the meaning of a piece of music | Talk about the intentions of self and others, and be able to describe their personal responses using descriptive language<br><br>Reflect on the intended effect of a piece of music | Link single cause and effect, for example minor key for sad<br><br>Make assumptions about intent based on direct experience/evidence<br><br>Create a simple hypothesis about causes and/or intent | Identify similarities and difference in music, for example mood and pace<br><br>Sort, group and sequence musical styles using two variables at a time and provide reasons for decision<br><br>Sort and group musical ideas and styles, such as classical and orchestral |
| *Concrete transitional* | Make and/or interpret style allusions, for example the use of 'Dies Irae' in the 'Fantastic' Symphony<br><br>Construct and explain alternative responses to music<br><br>Use different sounds to represent 'hidden messages' in music based on universals, such as drum roll for threat/danger/suspense<br><br>Use given codes systematically, such as musical notation, keys and modes | Recognize and describe a range of musical styles and structures, such as blues<br><br>Recognize the effect of context on the way music is created, performed and heard<br><br>Construct and justify alternative interpretations and accounts of a piece of music<br><br>Select the appropriate elements of music to realize a stated intention | Evaluate how variables affect music, such as loud, soft, tempo, instrumentation and context<br><br>Justify opinions and actions<br><br>Appraise a piece of music with an awareness of intention, form and structure<br><br>Refine work and opinions in the light of feedback | Find and test solutions to musical problems, such as how to represent a landscape in music<br><br>Use a limited range of variables, such as rhythm, pitch and instrumentation to create a particular effect<br><br>Make justifiable assumptions about a composer's intention<br><br>Compose a piece of music in a recognized style or genre | Compare and contrast pieces of music using more than two variables simultaneously<br><br>Re-classify in the light of new evidence<br><br>Recognize, identify and categorize musical structures, conventions and styles |

| Formal operational | | | | |
|---|---|---|---|---|
| Look for and interpret hidden messages in music without guidance or help | Make explicit implicit meanings in own and others work | Use argument and counter-argument in order to evaluate the musical compositions of self and others, and be able to justify their arguments by referring to their musical knowledge | Purposefully experiment with musical rules in order to achieve a desired effect | Make rich comparisons of two or more pieces of music, identifying multiple variables, such as context, style and instrumentation |
| Create and systematically use coded methods for 'writing' or 'reading' music, such as graphic scores | Understand how genre and style effect meaning | Critically analyse the effect of such features as instrumentation, structure and style on the success of a piece of music | Use a complex range of variables, such as melody, style and pace, to create a musical composition | Make justifiable connections between own work and the work of others using three or more musical dimensions |
| Create musical metaphors juxtaposing styles and genres, such as Jimi Hendrix 'Star Spangled Banner' | Explore systematically the use of genre, style and structure to achieve desired effects, such as the creation of mood and the use of instrumentation | Make justifiable connections between own work and the work of others | Speculate on a composer's musical intentions and evaluate his/her success, for example by evaluating the choice and effectiveness of such aspects as use of instruments, style and so on | Recognize that a musical performance consists of multi-variables and be able to categorize aspects of a work using three or more variables |
| Combine two or more rhythmical patterns to create a new musical meaning | Explore the effect of transferring or transposing different elements of music | Give multiple and justifiable interpretations of a piece of music using a variety of musical dimensions/elements | | |

**Table 9.3** Taxonomy for drama

| Piagetian level | Symbolic representation | Frames of reference | Critical reflection | Intention, causality and experimentation | Classification | Narrative seriation |
|---|---|---|---|---|---|---|
| Concrete | Use gesture and mime to suggest place and character<br>Use stereotypes, recognizing that they are culturally determined<br>Use of simple signs and symbols to aid narrative or characterization, for example a cloak for a king or queen | Recognize and describe basic features of a piece of drama, such as flashback<br>Accept and offer alternative accounts, recognizing that the interpretation of a person's behaviour is dependent on context<br>Recognize and understand stereotypes within a defined context<br>Describe events from different viewpoints | Reflect on the motives of self and others and respond using descriptive language<br>Comment on the use and impact of style and structure | Link a single cause and effect<br>Make assumptions about motivation and/or artistic intent based on evidence and/or direct experience<br>Create a simple hypothesis about causes | Recognize that a piece of drama consists of a number of variables, such as movement and dialogue<br>Recognize the elements of style and genre, for example forms of characterization and non-linear narrative<br>Sort dramatic work into groups using given criteria, such as is it true? | Sequence events into a justifiable order<br>Awareness of beginning middle and end of narratives<br>Tell a story or create a drama from a particular point of view |
| Concrete transitional | Use non-verbal methods to create meaning and character<br>Recognize that the relative position of characters conveys the nature of relationship and narrative<br>Use objects and characters in a non-naturalistic way to convey meaning<br>Use simile and analogy to carry meaning, for example particular characters representing different viewpoints in an argument | Recognize and describe a range of dramatic styles and structures, for example direct address and abstract<br>Use a range of dramatic styles to enhance meaning and to re-shape meaning, for example flashback and soliloquy<br>Represent the same story in a variety of styles<br>Construct alternative interpretations, taking into account different viewpoints | Justify opinions and actions<br>Recognize and explain bias and propaganda<br>Refine work and opinions in the light of feedback<br>Identify and reflect upon the use of dramatic structures to create meaning | Find and test solutions to dramatic problems, such as how to show a character ageing<br>Use dramatic/theatrical techniques in order to create an intended effect, such as silence, voice tone and level<br>Link a character's motives to his/her actions and relate this to the consequences of his/her actions | Compare and contrast pieces of work, ideas, arguments or outcomes<br>Re-classify in the light of new evidence<br>Recognize dramatic conventions and styles as a means of categorizing the component parts of a drama | Re-order events in order to change their original meaning or create a new story<br>Use complex narrative techniques, such as flashback<br>Speculate on a number of different endings |

| | | | | | | | |
|---|---|---|---|---|---|---|---|
| | Use style allusions to generate meaning, such as top hat for posh | Make explicit implicit meaning in own work and the work of others | Construct alternative endings of own work and the work of others | Use deductive reasoning to piece together evidence to form a judgement about a piece of drama | Construct and justify logical, critical arguments and counter-arguments about a piece of drama | Analyse part or whole relationships in terms of intent and causality | Make rich (multi-layered) comparisons of two or more pieces of drama |
| | Use icons to carry meaning, such as a flag for nationalism | Explore the relationship between style and genre and their impact on meaning | Construct alternative realities and their defining parameters for own work | Make clear and justifiable connections between their work and the work of others | | Create more complex hypotheses involving a number of variables | Select appropriate conventions and styles in order to achieve a desired effect |
| | Recognize the use of metaphor | Juxtapose apparently conflicting or contradictory genres and styles to achieve a novel effect, such as the use of a game-show format in a trial | | Understand and evaluate the dramatic intentions of self and others and con-struct arguments to justify critical conclusions | | Use a range of styles and structures and theatrical techniques in order to create an intended effect, for example the use of lighting to create mood and atmosphere | Recognize that a drama performance consists of multi-variables and be able to categorize aspects of a work using three or more variables |
| *Formal operational* | Create dramatic impact by using the relative positions of characters and the performance space to create meaning | | | | | Identify and evaluate the intentions of others | Recognize that all theatrical |
| | Create metaphors and analogies to communicate meaning | | | | | | |
| | The ability to recognize and speculate on the use of symbols by others | | | | | | |

Tell the same story or create a drama from a variety of different viewpoints

Create a narrative which carries more than one meaning at the same time, for example metaphor and parable

Recognize layers of meaning in others' narratives

## Derivation of the reasoning patterns defined by the Arts taxonomies

In discussions with expert Arts educators it became clear that, underlying many important concepts in the Arts are some deep logical assumptions, which can be described using Piagetian reasoning patterns. For example, the visual Arts clearly promotes proportionality and spatial temporal thinking. Music develops spatial-temporal thinking and formal logic and drama is a good vehicle for frames of reference and causality-type thinking. It is also clear that understanding simile, metaphor and paradox (an 'outcome of frames of reference' type thinking) is associated with language development, and in turn is associated with the development of formal logic.

The six reasoning patterns that we have identified and described within the three taxonomies are:

1 classification;
2 frames of reference;
3 symbolic reasoning;
4 critical reflection;
5 intention, causality and experimentation; and
6 narrative seriation.

Here we justify each of our chosen reasoning patterns and indicate how they were derived.

### 1 Classification

This is closely related to descriptors of this reasoning pattern found in the CASE and CAME projects as well as in Fusco's taxonomy (1983). It is the ability to group attributes or objects by one attribute and to shift to another attribute and regroup, according to new evidence, direct experience or need. Within this is the ability to rank or order objects using consistent criteria, such as chronology, loudness and size.

### 2 Frames of reference

Initially Fusco's taxonomy provided a working definition as 'the ability to co-ordinate two systems, each involving a direct and inverse operation but with one of the systems in a relation of compensation or symmetry with respect to the other' (1983: 9). This definition implies probabilistic reasoning and combinatorial reasoning. It describes a relativity of thought. We redefined this type of reasoning within the Arts to include inverse mental operations, that is reciprocity ('if this is that, then that is also this') and notions of equilibrium, balance and symmetry in a completed piece of drama, music or art. It is dependent on relational aspects and involves mental operations that attempt to reconcile conflicting information and reach closure, although firm conclusions are not necessary. Implicit assumptions must be made and can be justified. It involves elements of manipulating space/time continua in music and drama and objects relative to each other in visual Arts.

### 3 Symbolic reasoning

Piaget recognized the essential interplay between language development and other areas of symbolic action for young children. He and Inhelder describe how symbolic play leads to children's understanding of the implicit organization of language structures between the ages of 2 and 5, that is pre-operational to early concrete stages of development (Gallagher and Reid 1981). There has also been considerable work in the development of symbolic representation as part of mathematical deductive thinking, in the shift from concrete generalization to abstract, formal models (Adhami et al. 1998). In the Arts symbolic representation is usually described as part of the process of emotional and social development, rather than cognitive development, linking the use of symbols to increasingly sophisticated ways of communicating. Building on this, we define symbolic representation as the use of a wide range of visual and auditory symbols to create perspective, imagery and communicating ideas.

### 4 Critical reflection

We have created a tighter and more rigorous description of what often appears as 'evaluation skills' in thinking skills programmes (McGuinness 1999) and in the framework for English Years 7 to 9 (Department for Education and Skills 2001). For us, it is thinker as 'critic', in other words the development of judgement. Peel's (1971) description of the development of adolescent judgement provides a useful framework for the shift from egocentric ways of judging to a sophisticated process of judging thoughtfully. He talks of 'restricted judgement' which is often tautological, premise denying and irrelevant. This matures to 'circumstantial judgement', which is still bound solely by content of the context or situation and often at first takes into account only one element. This type of judgement is usually very descriptive with some explanation. At its most mature, judgement becomes what he calls 'imaginative comprehensive judgement'. This involves invocation of independent ideas and consideration of all aspects of the context or situation under analysis. At this level, comprehensive explanations are offered for reaching judgmental conclusions.

### 5 Intention, causality and experimentation

This reasoning pattern implies the act of making in each of the art forms, that is performance and improvization in drama, composition and performance in music, and creating a piece of art. There is an interplay between 'thinking through' actions before implementing them and systematic experimentation in order to reach desired outcomes. This is a mental operation beyond direct verification, depending on deduction, implied consequences and chains of inferences. It involves hypothesizing: 'If I do this rather than that then it is likely that . . .' or 'another way of achieving this effect might be to do . . . but then that would lead to . . .'.

In order to move forward in the mental process it is necessary to have the will to conclude what is or is not a causal relationship, and if the outcome of actions based on intentions is going to be positive or negative. At its lowest level it is based on 'trial and error'; at its highest level, it is fully integrated with formal modelling (see quote from Eliot on p. 149).

### 6 Narrative seriation

Fusco's description of seriation proved to be too restrictive and failed to capture the important thinking skills associated with creating and recreating stories and narratives. Seriation is described as:

> The ability to order one set of objects according to some relevant dimensions and next to be able to order a second set of objects along a relative dimension in relation to that set of objects.
>
> (Fusco 1983: 158)

It is apparent that this describes some aspects of the manipulation of variables within a visual Arts context, but these are better located within the reasoning pattern of 'frames of reference' as we describe it. It does not seem to apply to the realm of music at all.

In drama the need to have the ability to use narrative forms gives us a description of this reasoning pattern within our taxonomy as:

> The ability to sequence and re-sequence actions to create a narrative and to be able to manipulate different component parts of that narrative relative to each other to give multiple meanings and layers of complexity.

It is more than being able to tell a story well from beginning to end.

## Can formal modelling within the Arts be described?

Initially, we used a working definition of this as a separate, identifiable reasoning pattern based on the CASE materials (Adey, Shayer and Yates 1995). We accepted that mental modelling can take many forms, that a model gives a representation of something else. A formal model has 'moving parts' that are abstract entities, they must be imagined. It gives the thinker a 'microworld' where he can speculate and predict the outcomes of actions, or cause and effects. Formal models require the mental manipulation of many variables together, as well as other mental skills, depending on the purpose of the model required. Map-making is one form of modelling. It involves the interaction of two factors: an individual's expression of codes (encoded ideas) and the social conventions of different maps for different purposes. Stories use both explanatory and descriptive models to draw the reader in. Science fiction stories involve the 'willing suspension of disbelief' when we are invited to enter mentally another world with rules that are internally consistent to that world. Designers are practised in visual modelling and can juggle the conflicting demands of form and function. Engineers use mathematical models. Scientists have models to explain phenomena such as solid, liquid and gas states, energy transfers and photosynthesis. Creating mental models requires far more thought than using them. In drama formal modelling is required to produce high-quality improvizations and performance. In music it is the complete act of composition, where a musician can model the whole piece and all its interrelated component parts inside her head. In visual art it is constitutive in the act of making. Formal modelling within the Arts is not recognizable as a discrete reasoning pattern. It is a complex interplay between all the reasoning patterns. It constrains creativity to be exercised at a deeper level (the poet Eliot wrote that 'some creative writers are superior to others solely because their critical faculty is superior'[2]). At a concrete level, the progression of specific thinking skills is not interrelated, but at what we call the concrete transitional level there has to be *some* integration. By the formal operational stage, the thinker can express any strand in more than one way and can generalize by making links and connections.

Creativity often depends on combining existing elements, reinterpreting in unexpected ways or applying elements in novel ways. It involves making unusual connections, seeing analogies and relationships, and juxtaposing pieces of information that are apparently initially unconnected. It is integral to imaginative activity and the Arts as a whole are defined by it:

> Imaginative activity in our terms is not the same as fantasizing or imaging, although it may involve both. It is not simply producing mental representations of things that are not present or have not been experienced . . . Imaginative activity is a form of mental play – serious play directed towards some creative purpose. It is a mode of thought which is essentially generative: in which we attempt to expand the possibilities of a given situation; to look at it afresh or from a new perspective, envisaging alternatives to the routine or expected in any given task.
>
> (National Advisory Committee on Creative and Cultural Education, 1999: 29)

## An example of the thinking Arts lessons

The style in which the thinking Arts lessons are conducted can be seen as follows.

### Visual Arts lesson 3

*Symbolic representation*
The lesson deals with the way in which objects and contextual events can be

open to multiple interpretations and addresses universal symbols. The lesson should help pupils to move towards the ability to read hidden messages and understand symbolism.

The lesson requires:

- Reproductions of 'The Arnolfini Wedding' by Jan van Eyck and 'Mr and Mrs Ossie Clarke and Percy' by David Hockney;
- word bank cards; and
- room response sheets.

*Concrete preparation phase (5 minutes)*
Introduce lesson to whole class, pointing out that artists can challenge our accepted way of thinking about things. Explain that this often involves the artist choosing carefully the objects they choose to put into their pictures.

*Whole class*: Discussion about portraits. Artists often depict people alongside the possessions they value in their personal surroundings. The two pictures are very similar in many ways, but they were produced centuries apart.

*Construction phase (15 minutes)*
Put into groups of about 5. Discuss what is similar in the two pictures. Are there common objects? Which objects do you think are important? What are the people looking at? Why do you think the artists have chosen the 'objects' that appear in their paintings? Is the room the people are in significant? Do you think the artists had a reason for including certain objects, placing them alongside the two people? What could the objects symbolize about the lives of the people?

Give out the Word Bank (see Figure 9.1) sheet to help each pupil organize ideas. Do the prioritizing exericse. Feed back and justify the order to the whole class.

Some of the objects have special meanings. What could these be? In the Van Eyck picture the little dog represents domestic fidelity; the crystal prayer beads suggest faith; near them, the convex mirror may be the benevolent, observing eye of God.

Focus on one of the paintings, choose three objects that express a particular idea. How do these objects inform us about the meaning of the picture?

*Working individually*: Imagine yourself in a room full of objects you treasure. The room response sheet (Figure 9.2) represents this room. You are to record the objects you value in the boxes marked 'A'. The objects you choose will reveal something about yourself. Explain that these objects are a sort of self-portrait.

*Cognitive conflict phase (12 minutes)*
*Whole class, teacher as narrator*: Imagine the police have entered your imaginary room and told you that you have 5 minutes to gather up only five possessions. You will never return to the room again; your security has gone forever, you will be a homeless refugee.

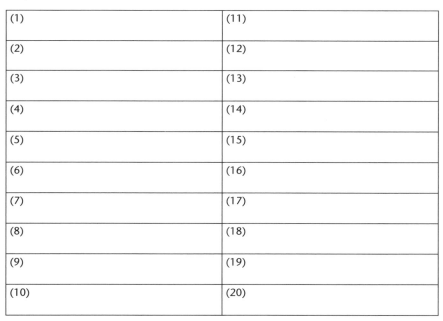

| Objects | Themes | Purpose |
|---------|--------|---------|
| Man | Togetherness | Celebration |
| Women | Love | Announcement |
| Cat | Joy | Record |
| Dog | Gloom | Describe the feeling |
| Flowers | Family | Describe a relationship |
| Mirror | Pets | |
| Window | Relationships | |
| Lamp | Marriage | |
| Light | Domestic | |
| Furniture | Ordinary | |
| Couple | Home | |

Put the words in the order of importance that you think best describes your feelings about the pictures.

| (1) | (11) |
|-----|------|
| (2) | (12) |
| (3) | (13) |
| (4) | (14) |
| (5) | (15) |
| (6) | (16) |
| (7) | (17) |
| (8) | (18) |
| (9) | (19) |
| (10) | (20) |

**Figure 9.1**   Word bank sheet

*In groups*: Discuss what these objects mean to you, what they reveal about your life, what they represent and symbolize. How will the choice of objects be useful in your new life? What value do you attach to them?

Is this set of objects the same as those recorded on the room response sheet under A? Record the newly selected objects under the original objects. If you have chosen different objects, why have you done so?

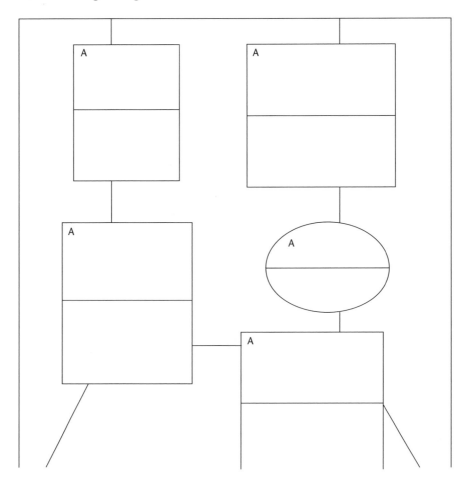

**Figure 9.2** Room response sheet

*Construction phase (10 minutes)*
Teacher reminds the class that the lesson focus is how artists can teach us about communicating using symbols, and how objects can be imbued with other meanings which can often be universal, for example a skull indicates death. An artist uses everyday objects and adds other meanings which are not immediately obvious. The word 'symbol' derives from the ancient Greek 'symbolon', a token composed of two halves, used to verify identity by matching one part to the other. It has come to mean a concrete sign or image that represents some other, more abstract thing or idea by convention, analogy or metaphor. Words describe and interpret signs, but they cannot substitute for them.

Signs and symbols are important ways of communicating in the world around us and in other areas of study, for example maps in geography and notation in music. Road signs provide immediate information.

*Working individually*: Create a picture from the five objects you have finally selected to form a portrait of yourself, which shows the importance of each object for you.

At a concrete level, pupils create naturalistic representations, using simple symbols and signs with a one to one match, for example important objects are drawn extra large, such as a dove to signify peace. At the transitional level, they use symbols carrying hidden meanings. They develop their own personal symbolic language and can use simile and analogy in pictures they create, for example a favourite teddy bear dressed in their own favourite clothing holding open a photograph album. Formal operational thought shows itself in pictures that use symbolic objects to convey multiple meanings, for example a disproportionally large bird in flight indicating a wish to leave home, world peace or a favourite family pet.

*Metacognitive phase (8 minutes)*
*In groups at first then as a whole class*: Think back over the lesson. What made you think differently during this lesson? Why? Are there links between the pictures you analysed and your portraits? What was the easiest/hardest part of the activities? Were the activities important in gaining an understanding about symbols and meanings in art? If so, why?

At a formal level, nuanced judgements will be made. Pupils will explain their thinking about hidden meanings of symbols and speculate on the intentions of others in using symbolic imagery. They will recognize the profound universal uses of symbols (a candle symbolizing the passing of time perhaps?) and show empathetic understanding. They are at a stage where they can use and interpret metaphor and also multiple meanings. They will speculate on intentions for the use of symbols.

## Next steps

Having completed the research and development phase and the pilot phase of the project, the 30 lessons and the teacher in-service course will now be tested on a large scale, in approximately 20 schools in Wigan LEA and several more in Hammersmith and Fulham and Harrow LEAs. This phase will provide empirical long-term data on pupils' performance to evaluate the CA effect on raising attainment. The first data analysis is expected by 2003.

## Acknowledgements

The authors of this chapter wish to thank the Wigan LEA ARTS project team and, in particular, the team leaders Harry Mcloughlin, Nigel Leighton and Lorna Pout.

## Notes

1 The Arts Reasoning and Thinking Skills materials are available from the Wigan Arts Advisory and Support Service, The Professional Development Centre, Park Road, Hindley, Wigan, WN2 3RY.
2 In the essay *The Function of Criticism*, in T.S. Eliot (1932) *Selected Essays*, p. 30. London: Faber.

# 10 DO ENHANCED TEACHING SKILLS REQUIRE SPECIALIZED VOCABULARY? THE ICI BRIDGING PROJECT

## Reed Gamble and Michael Shayer

### Introduction

In Chapter 8 it was shown that objections by practising teachers to the use of technical vocabulary ('jargon') can be overcome when they find that theory-laden language assists in the planning and conduct of specific lessons, and also in reflection on how they can be improved further.

Such a technical language for the CASE project has been in use for 10 years. Yet reflection on practice has shown that the term 'bridging' (drawn initially from the practice of Feuerstein's 'instrumental enrichment' intervention with early adolescents) lacks definition, leading to little occurrence in teaching. By encouraging divergent thinking by pupils on how some newly acquired skill or concept might be applied in contexts different from those in which it was learnt, transfer might be enhanced. However, can we extend the definition to include any process by which the intervention style of the CASE lessons can be incorporated in the conduct of good instructional science lessons? ICI has offered funding for the conduct and publication of an applicable research project, and this will be described in some detail later in this chapter.

With much of the preceding CA research, however, there can be read in the naïve assumption that it is merely necessary to *publish* work that contains good and useable ideas and the world will gladly recognize and adopt them. This entirely neglects the *political* aspect of any proposed change, so first this will be discussed.

### Current politics of educational change

Education in 2001 is canonical, hierarchical and authoritarian – accompanied by all the attributes of power (legalized frameworks, able to provide 'reward and punishment' via Ofsted and publication of KS3 results, ASTs and so on). This approach has some clear advantages. For example, it has taken a lot of the slack out of the system, by providing teachers with a well-developed and structured curriculum and with assessment via Ofsted a means of judging quality. Such an approach could be highly effective in developing an efficient and effective national education system.

However this approach, like all others, is based on a belief system or set of beliefs. Beliefs are enablers, clearly, but they can often *disable* us from developing different thinking. Belief can sometimes equal blinkers.

Every man prefers belief to the exercise of judgement. (Seneca)

So, we have the search for the 'Holy Grail' of the perfect curriculum. Implicit in this term is some believed notion of how children learn, resulting in a prescription for improving learning being based on mandatory sequences in heavyweight lesson planning, and so on. That notion is none other, psychologically, than behaviourism. Children, like pigeons and rats, can be taught any behaviour one chooses provided it is broken down into small enough steps, each of which can be drilled until automatic. Get the sequence right – but right only in the sense that each step incorporates all the preceding steps, and that there is no confusing redundancy or irrelevance in any of them – and the desired behaviour will eventuate (stimulus-response). The implicit model of the brain with its neurones and synaptic connections is a *tabula rasa*, upon which the teacher is exhorted to write by putting the desired knowledge in front of the children. And the teacher is not trusted to use his own judgement as to how to induct his pupils into the disciplines of physics, biology and so on; he needs to be given a precise list of Statements of Attainment (SoAs) and their suggested sequencing.

This leads to a sociological model as shown in Figure 10.1. Political, legal and legitimate power in the education system lies in the circles. Professionals and others employed in these zones will obviously believe that further

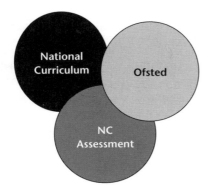

**Figure 10.1** Power zones in education

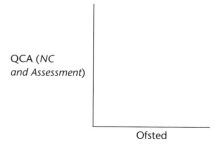

QCA (*NC and Assessment*)

Ofsted

**Figure 10.2**  Learning map A

development and refinement of what they do will, and must improve learning. This approach leads to Figure 10.2.

This is where science teachers tend to operate when thinking about teaching and evaluating KS3 science. The concepts they think with are:

1  curriculum SoAs (continuity, coherence, progression, and so on);
2  assessment (validity and reliability); and
3  Ofsted (quality of learning and quality of teaching).

These are all, apparently, just empirical matters to be verified by experience only. Apparently no additional theory is involved – the behaviourist theoretical assumptions are hidden both from the political administrators and from most teachers. The system is believed to work well as distant, heavily top-down policies ensure the quality of education.

Suppose, however, that the behaviourist model is inadequate on *two* grounds: it has no model of the *child* (which might lead to the prediction, irrespective of their prior knowledge being the same, that a given learning task was within the capacity of one or totally inaccessible to another), this is the Piagetian aspect; and it has no model of the *social aspect* both of cognitive development and also science learning itself, this is the Vygotksian aspect.

Then if the limiting factor to learning is the cognitive level of the pupils, the above approach has little further to offer. The locus of attention needs to move from the quality of the educational system to the cognitive realities of the classroom and the cognitive demands of the task in question, in other words from Figure 10.2 to Figure 10.3. The move is from policy to pupil.

Learning map A (Figure 10.2) does have some implicit assumptions about cognitive aspects, but has to handle them by notions such as 'differentiation', which in its turn implies that the differences between children are differences only in their prior knowledge.

Learning map B (Figure 10.3) similarly has implicit assumptions about the quality of educational system (the Piagetian and Vygotskian models of cognitive development referred to above), but approaches explicitly the issues of how children learn, develop and collaborate in their learning, and also models quantitatively knowledge itself. Learning map A has nothing to say about these.

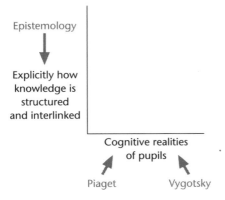

**Figure 10.3** Learning map B

A physicist is tempted to ask whether perhaps neither Map A or B is wrong, and rather they are analogous to the wave-particle duality account of fundamental particles? Let us try this assumption. Initially (analogous to learning map A) physicists found the particle model of electrons intuitively appealing. It meant they could still think in common-sense and Newtonian terms. Likewise, they could handle gamma rays as transverse waves, and again think in traditional ways about them. However, then they were asked (analogous to learning map B) to deal (with great difficulty) with the notion that electrons could also be diffracted and hence had wave properties, and some of the behaviour of gamma waves were those of discrete particles. This is both counter-intuitive and more difficult conceptually (and was strongly resisted by some contemporary physicists). Eventually, the convention was established that each model would be used in the contexts to which it was appropriate (the Copenhagen solution).

So perhaps one could say – while stigmatizing the antics of politicians such as Kenneth Clarke at the DES saying he had no use for 'barmy theories' and 'elaborate nonsense' and Chris Woodhead after leaving Ofsted likewise dismissing thinking skills as fashionable progressive nonsense, as analogous to that of the more hidebound physicists of the 1920s – that the educational system has an appropriate use of learning map A for the process of exercising democratic control over the values to be promoted by schooling and the competencies of the agents (teachers and so on) and institutions (schools and so on) involved. However, unless learning map B is used for thinking about the processes of learning and teaching by all concerned (and that includes the three parties involved in learning map A) most of the acts of judgement employed in learning map A will be flawed.

Perhaps one needs to think of three zones of learning as shown in Table 10.1. Bear in mind that at least 50 per cent of the KS4 NC is presently in zone 3, that is without at least 2 years' intervention for CA (for example CASE), from the beginning of KS3 many pupils will have little or no chance

**Table 10.1**  Zones of learning

| 3 Zones of Learning | Relation between student and task levels |
|---|---|
| Zone 1 | Cognitive level of students > cognitive demand level of task (learning map A) |
| Zone 2 | Cognitive level of students ≤ cognitive demand of task (learning map B) |
| Zone 3 | Cognitive level of students < cognitive demand of task (for example the need for CASE) |

And in each of these one needs to think of students' motivation as well.

of achieving grades which will serve them for entry into post-KS4 education. Think of the effect of that on students' self-esteem and hence their motivation. Zone 1, of course, describes the teaching problem for pupils in the top 20 per cent of the ability range entering traditional grammar schools, or in comprehensive schools in equivalent forms produced by setting from Year 7 onwards. This leaves a further 30 per cent of students in Zone 2, for whose learning present map A planning is inadequate. This describes the background to the ICI initiative on which this chapter is reporting.

Before concluding this section on the politics of education, it is perhaps worth remembering Max Planck's comment on the unwillingness of most academics of the 1920s to accept the new physics: 'A new scientific truth does not triumph by convincing its opponents and making them see the light, but rather because its opponents eventually die, and a new generation grows up that is familiar with it' (quoted in Kline 1986). Empirically, we find that most teachers' belief systems about children's learning can be changed. Politicians and administrators are a more difficult case, and for some Bohr's comment does apply. However, if we describe briefly a model which has been used successfully for developing teachers' thinking and behaviours, it may be possible to conjecture how to approach the others.

In Figure 10.4 the sequence of change is shown. Simply put, pupil outcomes are produced by classroom processes. Yet the *only* thing that sets up classroom processes are what pupils see, hear, notice or in some other way 'pick up' from the teacher.

So voice tone, gesture and body language are important aspects of teacher behaviours. Small changes in teacher behaviours lead to surprisingly large changes in classroom processes, so it is these which need to be changed. Given a very sparse present lexicon of teacher behaviours, the development of a suitable technical/practitioner vocabulary has been necessary.

If we consider teacher development in CASE as progressing along the novice to expert continuum, the main observed blocker is most teachers' initial inability to develop new teacher behaviours which enable and drive CASE classroom processes. This deficit situation can almost always be traced back to the very top of the model, that is thinking and beliefs. Without

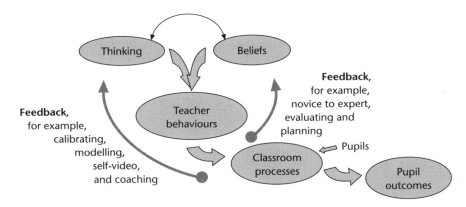

**Figure 10.4** CASE-North training model

significantly changing most teachers' thinking (as a basis for action) and beliefs – and there is a lot of evidence that both of these are often very resistant to change – they will continue with their existing teacher behaviours, which will result in existing classroom processes rather than any CASE type processes. Thus, it is here that one must start.

Bearing in mind that much thinking about teaching and learning is subconscious or even unconscious, the training starts with straightforward things that can be seen in videos of lessons and so consciously addressed. The following feedback loops are structured into the training within the model as shown in Figure 10.4, using a suitable vocabulary.

1 *Calibration*: What do CASE processes look like in Act 2 and Act 3 (see Figure 10.6)? What does their absence look like? How can you tell? Suitable group video observation exercises of real novice and expert lessons enable teachers to calibrate for the presence of CASE processes. This is clearly important as it is the only way to evaluate the success or otherwise of a CASE lesson. Just getting the operational detail right (such as providing a well-planned and well-disciplined science practical that works well) is not adequate on its own. The main, and really only, criterion for success is the operationalization of both axes of learning map B and their effective interaction.

2 *Constructing novice and expert CASE teacher behaviours*: Using the same videos and explicitly linking to (1) above, teachers are asked to describe both.

3 Given the ability to describe both kinds of behaviours, teachers can then plan the process of moving from one to the other. The novice end of the continuum provides a well-described and structured situation to move away from, and the expert end gives a scenario to work towards. The interaction between (1) and (2) provides the framework enabling teachers to evaluate videos of their own lessons, and hence to prepare for coaching.

4 Finally, teachers can be asked to reflect on the effect of some commonly held science teacher beliefs about teaching and learning on teacher behaviours and, thus, on the resulting classroom processes. They can then decide to choose different behaviours to suit different teaching situations.

This training model, delivered over a period of 2 days, has been used by the CASE North management team for the initial training of some 100 teachers as coaches for their schools in the North of England.[1] Subsequently, it is reinforced by coaching in the schools over the period in which teachers are developing their CASE art.

In order to illustrate the further scope of the ICI bridging project, it is first necessary to give more detail of the theoretical basis of the original CASE programme of research and development.

## Piaget, Vygotsky and the CASE model

The Piagetian aspect in the context of a 'thinking science' (Adey et al. 1995) lesson can be seen in Figure 10.5, showing the structure of lesson 27: floating and sinking, normally taught near the end of the 2-year intervention period, in Year 8.

In this lesson pupils are shown a two-way matrix of jars that vary by size in one dimension and weight in the other. After being shown one demonstration in which size only was varied, and the other in which weight only was varied (some sinking and some floating), they are then asked to predict whether other bottles jars will float or sink. Their predictions are mostly false, and this is where the cognitive conflict begins. After this they have to collaborate to argue to a more sophisticated model where it is the weight to volume ratio is the crucial concept.

The squares to the right indicate the various levels of understanding which different pupils in the class might attain in the process of working on the problem. At least four levels of achievement are possible, each of which can be acknowledged.

The Piagetian aspect of this is clear from Figure 10.5. The current level of each pupil can be assessed in Piagetian terms, as can each intellectual step of the lesson context. It can be seen that no less than five episodes of bridging occur in the context of this one lesson.

However the Vygotksian aspect determines the whole-class management strategy of the teacher. Two quotations from Vygotsky introduce two essential concepts. First:

> there is a gap between any student's . . . actual developmental level as determined by independent problem-solving and the level of potential development as determined through problem-solving under adult guidance or in collaboration with more capable peers.
>
> (Vygotsky 1978: 163)

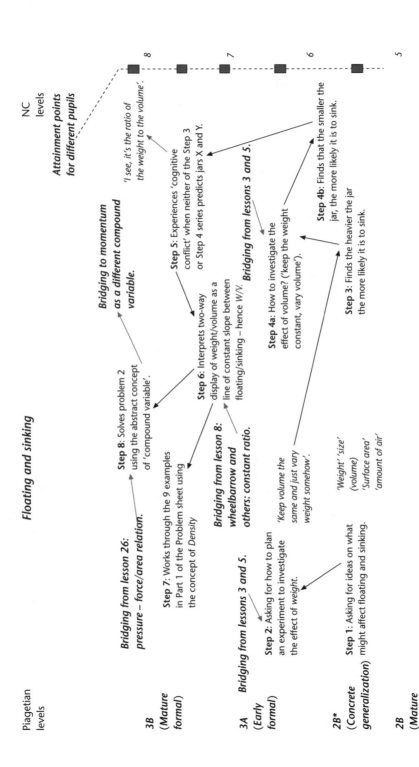

**Figure 10.5** Structure of thinking science lesson 27

Here he describes the concept of the ZPD. Children's assured competencies, as typically tested by performance on psychological tests where – in one sense of the word – they have no time to *think*, is not all there is to know about the children's present minds. There are in addition many half, quarter, three-quarters completed strategies already operative which are only waiting for either the appropriate mediation or children's own mindful accommodation to the situation which requires them, for their completion. Cognitive development then mostly consists of converting these potential, partially completed skills into present assured competencies. For how this may come about we need the second quotation:

> Any function in a child's cultural development appears twice, or on two planes. First it appears on the social plane, and then on the psychological plane. First it appears between people as an interpersonal category, and then within the child as an intrapsychological category.
>
> (Vygtosky 1981)

Vygotsky goes on to explain that the meaning of this is that much of cognitive and also language development takes place through the child seeing a successful performance in another ('the social plane') and instantly internalizing it. The nearer the 'successful performance' is to the child's present partially completed strategies, the greater is the probability of the instant internalization. However, with adolescence the word 'nearer' takes on an extra connotation. Since at this point in their lives they are in the process of inserting into the present adult world newly created adult presences which are not just an imitation of present adult models, it is far more likely that it will be the style of successful performance from a peer who has just got there that will be internalized. Teachers' 'successful performances', polished by time and familiarity, are often too far from where the adolescents presently are to be easily internalized and assimilated. Thus, there is both a Piagetian and a Vygotskian contribution to the teaching skills which are used.

The Vygotskian aspect of CASE can be seen in Figure 10.6. The Concrete preparation phase (Act 1) is essentially a 'raising of consciousness' in relation to the subject matter of the activity, and its success depends on the extent to which the teacher engages as many pupils as possible in constructing ideas to be used in the task ahead. The possibility of cognitive conflict (the Piagetian aspect) is both implicit in the processing of the task itself, and can also be made explicit in the Construction phase (Act 2) by tactical questioning from the teacher as she 'floats' from group to group. During this period of work on task, there is the opportunity for some of the pupils to construct more powerful strategies. An essential phase of each CASE lesson is the period of whole-class discussion which follows group work on task (Metacognition in Act 3), and for this to work it is not essential that *all* groups have completed *all* aspects of the experiment and questions on the worksheet. Managing this phase of the activity requires the teacher to be very aware of the working of the ZPD described above. By questioning and chairing the discussion, she has to ensure that every interesting insight, or difficulty encountered, in

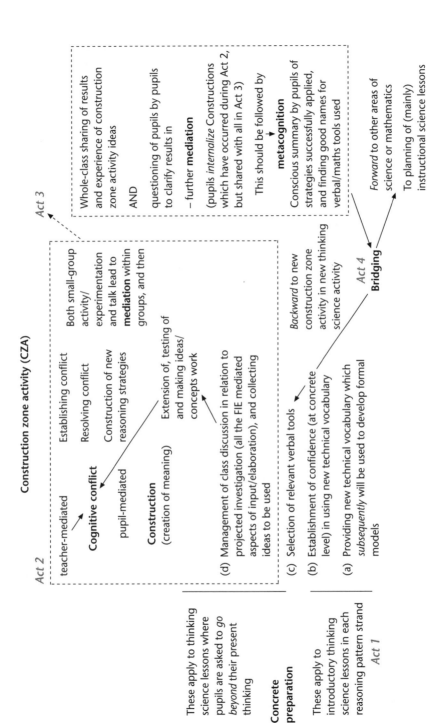

**Figure 10.6** Technical terms used to describe phases of CASE and a CAME lessons

each of the working groups now is made available for all the pupils in the class, in their own language. Sometimes this is shown on the actual apparatus itself by the pupils, or on notes scribbled on the board. This will maximize the probability that each pupil will find in some other's 'successful performance' just what he needs to complete his ZPD.

This model of the CASE classroom/laboratory relates to another Vygotsky quote:

> the only good kind of instruction is that which marches ahead of development and leads it; it must be aimed not so much at the ripe as the ripening functions.
>
> (1986: 188)

But if one bears in mind the range of mental ability in a typical mixed-ability class, the questions immediately arise: 'Whose level of development are we to march ahead of?' 'Whose ripening functions do we have in mind?' Hence the multiple levels of cognitive achievement present within each CASE lesson, as shown in Figure 10.5. So the lesson has to be conducted in such a way that all have the chance to complete their ZPD from whatever level it presently is at – a very sophisticated teaching skill.

It is at this point of the development and theory and practice that the work of the ICI bridging project began. If we extend even further the concept of bridging to include metacognitive awareness of strategies of problem-solving by pupils, then it is possible to see that it covers all aspects of thinking useful for them in addressing new tasks. By a similar argument, for the teacher it covers most aspects of planning and class management needed for addressing pupils' learning tasks for any new and difficult science lessons that are on the curriculum. Our task, then, was to invent and construct a sample of lessons which illustrate the varied ways in which aspects of the CASE teaching art might be applied to the context of ordinary science lessons – in fact to distinguish the concept of 'instruction' (Zone 1 in Table 10.1) from the concept of 'intervention' (Zone 3) and then to show how they can both contribute to lessons occurring in Zone 2.

## The ICI bridging project

From 31 March to 2 April in 2000, 20 experienced science and CASE teachers (some presently LEA advisers) met together for a writing weekend sponsored by ICI and called the 'Stanhope conference'. They were to share ideas on how the CASE art has developed, and then to design a set of possible bridging lessons, with enough detail to enable them to be trialled in schools and further refined in the light of experience. The set of specimen lessons were to exhibit as many aspects of the bridging art as possible in a variety of contexts in physics, chemistry and biology. Later, eight of the lesson plans generated at Stanhope or elsewhere were trialled, and detailed notes made of the conduct of the lessons by Michael Shayer or Reed Gamble. These notes were used to generate the descriptions of the CASE bridging lessons in a book (Shayer and Gamble 2001).

### Possible types of bridging lessons

At Stanhope, several possible models for this were conceived:

1 *The full model: a new CASE lesson*

The original 'rules of the game' for CASE lessons were to find a science context involving at least one reasoning pattern and then to construct the full four-Act model and the underlying reasoning patterns, with suggested technical language if relevant.

The next stage was to think in terms of differential outcomes, so each pupil could move up a step (at least) and to 'throw away' the explicit conceptual and procedural learning element. (Remembering that this is an art, not a procedure!)

It was desirable, occasionally, to wake students up to metacognitive rather than immediate NC aims.

2 *Bridging through reasoning patterns*

This is the next strongest model. It is for a specific science-learning context, where one, at least, of the reasoning patterns is a necessary condition. During the concrete preparation, use the reasoning pattern strategically, ensuring that the pupils themselves 'construct' it into the context in which they are going to work, and have already formulated some possible strategies for applying what they recall about it. Use the full three-Act model, but don't throw away the desired learning outcome, with its concepts and procedures. Endeavour to conduct the lesson so pupils construct (each in their own way) the overall lesson aim. So, a final Act 4 may not be relevant.

3 *Bridging through collaborative learning (Vygotskian aspect)*

There may not be a specific reasoning pattern involved, but the four-Act lesson model with an extended concrete preparation phase may be used to plan and structure the lesson focused on desired learning outcomes. So here the Vygotskian basis only is used to facilitate collaborative learning.

4 *Bridging in concrete preparation*

Here only the concrete preparation style of lesson introduction is used. The rest of the lesson is taught as normal. Either a specific reasoning pattern and its terminology and procedures is invoked explicitly during concrete preparation, or there is a bridge from previous relevant scientific knowledge, until pupils have constructed for themselves what it is that they will use in the instruction phase. This may, rightly, be called just 'good teaching', but getting pupils to access an extra level of abstraction in their learning can empower them substantially. An Act 3 may be added optionally instead of running the lesson until just before the bell.

All of these require, implicitly, that teachers look at science lessons 'through CASE eyes', which sounds simple enough, but in fact is unlikely to be done at the level of simple intuition. The thinking science lessons (see Adey et al. 1995) to some extent have the CASE methodology implicit, and as long as the teacher follows the lesson plan and suggested timing, the lesson may work without the teachers explicitly possessing the underlying theory(theories) involved. But to abstract from CASE practice to any of the contexts for the lessons which follow, teachers must at least be conscious of the Vygotskian aspect which lies behind the four-Act model, and preferably also have a student-curriculum matching model derived from Piaget[2] in their heads.

*Conduct of the applicable research*
All these lessons were taken through a full cycle of applicable research, that is the initial plans produced at the Stanhope conference were regarded as testable theories (of what good bridging lessons might be). The first trial was then the experimental test. Following this, the feedback from the reality test was used to refine the original theory. As no scientific theory is the last word, the further application is then in the hands of teachers. The way in which the collection was intended to be used can be shown in a quotation from the book:

> Please do not look on this as a new small stable of tried and tested thinking science lessons, to be added to the existing corpus in the Nelson *Thinking Science* manual! We do, in fact, think they are good lessons, but their purpose is other. They have been chosen to exhibit, in a wide range of contexts, the various professional skills which are involved in applying some of what is involved in the original set of *Thinking Science* lessons to a variety of new learning contexts.
>
> Each of these lessons has a different context and different purposes. We suggest that you select two or three of these lessons that seem relevant to your own classes, teach them yourself, and then re-read the commentaries and the Piagetian diagrams in light of your own experience of the lesson and your own pupils' engagement with it. Only in this way will the rather abstract descriptions of the art come to life in your own practice. There is a specialized technical language ('concrete preparation', 'construction' and the like) through which CASE teachers can compare and exchange their teaching experience with each other, and we make no apologies for adding to it in this publication. But it makes sense only when applied to describing specific experiences with real learners: the abstraction only links two contexts when it can be intimately related to each separately.
>
> The next step might be to find some part of the curriculum – anywhere between Years 7 and and 11 – that you know is a problem for your classes, and see if you can devise a teaching plan that parallels one of these that you have taught, but in your chosen new context. This would be 'bridging' in two senses: for your pupils because some of the CASE art they are familiar with from their thinking science lessons would be applied in a new context, and for you because it involves taking the

teaching principles from one context and re-contextualizing them in the new.

Better still – particularly if your department is tending to get a little stale in their use of CASE, or if your gifted teachers have left for promotion elsewhere and there are new members of the department who have not yet got into the CASE style of teaching – if two or three members of your department can collaborate (in every way parallel to the way you are asking you pupils to collaborate in their learning) by teaching some of these bridging lessons separately, and then discussing their experience, their teaching art should then have further possibilities of development.

*Two examples of the lessons*
The first example, Photosynthesis for Year 7, in the end came to have a paradoxical teaching aim, namely how to programme out of the lesson plan the intervention element, so as to design a lesson with instructional aims, yet using aspects of CASE theory to do it. The aim was to give a first general introduction for a Year 7 class to the whole subject of Photosynthesis.

The lesson was intended to be a Type 2: bridging through a reasoning pattern. It is true that control and exclusion of variables is involved by implication, but this is not stressed during the concrete preparation phase and the lesson is handled more as a Type 3: four-Act lesson using Vygotskian aspect.

The activity is run as a circus, with nine stations, with workcards (some with the corresponding apparatus). Each station has a traditional experimental set-up for this part of biology, for example:

- two geranium plants, one that has had a stencil placed over a leaf, another to start the activity;
- pond weed in a beaker, preferably left in the light so that bubbles of oxygen appear;
- a variegated leaf tested for starch;
- a 'stencilled' leaf tested for starch;
- two dishes of cress seeds, one on cotton wool, the other on soil with a data card to show increasing mass over growth period; and
- one dish of dried-out cress seedlings.

The pupil workcards have:

- pictures of pond weed with lights, showing oxygen bubbles;
- pictures of pond weed, with added carbon dioxide;
- data on crop production at different temperatures; and
- details of experiment in which cress seeds are grown without oxygen with date or mass change over growth period.

A Worksheet shows the van Helmont experiment, where a tree was grown in a bucket for 5 years, with everything weighed before and after.

For each station the pupils must answer on their worksheet:

- What is the input variable?
- What is the outcome?
- What is the relationship?

After the concrete preparation, pupils in groups of three or four progress through the circus, and do as many stations as possible in the time. Six stations, on average, are covered by any one group. Essentially, the task for the pupils is to construct their own beginning model of what plants are and how they promote their life through interaction with the environment. 'Correct' terminology and concepts would come in later lessons, so in this lesson there is no pre-determined learning outcome to be achieved by all. Rather it is the whole process by which biologists approach the description of the vegetable world that is being initiated, and here the aim is individual and collaborative construction of the biological model, with questions raised and accepted for later consideration.

In Figure 10.7 the Piagetian aspect of the lesson is shown. It can be seen that there are three different cycles of knowledge involved in the biologist's model of photosynthesis at increasing levels of sophistication. Since the bulk of Year 7 pupils can be assumed to be at the 2B concrete, or 2B* concrete generalization level, with maybe 10 per cent into 3A early formal, here Piagetian theory is used to constrain the selection of concepts to be used or invoked in the conduct of the lesson. For example it is quite reasonable for a 12-year-old to think that light might have something to do with the increase in weight in the van Helmont experiment, but it will only be when he has learnt enough physics to realize that electromagnetic waves have no weight that he will know what it means to say that they contribute only the energy for the chemical reactions. For both the physics and chemistry of this distinction he will need at least early formal thinking, and some year or two of further accumulation of specific knowledge, as shown in Figure 10.7.

Yet the reasonable aim of the lesson is to register in the pupils' minds the many variables which in one way or another are involved in photosynthesis. If, by the end of the lesson, they construct their own working model of what is involved in plant growth, then that would be a valuable end in itself, stimulating their interest by constructing their own ideas, which might then be refined further by subsequent lessons giving them the essential information they need to distinguish between the relative contributions of each of the necessary conditions.

The Vygotskian aspect of the lesson is shown in a two-page-spread lesson 'crib' for the teacher to glance at immediately before (and possibly during) the lesson (see Figure 10.8).

Hence a purely instructional aim for a lesson can be enriched by applying CASE teaching skills, as Jerome Bruner's famous statement exemplified: 'Any idea or body of knowledge can be taught to any pupil at any level of development in some intellectually honest way' (Bruner 1977: 62).

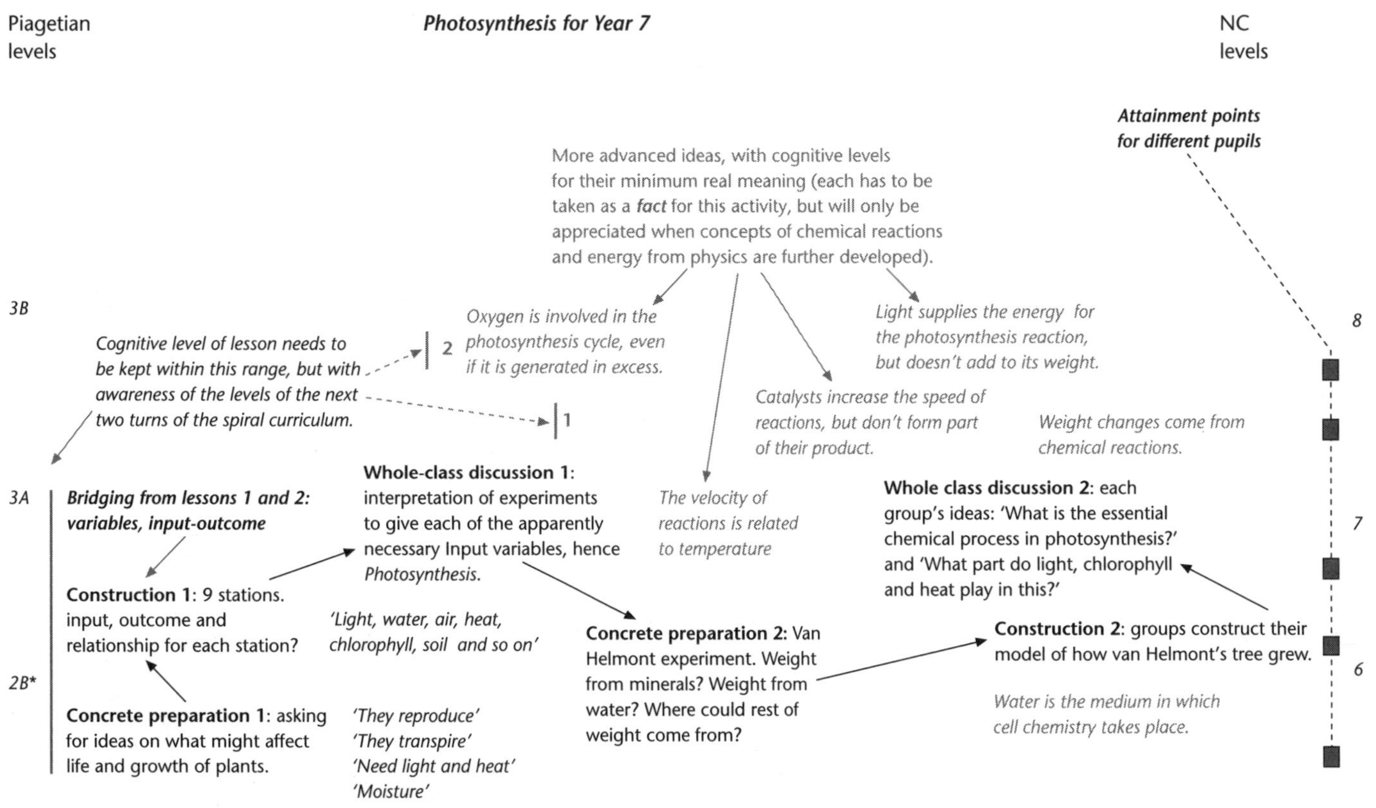

**Photosynthesis for Year 7**

Piagetian
levels

NC
levels

*Attainment points
for different pupils*

8

7

6

5

3B

*Cognitive level of lesson needs to
be kept within this range, but with
awareness of the levels of the next
two turns of the spiral curriculum.*

More advanced ideas, with cognitive levels
for their minimum real meaning (each has to be
taken as a **fact** for this activity, but will only be
appreciated when concepts of chemical reactions
and energy from physics are further developed).

*Light supplies the energy for
the photosynthesis reaction,
but doesn't add to its weight.*

*Weight changes come from
chemical reactions.*

*Oxygen is involved in the
photosynthesis cycle, even
if it is generated in excess.*

*Catalysts increase the speed of
reactions, but don't form part
of their product.*

2

1

**Whole-class discussion 1:**
interpretation of experiments
to give each of the apparently
necessary Input variables, hence
Photosynthesis.

*The velocity of
reactions is related
to temperature*

**Whole class discussion 2:** each
group's ideas: 'What is the essential
chemical process in photosynthesis?'
and 'What part do light, chlorophyll
and heat play in this?'

**Construction 2:** groups construct their
model of how van Helmont's tree grew.

*Water is the medium in which
cell chemistry takes place.*

**Concrete preparation 2:** Van
Helmont experiment. Weight
from minerals? Weight from
water? Where could rest of
weight come from?

3A

*Bridging from lessons 1 and 2:
variables, input-outcome*

**Construction 1:** 9 stations.
input, outcome and
relationship for each station?

*'Light, water, air, heat,
chlorophyll, soil and so on'*

2B*

**Concrete preparation 1:** asking
for ideas on what might affect
life and growth of plants.

*'They reproduce'
'They transpire'
'Need light and heat'
'Moisture'*

2B

**Figure 10.7** Structure of Photosynthesis lesson

---

**Photosynthesis for Year 7**

---

**CASE aims**
- To develop pupils' concepts of inputs necessary for plant growth.
- To give a minimum meaning to the concept of photosynthesis in terms of water and carbon dioxide giving plant food.

**Resources**
- geranium plants, one with stencil
- pond weed in beaker
- variegated leaf tested for starch
- 'stencilled' leaf tested for starch
- two dishes of cress seeds, one on cotton wool
- one dish of dried-out cress seedlings
- workcards and pupil worksheets
- van Helmont diagram

**Organization**
- groups of three or four on mixed-ability tables alternated with whole-class discussion.

**Vocabulary**

| | |
|---|---|
| energy | carbon dioxide |
| catalyst | photosynthesis |
| input | outcome |
| relationship | chlorophyll |

**NC reference**
- KS3 Sc2
- 3a
- 3b (plus relevant words)

**Whole-class preparation 1 (10 minutes)**                                          1
- 'You'll be working together in groups, three or four brains working together. You've been working on plants, about food chains, etc. What's at the bottom of every food chain?'
- 'Look around at the green plants around the laboratory. Are the plants alive? How do you know?' Explore connections between the different descriptions.
- 'But for nutrition, they are different from animals.' 'Yes?'
- 'So how do plants get their food, what are the inputs essential to the process?'
- 'What are the input variables? 'Do you remember that from other CASE lessons?'
- 'So what are your ideas about photosynthesis?'
- Explain how they are to work on the circus and how much time they have for it.

**Figure 10.8**  Teachers' spread for Photosynthesis lesson

**Concrete preparation 2 (4 to 5 minutes)** 4
– Give out diagram of van Helmont experiment.
– 'How much weight did the minerals in the soil contribute to the final plant?'
– 'van Helmont thought most of the weight of the plant food created came from the water – is that reasonable?'
– 'Could carbon dioxide be the other thing that combines with water to make plant food, but van Helmont missed it?'

**Construction 1 (20 to 25 minutes)** 2
– Give out worksheet 1.
– 'There are nine stations, and I want just one person to act as a scribe. Your worksheets are just to record your ideas, they are not 'neat and tidy' work. Start at the one you are at, and as soon as you have finished talking it through with each other, move on to the next. At each station you need to decide as a group what is the input, what is the outcome, what is the relationship?'
– Remind them about the time they have, and that you want their ideas about what is involved in photosynthesis expressed on a poster they can talk to/with.

**Construction 2 (5 minutes)** 5
– Discuss with each other where the weight and bulk of the plant food came from in the van Helmont experiment.
– Discuss with each other what part you think the light and the chlorophyll play in photosynthesis (and heat also if you like).

**Class discussion 1 (10 minutes)** 3
Get each group to talk to their poster and explain their ideas.
– 'Be prepared to tell me your evidence.'
– Group class so all can see each other's posters, and also hear.
– Ask strategic questions if pupils do not.
– 'What about the experiment without the soil?'
– 'How about light?'
– 'Why is carbon dioxide important?'
– 'What do the experiments tell us about water?'

6

**Class discussion 2 (5 minutes)**
– Collect ideas quickly. Let the pupils discuss each other's arguments about what part each input plays.
– End the lesson by asking explicitly how to express what goes on in photosynthesis by a simple word equation.

**Figure 10.8** (*cont'd*)

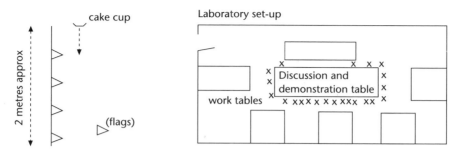

**Figure 10.9** Trial of Cup Cakes lesson

The second example, Newton's laws for Years 9 and 10: Cup Cakes has in common with Photosynthesis that it is intended to serve as a thinking introduction to what is a large field of knowledge to come. There is no one aim for all pupils – as with all thinking science lessons, each pupil can attain in a worthwhile way at his own level. Whereas Photosynthesis was a Type 3: Bridging through collaborative learning (Vygotskian aspect), Cup Cakes is a modification of a Type 1: the full model, a new CASE lesson, because the underlying theory is very demanding. It differs from a thinking science lesson in that it has mainly an instructional aim.

In contrast to Photosynthesis, the processing level of Cup Cakes is all within the range of early to mature formal level. Yet it has in common with Photosynthesis that, as in all CASE activities, there is no one aim for all, but it is to be conducted so that each pupil gains something at his own level. Whereas in Photosynthesis there are many variables to be sorted according to their relevant kind of contribution, even though the overall processing level in cognitive terms is low, in Cup Cakes the complexity is vertical, rather than horizontal (see Figures 10.5 and 10.7), so the processing level is very high even if the variables are few and simple (force, time and distance – mass is controlled by treating cup cakes as all the same, assuming the factory has good quality control). Thus, there are quite different problems for the teacher to consider.

The apparatus for the experiment consists of a bamboo pole, fixed vertically to retort stands, with four paper flags each at equal distance from each other (50 cm), and the first flag 50 cm from the top. (See Figure 10.9.) The paper cups for cakes have the interesting property of being self-orientating as they drop in air, so they drop like a parachute. So if they are dropped freely from the top of the pole they can be timed as they pass the first, second, third and fourth flags. The problems for the pupils are first to describe the time/distance relationship as the cups drop, and then afterwards to account for what they have described in terms of the forces acting on the cups at each point. Sets of apparatus are provided, so there are five students in each working group: four are given the task of timing to the different flags as the fifth drops the case. Normally the cup cake case attains terminal velocity between the second and the third flags.

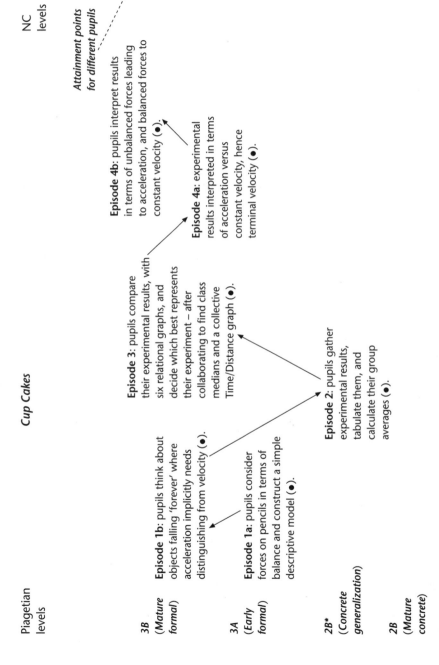

**Figure 10.10** Structure of Cup Cakes lesson

There are two necessary conditions for the development of the pupils' understanding of the lesson context: the mathematics of the processing of relational graphs, and the physics of the Newtonian concepts. To cope with the latter pupils need to know that a body on which there is a net force will accelerate, they need to have the model of action and reaction being equal and opposite, and they also need to construct the understanding that a body on which there is no net force will continue at constant speed (including the value zero). All three of Newton's laws are involved. The lesson agenda can be seen in Figure 10.10.

The lesson begins with the teacher dropping a pencil on the bench, and asking the pupils 'What forces are acting on this?' She, of course, gets the answer, 'None'. She continues to ask until the pupils construct an equal but opposite model, which is left on the board as a diagram. They then carry out the practical exercise, and each group records three runs (after a few practice runs) which are then pooled in an EXCEL spreadsheet to obtain class medians, again recorded in a table on the board. Then follows the second three-Act sequence. First they are given a whole-class discussion episode on strategies for reading relational graphs (Episode 2). Then they are given six different possible graphs, and asked to decide which of them best fits the median class data. They then have a whole-class discussion on the mathematical interpretation of the data (hopefully finding that the latter part is linear and hence constant velocity). The final three-Act sequence is then focused on the physics. Can they relate the experimental findings to the model they used on the pencil at rest on the bench? This may lead to them making a forces diagram for the cup cake CASE at terminal velocity, comparing it with the diagram made at the beginning for the forces on the pencil on the table, and hence constructing for themselves Newton's first law.

Additional detail may be seen in the two-page spread which is shown in Figure 10.11.

Despite the suggestion that the activity be treated as with a full thinking science lesson, there is a subtle difference. Both Cup Cakes and Photosynthesis have in common that they are introductory episodes to complex areas of science which could never be assimilated in one fell swoop. Ausubel said that when students were to be introduced to a new field of learning they first should be given an advance organizer, that is they should be given a preview of the field at a higher level of abstraction from its specific content. In a sense, it could be said that these lessons act as advance organizers for the pupils, giving them some overview of the territory ahead. Yet unlike Ausubel's use of the idea as something given in abstract form by the teacher, here we manage the lessons so it is the pupils themselves who construct the overview. Their work is intended to set them out on the instructional path towards an eventual understanding of Newton's laws. In comparison in the specific thinking science lessons the overall thinking is always orientated to the underlying reasoning patterns involved in the activity – a different kind of abstraction.

---

**Cup Cakes for Year 9**

---

**CASE aims**
- To prepare for KS4 Advanced Forces Concepts
- To understand that the terminal velocity of a falling object gives the same Newton's 3rd law interpretation as an object resting on the bench

---

**Resources**
- tube containing glycerine and ball to drop
- cup cake cases and bamboo rod apparatus (8 ft bamboo canes from garden centre with four paper flags at 50 cm intervals, the first 50 cm from top); one apparatus for each group, clamped vertically
- four stopwatches/timers for each group
- computer with EXCEL on screen
- pencils to drop
- workcards and pupil worksheets

**Organization**
- groups of four on mixed-ability tables alternated with whole-class discussion.

**Vocabulary**

| | |
|---|---|
| force | acceleration |
| equilibrium | terminal velocity |
| input | outcome |
| relationship | uniform and non-uniform |

**NC reference**
- Sc4: 2b, c, d
- Sc4: 2a, e, h, i

---

**Whole-class preparation 1 (10 minutes)**                                   1
- Place a pencil flat in the middle of the demonstration table.
- 'What is the pencil doing?'
- 'Can anybody give me a sentence that has "forces" in it?'
- 'But there are forces acting on it. What can we say about them?'
- 'Can we now draw a diagram of the forces?'
- 'Can you add to the diagram the forces acting on the table?'
- 'If the pencil kept on falling or if someone falls out of somewhere?'
- 'Oh, so do you think something falling goes on getting faster and faster forever?'
- 'You've got to answer! Yes or No?'
- Explain how they are to work on the falling cup cake experiment and how much time they have, and that they are to take their results to the computer expert to get the best class result.

---

**Figure 10.11**   Teachers' spread for Cup Cakes lesson

**Construction 2 (5 to 6 minutes)** 4
- Give out worksheet with the six graphs.
- 'See the whole-class medians for flags 1 to 4 on the board: discuss in your groups which of the six graphs best fits the class data, and be ready with your reasons.'

**Construction 1 (20 to 25 minutes)** 2
- Give out worksheet 1.
- 'There are four flags, so there are going to be four people, each with their stopwatch (it's very difficult to stop and start a stopwatch quick enough). The first times from the top to the first flag, the second from the top to the second flag, and so on'. Try some practice runs first, and then make four recordings, and then take them to the computer expert so that we can get the best result from the whole class.'
- In EXCEL computer expert sorts each column and then arrives at the class median for each flag, and writes them in a table on the board.

**Class discussion 2 (5 minutes)** 5
- 'I want each group to tell me which graph it is, and why.'
- 'Don't be tempted to change your answer because another group says another idea. You stick to what you think.'
- 'So now (5 minutes) see in your groups if you can draw the forces on the cake cup (i) soon after you release it, then (ii) after flag three.'

**Class discussion 1 (4 to 5 minutes)** 3
- Show on the board the graph:

- 'What is happening to the object at section (a) where it is curving upwards?'
- 'Are you sure?'
- 'What is happening at section (b) where the graph is straight?'
- 'What is happening at section (c) where it is starting to curve down again?'
- 'So how do you think about the graph in relation to the two variables of time and distance? What is the best strategy?'

**Class discussion 3 (up to 10 minutes)** 6
- Collect ideas quickly. Let the pupils discuss each other's arguments about how the forces change as the cup reaches terminal velocity. Record them on the board as drawings.
- Then ask the class explicitly how they connect up these diagrams with the drawings they left on the board of the forces on the pencil lying on the bench.

**Figure 10.11**   (*cont'd*)

## Notes

1 The CASE North Initiative, supported by ICI, started in 1997 in two local education authorities (LEAs). It is now probably the largest cross-LEA science project that there has ever been in the North of England. Currently, 26 LEAs are involved, stretching from Cumbria to Hull and Northumberland to Lincolnshire. The training, developed by Reed Gamble, uses a novel approach of constructing and describing 'novice' and 'expert' teacher behaviours in the form of four acts and calibrating resultant classroom processes with a major role for peer coaching within this theoretical development framework.

2 See Shayer and Adey (1981). Available now from Science Reasoning, 16 Fen End, OVER, Cambridge CB4 5NE (tel: 01954 231814) and from Philip Adey, Centre for the Advancement of Thinking, King's College, Cornwall House, Waterloo Road, London SE1 9NN (tel: 0207 848 3079).

# 11 NOT JUST PIAGET, NOT JUST VYGOTSKY, AND CERTAINLY NOT VYGOTSKY AS AN *ALTERNATIVE* TO PIAGET

## Michael Shayer

## Introduction

As we know from investigations of the process of concept formation, a concept is more than the sum of certain associative bonds formed by memory, more than a mere mental habit; it is a complex and genuine act of thought that cannot be taught by drilling, but can be accomplished only when the child's mental development has itself reached the requisite level.

(1)

Throughout the history of the child's development runs a 'warfare' between spontaneous and non-spontaneous, systematically learned, concepts. (Cf the Alternative Conceptions movement.)

(2)

the development of non-spontaneous concepts must possess all the traits peculiar to the child's thought at each developmental level because these concepts are not simply acquired by rote but evolve with the aid of strenuous mental activity on the part of the child himself. We believe that the two processes – the development of spontaneous and of non-spontaneous concepts – are related and constantly influence each other.

(3)

recently psychologists have shown that a person can imitate only that which is within her developmental level.

(4)

Each school subject has its own specific relation to the course of child development, a relation that varies as the child goes from one stage to another.

(5)

Quotations from Piaget or from Western applied research from the 1960s and 1970s? No, all from Vygotsky, about 1930.[1] Having laid down his framework of thinking at the pure and applied level of research, Vygotsky then goes on to make recommendations for education at the 'applicable' level (Belbin 1979).

> Formerly, it was believed that, by using tests, we determine the mental development level with which education should reckon and whose limits it should not exceed . . . It turned out that a teaching system based solely on concreteness – one that eliminated from teaching everything associated with abstract thinking – not only failed to help retarded children overcome their innate handicaps but also reinforced their handicaps by accustoming children exclusively to concrete thinking and thus suppressing the rudiments of any abstract thought that such children have.
>
> (Vygotsky 1978: 89) (6)

In thinking about the relation between 'spontaneous thinking', that is the kind of thinking studied primarily by Piaget in the Genevan methodology, and 'non-spontaneous thinking', that is the explicit teaching of concepts and procedures characteristic of normal school instruction, Vygotsky suggests there is a subtle relation between the two:

> Since instruction given in one area can transform and reorganize other areas of child's thought, it may not only follow maturing or keep in step with it but also precede it and further its progress.
>
> (Vygotsky 1986: 177) (7)

In saying that:

> the development of scientific concepts runs ahead of the development of spontaneous concepts
>
> (Vygotsky 1986: 147) (8)

he is in no way saying that teachers may remain ignorant of children's level of mental development. Only three pages later he warns:

> Practical experience also shows that direct teaching of concepts is impossible and fruitless. A teacher who tries this usually accomplishes nothing but empty verbalism, a parrot-like repetition of words by the child, simulating a knowledge of the corresponding concepts but actually covering up a vacuum.
>
> (Vygotsky 1986: 150) (9)

His formulation of the learning paradox begins:

to introduce a new concept means just to start the process of its appropriation. Deliberate introduction of new concepts does not precede spontaneous development, but rather charts the new paths for it.
(Vygotsky 1986: 152) (See quote (3) above.) **(10)**

but

scientific concepts, like spontaneous concepts, just start their development, rather than finish it, at a moment when a child learns the term or word meaning denoting the new concept.
(Vygotsky 1986: 159) **(11)**

Thus far, one may doubt whether Vygotsky is describing schooling as he has seen it, or as he thinks it should or could be. It quickly becomes clear that more, much more, is needed, if learning, in relation to mental development, is to be optimal. Given the dual and reciprocal relation between cognitive development and conceptual learning within school subjects, that is as the former develops it makes higher levels of learning possible, but as children are challenged by new school learning demands they may be stimulated to re-process the learning in their own spontaneous manner of processing and hence receive a stimulus to further cognitive development, it follows that revolutionary teaching methods are needed. A first step is suggested. Since:

Scientific and spontaneous concepts reveal different attitudes toward the object of study and different ways of its representation in the consciousness.
(Vygotsky 1986: 161) **(12)**

it follows that:

The most promising approach to the problem [of reconciling laboratory studies of cognition with school achievement measures, necessarily superficial] would seem to be the study of scientific concepts, which are real concepts, yet are formed under our eyes almost in the fashion of artificial concepts . . . To uncover the complex relation between instruction and the development of scientific concepts is an important practical task.
(Vygotsky 1986: 161–2) **(13)**

In parenthesis, I would claim that this is exactly what we undertook, and for the same reasons, for secondary school mathematics and science in the 5-year CSMS research programme at Chelsea College, London in the 1970s (Hart 1981; Shayer and Adey 1981). I say this because Vygotsky was never able to undertake this programme of research before his early death in 1934. However, he did work on the other major problem, namely just how may schooling be optimized so as to overcome the learning paradox? His answer was:

the only 'good learning' is that which is ahead of development.
(Vygotsky 1978: 89) **(14)**

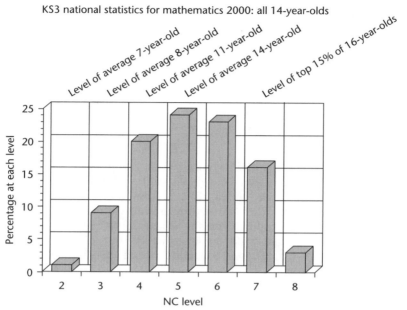

KS3 national statistics for mathematics 2000: all 14-year-olds

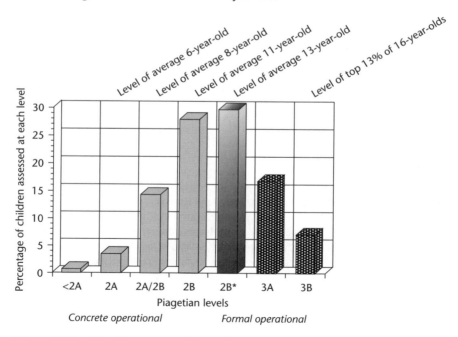

**1974/5 CSMS survey of 14,000 children between the ages of 10 and 16: data for 14-year-olds**

**Figure 11.1** The 12-year gap shown in two independent sources of evidence

the only good kind of instruction is that which marches ahead of development and leads it; it must be aimed not so much at the ripe as the ripening functions.

(Vygotsky 1986: 188) **(15)**

This presupposes reconciling all the statements cited above. On the one hand, mere 'cognitive level matching' leaves the children's mental development stagnant (see quote (6)); on the other, empty verbalism may result if the concept is too far ahead of the children. Moreover, a whole programme of applied research is needed first to enable teachers in each school subject to know just how far 'ahead of development' the learning they choose for their students should be. I would add, too, that we need to know a great deal more about differential cognitive development in the child population than either Vygotsky or Piaget were aware of in the early 1930s – the Cockcroft Report (DES 1982) referred to a '7-year gap' between the mental ages of pupils entering secondary school, but Figure 11.1 shows that for 14-year-olds the spread between the more and less able pupils is of the order of 12 mental-age years. But most important of all, without a theory of how 'spontaneous development' is related to the progressive inculcation of the child into the culture as embodied in school learning, there is no way in which Vygotsky's 'new formula' for teaching (his words) could be implemented; hence the notion of the ZPD.

## The ZPD

It is a strange fact that both Piaget and Vygotsky were introduced to research in psychology by being asked, in their respective countries, to undertake the replication of the new Binet test of intelligence in the 1920s. It is also strange that a concept tied specifically to the testing of individual children should be treated, later, by some authors (such as Lerman 1996) as a theory of the social origin of children's development. The essence of the method is this. The child is first given a standard intelligence test, such as the Binet, and his mental age estimated from his score. The psychologist then takes the child through some of the easier items on which he had failed, giving various hints and/or discussing the problems with the child. With this assistance, the child can then solve more of the items, and hence a new mental age can be calculated relating to the limit of the child's success with the mediation of the psychologist. The difference between the two scores represents the ZPD of the child. In Vygotsky's words:

> The [ZPD] of the child is the distance between his actual development, determined with the help of independently solved tasks, and the level of potential development of the child, determined with the help of tasks solved by the child under the guidance of adults and in cooperation with his more intelligent partners.[2]

**(16)**

Note that 'his more intelligent partners' is just speculative on Vygotsky's part – the research which was actually done was with the psychologist and the child only. Hence one aspect of the solution to the problem of teaching 'ahead of development' is the recommendation to teach to the limit of the ZPD of the students, but no further. Note that this presupposes the availability of the applied research of the cognitive demand level of the specifics of the school curriculum, which had been done neither at the time when Vygotsky was working, nor until the 1970s, and is far from being universally accepted as feasible even now (Collis 1975; Hart 1981; Shayer and Adey 1981).

It is interesting that in the original paper/lecture in which the ZPD was presented he gave an interpretation of it that has shown to be, at least partially, wrong:

> Taking an example of a child, tested at the age of 4 giving an independent mental age of 4.5 years, but having a ZPD extending to 7 years after mediation, Vygotksy predicted that over the next three years the child would reach an unassisted mental age of 7, as predicted from the earlier ZPD, *but that the ZPD of 7 would have remained static at 7.*
> (van der Veer and Valsiner 1991: 343 and 344, original emphasis)

When this process of dynamic testing was initiated to children in a special school at the age of 12, it was found, 2 years later, that the ZPD of control children had indeed moved up but little. But those who had received the Feuerstein IE intervention (in other words, taught just as Vygotsky recommended) had reached the level predicted from their ZPD 2 years earlier, but now they had a new ZPD reaching about 2 mental-age years even further ahead of their new unassisted score (Beasley and Shayer 1990).

The educational application Vygotksy cited was this: with children tested by his clinical interview at ages 10, their unassisted score on the Binet predicted less well their school achievement 2 years later than their ZPD score, that is the difference between their unassisted score and their post-mediation score. Hence the theory that the ZPD is a better predictor of potential achievement than the child's IQ score itself. It follows from this that the experimentally grounded source of the theory of the ZPD is in terms of the behaviour of the individual child, and so this sense of the concept is indicative only of partially formed skills or schemes possessed by that child himself (not in his social milieu, but mostly derived therefrom), as revealed in the dynamic assessment interview. In the mediation process the children – admittedly in social interaction with the psychologist – construct from their partially achieved skills or concepts the completed skill or scheme required to solve the test items. The less the mediation required for success, the nearer to 100 per cent competence the child is. In our replication of this testing process it was possible to differentiate 10 different levels of mediation (ranging from 'Just look again' at one end to giving the solution and the reason for the solution at the other end), and also to describe the qualitative cognitive functions in which the child was strong or weak (Beasley 1984; Beasley and Shayer 1990). We also verified the better predictivity of the ZPD, but with the proviso *only* with those children who have received the IE intervention, that is only those children who have received the kind of instruction designed to realize the children's potential, aimed ahead of where they presently are (Shayer and Beasley 1987).

So what is the connection between this testing process, conducted on individual children, and a theory of optimal teaching in school, and with classes, and also with a more general theory of child development? Unfortunately, Chapter 6 of *Mind and Society* is somewhat unhelpful for answering this question because it appears to be a palimpsest of extracts from several different papers, given on different occasions and with different contexts, with no indication of where one begins or another ends. Nor is the reference given (we have only a mention in the preface of a 1935 book with an English title, which does not exist in English). The only further hint of a connection is the recommendation:

> We propose that an essential feature of learning is that it creates a [ZPD], that is learning awakens a variety of internal developmental processes that are able to operate only when the child is interacting with people in his environment and in co-operation with his peers. Once these processes are internalized, they become part of the child's independent developmental achievement.
>
> (Vygotsky 1978: 90) **(17)**

Here the ZPD is taken out of the context of individual testing, and displaced to the context of school learning as a social process. We may then perhaps make the further connection to the thought in a paper with a quite different context, *The Genesis of Higher Mental Functions*, in which he states:

> We could formulate the general genetic law of cultural development as follows: any function in the child's cultural development appears twice, or on two planes. First it appears on the social plane, and then on the psychological plane. First it appears between people as an interpsychological category, and then within the child as an intrapsychological category. This is equally true with regard to voluntary attention, logical memory, the formation of concepts, and the development of volition.
>
> (Vygotsky 1979: 163) **(18)**

In this paper (perhaps written several years earlier) the distinction he made, in *Thought and Language*, between spontaneous and non-spontaneous was not there in his thinking, and 'development' is being taken rather globally. But the following statement seems to link quotations (17) and (18):

> the connection between the child's natural behavioural development based on organic maturation and the types of development we have dealt with . . . has a revolutionary rather than an evolutionary character. Development does not take place by gradual alteration or change, by the accumulation of small increments, the sum of which finally provides some kind of essential change: from the very beginning we observe a

revolutionary type of development. In other words, we see sharp and fundamental changes in the very type of development, in the motivating factors of this process.

(Wertsch 1979: 171) **(19)**

The kind of 'jumps' in performance one sees when mediating children in the dynamic assessment of their ZPD are revolutionary (although the child may be already three-quarters of the way there, even if one could not see it) like, possibly, similar jumps made by individuals when collaborating with their peers when they internalize some successful performance to which they may have contributed but have, nevertheless, witnessed in a peer and immediately internalized (completed their individual ZPD). Between collaborating peers it would be meaningful to postulate a collective ZPD from which each child can draw as from a collective pool, and quotation 17 above is suggesting that it should be part of the teacher's art to offer a learning situation in which the instruction 'marches ahead of development and leads it; it must be aimed not so much at the ripe as the ripening functions' (Vygotsky 1986: 188). This is the point where it is necessary to compare Piaget's and Vygotsky's position on development.

## Piaget and Vygotsky's view of mental development

A major difficulty in interpreting Vygotsky's work derives from what, in my opinion at least, is his major virtue. Each time he gave a lecture or wrote a paper, he updated his thinking according to the particular context he was inquiring into at the time. Instead of trying to make himself consistent with what he may have published earlier, or trying to defend himself against other academics (or anonymous referees!), he thinks afresh according to how he saw things at the time (Piaget, I am afraid, was quite different, appearing to show he had always thought of everything and was never inconsistent, only evolving). This dialectical method is quite delightful, but it means the reader has to try to gauge what were the issues Vygotsky was trying to address, and to what extent his thinking had become more powerful. It is more like trying to compare the Verdi of *La Traviata* with the Verdi of *Otello* and *Falstaff*, asking not only the question 'What has been deepened and developed', but also 'What has been lost?'

In his papers from around 1926 until his death in 1934 two closely related, interwoven but not identical themes are What is the relation between children's 'spontaneous' thinking (which is what he claimed Piaget studied) and their 'non-spontaneous' or learning-related thinking and What is the relation between action and 'the Word'?

If you look at quotations (2), (3), (7), (8) (10) and (11), and couple them with (4) ('recently psychologists have shown that a person can imitate only that which is within her developmental level') you can see a paradox. From quotation (6) one sees rejected the idea that one should teach only at the level of children's current competence. Likewise, quotation (9) rejects as useless teaching which is too far ahead of where the children are. But if it is true that 'the development of scientific concepts runs ahead of the development of spontaneous concepts', it is also true that teaching at what has been called the 'N + 1' level, where N is the child's current mental level, can challenge the children's thinking in such a way that their 'spontaneous' thinking moves ahead:

> to introduce a new concept means just to start the process of its appropriation. Deliberate introduction of new concepts does not precede spontaneous development, but rather charts the new paths for it.
>
> (Vygotsky 1986: 152) **(20)**

So, on the one hand, it is conceded that 'natural' or 'spontaneous' thinking inevitably lags behind the intellectual challenge of schooling, but on the other it is asserted that in providing children with new tools for thinking the learning demands of school act as a kind of leading edge impelling their spontaneous thinking to more powerful schemes (to use Piaget's word). Vygotsky never resolved this paradox, but sometimes to locate a valid antithesis to a thesis is itself a great achievement from which others can then benefit.[3]

With action and 'the Word' (Vygotksky did use the Greek and biblical sense often in his thinking) one thinks first of Vygotsky's criticism of Piaget in *Thought and Language*, and of Piaget's later response to that criticism in 1963 (retranslated in Piaget, 2000). It is rather pointless to try to takes sides on that exchange, because on Vygotsky's part he had access only to the work Piaget had done up to 1924, and Piaget did not read Russian so had even less access to the bulk of Vygotsky's later thinking. Piaget's early work was open to the criticism of being focused too much on children's words and too little on their action. He admitted this later in his life (see footnote 15 in Piaget 1933/2000 for references), and in Piaget (1933/2000: 242) admits by implication that it was only after he had completed the study of his own three children's development from birth, as reported in *The Origin of Intelligence* – during much of which time there were no words to observe and study – that he was able 'to locate the beginnings of thinking in a context of adaptation which has a more and more biological sense'.

I claim instead that by 1933 the two had reached an almost identical position – in the case of Vygotsky a synthesis achieved possibly by further reflection on his criticism of Piaget taken as antithesis; in the case of Piaget the antithesis being the activity of meticulous recording of his children's actions before they were able to speak. Under the heading, *Word and action* (in 'Tool and Symbol in Child Development' in van der Veer and Valsiner 1994: 166–70, original emphasis) Vygotsky begins by rejecting 'In the beginning was the Word' as applying to the development of children's minds. He then quotes from Goethe's *Faust*, but with the subtle change of italicization: '*in the beginning* was the deed' and goes on to reject the idea that speech and action evolve independently of each other or in parallel. He objects (to the positions others had taken):

Yet we were able to observe on a factual basis how, in the process of development, the child's action becomes social, and how, in losing speech because of aphasia, its practical action falls to the level of its elementary zoopsychological form.

Finally he says:

We cannot dwell . . . on either the evangelical or Goethean formula, no matter which word we accentuate.

and hence

We have attempted, throughout the article, to show how the *word*, itself intellectualised and developed on the basis of *action*, raises the action to a higher level, subjects it to the power of the child, puts upon the action the stamp of will. But since we wanted to express all this in one short formula, in one sentence, we might put it thus: if *at the beginning* of development there stands the act, independent of the Word, then at the end of it there stands the Word which becomes the act, the Word which makes man's action free.[4]

(21)

Although Piaget would never have expressed himself like that, I can hardly slip a piece of paper between this position and that of the man involved in researching *The Growth of Logical Thinking* (GLT) (Inhelder and Piaget 1958) and *The Early Growth of Logic* (EGL) (Inhelder and Piaget 1964).

Finally in this section, a point which is very obvious, although I have never seen it expressed by any commentator, be they either pro- or anti-Piaget, if you want to see the detailed specifics of what is present in various children's ZPDs, if you want evidence that partially achieved schemes are present in children's minds before they finally achieve them, you will not find Vygotsky ever bothering to show you. Instead you will see them re-corded in fascinating detail in every work associated with Piaget.

## For cognitive development, follow Piaget

Even Cole and Wertsch (2000) concede:

There is little doubt in our view that there is still much to be learned from both Vygotsky and Piaget, and in many cases the strengths of one theorist complement the weakness of the other. However, we believe that discussions of these two figure's accounts of mind and its bound-aries are not well served by overly rehearsed debates about the primacy of the individual or the social. Instead, we have argued that the more interesting contrast between them concerns the role of cultural artefacts in constituting the two poles of the individual-social antinomy. For Vygotsky such artefacts play a central role in elaborating an account of what and where mind is. In pursuing the line of inquiry, he focused on a set of issues and phenomena that do not appear to have any clear counterpart in Piaget's thinking, and consequently may be more appropriately characterized as being different, rather than directly in conflict with those at the centre of Piaget's project.

In this spirit, I claim that, provided one takes *The Origin of Intelligence* as marking the beginning of the thoroughly well-grounded life-work of Piaget studying all stages of development (excepting ages 3 to 5) of children from birth to the end of adolescence, then it is the strength of this person that one should rely on. However, first, it is necessary to clarify what it was that Piaget had described. Vygotsky (1986: 154) claimed that Piaget only described the genesis of children's 'spontaneous concepts'. Yet in the previous section we have seen that the relation between 'spontaneous and non-spontaneous, systematically learned concepts' – as Vygotsky rightly states – is an interaction in the process of development. Piaget *never* presented these concepts as 'firmly divided and self-contained entities whose interaction is impossible' – Vygotsky was wrong about that (1986: 154). What can be said is that Piaget selected tasks for children little likely to be contaminated by the children parroting 'teacher's right answers'. But the purpose of this was to get below the surface of younger children's performances to find the extent to which they could construct classes, relations and so on in a wide variety of contexts. If one looks at Piaget's sampling unit as being not the individual but a set of children sufficiently varied both in age and ability to elicit both successful understanding and all the steps in the ZPD leading up to the achievement of the scheme studied, one can then view the Genevan methodology as focused on the *qualitative* detail of the study of the ZPD phenomenon, as distinguished from the *quantitative* side which Vygotsky described in his psychometric phase. It is interesting that both used the term 'genetic' to describe their approach to development. Piaget's own view of his methodology as being the study of 'the epistemic subject' (but see Shayer 1993) is compatible with this description of his sampling unit, within which enough detail can be given to describe all steps or alternatives of development of that 'subject'.

Looking then on Vygotsky and Piaget's approaches to development as different in the way suggested by Cole and Wertsch, one can see that Vygotsky's emphasis on 'non-spontaneous' concepts was a concern with the dynamics of development (that which drives it) and Piaget's with the statics of development, where they actually are when removed from sources of stimulus – exactly what Vygotsky said one needed to know in order to have a good model of 'instruction' (quotations (4), (13), (14) and (15)). Hence the Genevan methodology where the psychologist, while supporting the children by approving all they do and say, deliberately avoids mediation, and in fact by offering counter-suggestions to gauge the stability of a child's concept, could be described as sometimes offering negative mediation. In this sense, one could call the Vygotskian dynamic assessment process, where a variety of mediation is offered to each child, as being focused on the *individual*, and Piaget's as focused rather on the *population*.

There could have been some justification at the time in Vygotsky viewing Piaget's work with younger children thus:

> In schoolchildren of eleven to twelve, the nonspontaneous concepts completely replace the spontaneous, and with this, according to Piaget, intellectual development reaches its port of arrival. The real culmination of the developmental process, i.e. the formation of mature, scientific concepts in adolescence, simply has no place in Piaget's model.
>
> (22)

However, this could only have been true with respect to the development of concrete operations. I don't recognize this myself as a valid description, but if one looks at the characteristics of the concrete generalization level one might be forgiven for interpreting it as children having the capacity to use all the concrete operational schemes that Piaget describes fluently in any school learning they are offered, and hence the gap between development and learning capacity to have disappeared. But as soon as one looks at GLT, 20 years later, it is possible to see that many of the aspects of development which Vygotsky described apply more to the development of formal operations than to concrete operations.

In the various chapters researched by Inhelder and Piaget in GLT one can see, exhibited within the specifics of well-chosen contexts, the major underlying schemes (reasoning patterns) required for effective thinking in the biological and physical sciences. These presuppose without any doubt (the research was done on the selected population of Swiss gymnasia schools, perhaps the upper 20 per cent or less of the population) adolescents whose development had already long been established in a complex interaction between their mental development and their exposure to and (partial) mastery of the reasoning patterns needed to make their own the concepts of science. As Vygotsky put it:

> the development of non-spontaneous concepts must possess all the traits peculiar to the child's thought at each developmental level because these concepts are not simply acquired by rote but evolve with the aid of strenuous mental activity on the part of the child himself. We believe that the two processes – the development of spontaneous and non-spontaneous concepts – are related and constantly influence each other.
>
> (1986: 157) (23)

Thus, all Inhelder and Piaget are doing in GLT is to present adolescents with investigations, related to quite complex thinking underlying genuine mastery of science concepts, which reveal their development of reasoning patterns such as control and exclusion of irrelevant variables required in biological thinking, and proportion and equilibria of systems needed to model physical science. Vygotsky's criticisms of the limitations of spontaneous thinking all vanish as we see they relate only to the middle phase of the development of concrete operations in younger children. The 'spontaneous' thinking of the adolescent is a very different animal to that of the 8- to 10-year-old. As Inhelder and Piaget show in delightful detail, the 'spontaneous concepts' exhibited by these adolescents have already been brought 'up to the level of development which would guarantee that the scientific concepts are actually just above the spontaneous ones' (Vygotsky 1986: 195).

In claiming that if one needs the specifics of the levels of mental development it is to Piaget that one should turn, then one should remember that this delivers only the statics. To give Vygotsky the last word in this section:

> It became clear that the functioning of intelligence depends upon the structure of thought. Piaget's works are but the most explicit expression of the concern with the structural aspect of thought.
>
> (1986: 207)

## Fostering the dynamics of development: Vygotsky the leader

Before beginning this section, two points need to be made. First, for any reader, who cares to look, Chapter 6 ('The Development of Scientific Concepts in Childhood') in *Thought and Language* is heavy in comments (see quotes (4), (5), (6), (7), (13), (14) and (15) to begin with) about the importance of being able to gauge both the level of mental development of children and also the level of thinking that each step in each school subject requires. Here are two more:

> The development of a spontaneous concept must have reached a certain level for the child to be able to absorb a related scientific concept.
>
> (Vygotsky 1986: 194)

> To uncover the complex relation between instruction and the development of scientific concepts is an important practical task.
>
> (Vygotsky 1986: 162)

Second – and this is a lacuna in the thinking of both Vygotsky and Piaget – perhaps the most important implication of the survey of 14,000 children between the ages of 10 and 16 on Piagetian tests (Shayer et al. 1976; Shayer et al. 1978) is that the range of mental development in any one year group is far, far wider than anyone dreamed, as those teaching in comprehensive schools have learnt empirically the hard way (for example in a representative sample of 12-year-olds around 7 per cent test at the level of the average 6-year-old, and 10 per cent at the level of the top 30 per cent of 16-year-olds (early formal), see Figure 11.1). Bearing in mind his creative contribution to special education in the former USSR, I am sure that this would have been taken very seriously by Vygotsky, had his research revealed it. But in assessing his contributions to the theory and practice of teaching one needs always to remember that although they are developmentally orientated, his pedagogics assume that (children in special education excluded) each year group of children are fairly homogeneous in mental development. This is shown in his elaboration of his dynamic assessment process:

in this way the analysis of the [ZPD] becomes not only a magnificent means for the prognosis of the fate of the intellectual development and the dynamics of the relative success [of the child] in school, but also a fine means for the composition of classes . . . the level of intellectual development of the child, his [ZPD], the ideal [mental] age of the class, and the relation between the ideal [mental] age of the class and the [ZPD] . . . [form] the best means to solve the problem of the composition of classes.

(Vygotsky 1993/1935, quoted in van der Veer and Valsiner 1991: 340)

Well, perhaps he did know *something* of the problem of different abilities of same-aged children!

Piaget has been represented as studying (and promoting) only the individual, and Vygotsky as focusing on (and promoting) the primacy of social processes of learning (Lerman 1996). But this is to confound investigational method with intention. Neither engaged in applicable research in the classroom. I have already presented the paradox that Vygotsky's own reports of his work in dynamic assessment were focused only on the individual, whereas Piaget notoriously once said, truly, of the Genevan method 'I am not interested in individuals', for in fact his selection of a good sample of children was typical of the methodology of the biologist seeking to describe a species.

Les Smith (Piaget 1995; Smith 1996) has shown in meticulous detail that, at the abstract level at least, Piaget and Vygotsky occupied very similar territory with respect to the social origin of thinking. Any reader who doubts this is invited to sit the self-test given in Smith (1996), where one is requested to attribute to the right author 20 brief quotations, there being an equal number from Piaget and Vygotsky. Among a score of 'experts' who were given the test unseen at the time, none did better than 16 correct, and their mean score was 13 (mine was 12, but then I dodged two items, my uncertainty helping to make Smith's case). Both, in their own ways, stressed the importance of 'construction' by the individual (see quotation (3)) – in Vygotsky's case covered by the global term 'internalization', which sometimes means immediate appropriation of a concept made available by another collaborator in learning, and sometimes means (quotation (3)) subsequent work by the individual. This second meaning overlaps Piaget's contribution to the art of 'cognitive conflict', the pain and challenge that follow a person finding that his present concepts are not powerful enough to solve a dilemma.

One important insight from Vygotsky is that in 'spontaneous' thinking the movement in the child's mind is from particular instances toward some more general concept which links them, whereas in school learning, particularly that of science, the child first receives the concept at the abstract level, and then has to struggle to find out how it may be applied to different specific contexts. Quoting from West and Pines 1985, Howe (1996) describes this:

The metaphor is of two vines; one vine representing spontaneous concepts grows upward while the other vine, representing scientific concepts, grows downward. Under the influence of instruction that encourages integration and consolidation the two vines intertwine and grow together as conceptual understanding develops.

How then is one to draw on these various insights to create a general strategy for effective teaching in school? In different ways both Feuerstein through the Instrumental Enrichment programme and the workers involved in the CASE and CAME interventions have chosen an intermediate *tactical* solution (Feuerstein et al. 1980; Adey et al. 1995; Adhami et al. 1998). Although they express it differently (Feuerstein through the concept of 'cultural deprivation'), I believe that both sets of workers are addressing the problem shown by the CSMS survey quoted above that in any one year group or in any one class of 12-year-olds in a neighbourhood high school with a mixed-ability policy maybe no more than 20 per cent may be functioning at the level of their true mental potential, so that in Piagetian terms their mental levels may range from early to middle concrete right through to mature formal. Before one could dream of an ideal solution to school learning, first one must tackle the problem of the Western environment that has produced 'cultural deprivation' and hence so many people that cannot benefit from schooling once it goes beyond the primary level. Hence the notion of 'intervention' (drawn from medical terminology) as an intermediate tactic to increase by a large amount the proportion of children to a mental level at which they can process their learning during the course of ordinary instructional teaching (Shayer 1999a; 1999b). Perhaps in 30 years, when intervention methodology has been practised with all age groups from 5 through to 14, and most children realize their genetic potential, 'good teaching practice' will have evolved to a seamless integration of instruction and intervention.

Given the twin vine concept on the one hand, and the CSMS survey evidence of wide ranges of mental levels among the pupils on the other, then the first general principle one can enunciate is that any good intervention activity should be in a context that allows processing at several different levels. In this way, there are opportunities for all children in the class possibly to make 'revolutionary' jumps in thinking, each from where they presently are. 'All shall get prizes' would then not be a patronizing observation.

But in order to design activities having this characteristic (such as the 'Instruments' in the Instrumental Enrichment programme and the CASE and CAME lessons) it is essential that designers, and those who teach the lessons, are able to look at their curriculum through mental development (Piagetian) eyes, as Vygotsky originally argued was essential. If you cannot assess the range of mental levels of the children in your class, and simultaneously what is the level of cognitive demand of each stage of the lesson activity, how can you plan and then execute – in response to the minute-by-minute responses of the pupils – tactics which result in all engaging fruitfully?

There then arises the question 'How should the teachers conduct these intervention activities?' Quotations (17) and (18) are suggestive that some kind of collaborative learning should be beneficial, and in case a Western reader is put off by the language of:

Functions are first formed in the collective[5] as relations among children
and then become mental functions for the individual
(Vygotsky 1979: 165)

(who can totally resist using the jargon of the times?), she could also interpret it in the spirit of a later statement:

play also creates the [ZPD] of the child. In play the child is always behaving
beyond his age, above his usual every day behaviour; in play he is, as it
were, a head above himself. Play contains in a concentrated form, as in
the focus of a magnifying glass, all developmental tendencies; it is as
if the child tries to jump above his usual level. The relation of play to
development should be compared to the relation between instruction and
development . . . Play is a source of development and creates the [ZPD].
(Vygotsky 1933/1935, quoted in van der Veer and Valsiner
1991: 345)

Thus, the abstract formulation:

Research shows that reflection [by the individual] is spawned from argument
[in the collective]
(Vygotsky 1979: 165, 170)

implies a process nicely specific, indicating that the main source of mediation for adolescents is their peers, rather than 'scaffolding' by adults.

'How do I know what I think until I hear what I say?' (last page of *Howards
End* by E.M. Forster) applies even more to a group of children trying to find
an idea which will illuminate a science problem or a strategy by which to
attack a maths task, and could be complemented by 'How do I know what I
think until I also hear what the others say?' In fact, even 'until I hear what
*I* say' implies the response and stimulation of the others and the presence of
'the collective'. So the suggestion is that the teacher, in her role of mediator,
realize her role is that of manager of learning. As quickly as possible a
learning issue is presented to the class (concrete preparation), and then groups
of pupils (between three and five to each group) are given a few minutes to
come out with ideas which might be useful – perhaps using blank sheets of
paper to scribble models on and discuss (construction). But (quotation (18))
what if 'the interpsychological' has appeared in group 2, and a child whose
ZPD is sufficiently advanced to be affected by witnessing this is in group 7
on the other side of the room? There is no way the performance could
become 'intrapsychological' for him. Hence the importance of Act 3 of the
cycle (whole-class discussion or metacognition), where each group quickly
reports to the rest of the class the high points of their discussion, and others
are allowed to comment ('I don't agree with what John said, because . . .').
Bearing in mind the issue of different levels of mental development in the
class, and also different depths of interpretation of the agenda, the teacher
would be wise, at this point, to ask first the less able children to present any
solutions to the lower-level aspects of the task she has seen and heard during
the construction period. It is not always the less able pupils who benefit

from this! Sometimes the more able say that worried them too, but they didn't want to ask. If each group only present what hasn't already come up, this exchange can be brisk and not tedious. Ideally, every idea or strategy which has come up in the group discussion then becomes available, for any or everyone, increasing by a large factor the number of opportunities for each to complete their ZPD in respect of this or that concept.

The ideas developed in one three-Act cycle can then serve as concrete preparation for a second cycle during which the learning context can be deepened or extended.

It is not suggested that this teaching art, integrating the Piagetian (mental level) and Vygotskian aspects (class management) is as easy as current announcements by the DfEE about 'thinking skills' seem to suggest. You cannot hope for any success – previous research data show this (Adey and Shayer 1994: Chapter 3) – by giving teachers a few days of abstract training and then asking them to go away and apply it to their own subjects. Hitherto, whether it be Feuerstein Instrumental Enrichment, CASE or CAME, it has required several years with subject specialist research teams to generate portfolios of lesson contexts which fulfil all the criteria mentioned above. In this book three different recent developments of the art have been presented: to primary maths Years 5 and 6 (Chapters 7 and 8), to Performing Arts subjects (Chapter 9), to the next stage of the development of the CASE art, learning how to integrate the teaching skills practised in thinking science lessons which those teachers use in their 'ordinary' science lessons (Chapter 10), and in the intervention for Year 1 primary children (Chapters 2, 3, 4, 5 and 6). Each of these teaching programmes only becomes effective through PD delivered over a period of at least a year, where feedback is given to the teachers as they gain increasing experience of the problems which arise from the lesson activities.

## Notes

1 Quotations from (1)–(3) Vygotsky (1986: 149, 155 and 157). Quotations (4) and (5) from Vygotsky (1978: 88 and 91).
2 Note: this is not taken from the more usually quoted *Mind in Society* (1978), but from a (partial) translation of the original by van der Veer and Valsiner (1991: 337) See their reference to Vygotsky 1933/1935.
3 Cf Newton *thesis*: heavenly bodies attract each other with an inverse square law; *antithesis*: action at a distance is an unsatisfactory mystical concept – it would be over 200 years until Einstein resolved this.
4 The first sentence in this quotation differs from that given by van der Veer and Valsiner and was re-translated by Mundher Adhami. Van der Veer confirmed by email (11/10/01) that this version, giving the power to the *child*, is a better reading of the original Russian.
5 My Russian translator assured me that the Russian word is used much as 'group' is used in English, without carrying as heavy political overtones as the word 'collective' does in English.

# REFERENCES

Adey, P.S. and Shayer, M. (1993) An exploration of long-term far-transfer effects following an extended intervention programme in the high school science curriculum, *Cognition and Instruction*, 11(1): 1–29.

Adey, P. and Shayer, M. (1994) *Really Raising Standards*. London: Routledge.

Adey, P., Robertson, A. and Venville, G. (2001) *Let's Think!* Windsor: NFER-Nelson.

Adey, P.S., Shayer, M. and Yates, C. (1995) *Thinking Science: Student and Teachers' Materials for the CASE Intervention*, 2nd edn. London: Nelson 3rd edn. published 2001, Nelson Thornes.

Adhami, M., Johnson, D.C. and Shayer, M. (1998). *Thinking Maths: The Programme for Accelerated Learning in Mathematics*. Oxford: Heinemann Educational Books.

Alibali, M. and Golden-Meadow, S. (1993) Gesture-speech mismatch and mechanisms of learning: what the hands reveal about a child's state of mind, Cognitive Psychology, 25: 468–523.

Ames, C. (1986) Effective motivation: the contribution of the learning environment, in R.S. Feldman (ed.) *The Social Psychology of Education*. Cambridge: Cambridge University Press.

Anderson, M. (1992) *Intelligence and Development: A Cognitive Theory*. London: Blackwell.

Argyle, M. (1991) *Co-operation: The Basis of Sociability*. London: Routledge.

Askew, M., Brown, M., Rhodes, V., Johnson, D.C. and Wiliam, D. (1997) *Effective Teachers of Numeracy* (Final Report). London: King's College.

Baddeley, A. (1990) *Human Memory: Theory And Practice*. London: Lawrence Erlbaum.

Bandura, A. (1986) *Social Foundations of Thought and Action: A Social Cognitive Theory*. Englewood Cliffs, NJ: Prentice-Hall.

Barnes, D. and Todd, F. (1978) *Discussion and Learning in Small Groups*. London: Routledge & Kegan Paul.

Beasley, F. and Shayer, M. (1990) Learning potential assessment through Feuerstein's LPAD: can quantitative results be achieved?, *International Journal of Dynamic Assessment and Instruction*, 1(2): 37–48.

Beattie, G. (1983) *Talk: An Analysis of Speech and Non-verbal Behaviour in Conversation*. Milton Keynes: Open University Press.

Belbin, E. (1979) Applicable psychology and some national problems, *British Journal of Psychology*, 70(2): 187–97.

Biggs, J. and Collis, K. (1982) *Evaluating the Quality of Learning*. New York: Academic Press.

Birmingham City Council (1997) *Signposts*. Windsor: NFER-Nelson.

Bloom, B.S. and Krathnohl, D.R. (1956) *Taxonomy of Educational Objectives. Handbook 1: Cognitive Domain*. New York: Longmans.

Blurton-Jones, N.G. (1973) Non-verbal communication in children, in Hinde, R.A. (ed.) *Non-verbal Communication*. Cambridge, UK: Cambridge University Press.

Borkowski, J.G., Ryan, E.B., Kurtz, B.E. and Reid, M.K. (1983) Metamemory and metalinguistic development: correlates of children's intelligence and achievement, *Bulletin of the Psychonomic Society*, 21: 393–6.

Breckinbridge-Church, R. and Goldin-Meadow, S. (1986) The mismatch between gesture and speech as an index of transitional knowledge, *Cognition*, 23: 43–71.

Brown, A.L. (1987) Metacognition, executive control, self-regulation and other more mysterious mechanisms, in R. Kluwe and F. Weinert (eds) *Metacognition, Motivation and Understanding*. London: Lawrence Erlbaum.

Bruner, J. (1977) *The Process of Education*. Cambridge, MA: Harvard University Press.

Bruner, J. (1996) *The Culture of Education*. Cambridge, MA: Harvard University Press.

Calouste Gulbenkian Foundation (1982) *The Arts in Schools: Principles, Practice and Provision*. London: Calouste Gulbenkian Foundation.

Carroll, J.B. (1993) *Human Cognitive Abilities*. Cambridge, UK: Cambridge University Press.

Cattell, R.B. (1963) Theory of fluid and crystallized intelligence: a critical experiment, *Journal of Educational Psychology*, 54: 1–22.

Cavanaugh, J.C. and Borkowski, J.G. (1980) Searching for metamemory-memory connections: a developmental study, *Developmental Psychology*, 16: 441–53.

Clarke, D.M. (1994) Ten key principles from research for the professional development of mathematics teachers, in D.B. Aichele and A.F. Coxford (eds) *Professional Development for Teachers of Mathematics: The 1994 Yearbook of the National Council of Teachers of Mathematics*: 37–48. Reston, VA: National Council of Teachers of Mathematics.

Cole, M. and Wertsch, J.V. (2000) URL: http://www.massey.ac.nz/~Alock/colevyg.htm

Collis, K.F. (1975) *A Study of Concrete and Formal Operations in School Mathematics: A Piagetian Viewpoint*. Melbourne: Australian Council for Educational Research.

Cooney, T.J. and Shealey, B.E. (1996) On understanding the structure of teachers' beliefs and their relationship to change, in E. Fennema and B.S. Nelson (eds) *Mathematics Teachers in Transition*. Mahwah, NJ: Lawrence Erlbaum Associates.

Cornoldi, C. (1998) The impact of metacognitive reflection on cognitive control, in G. Mazzoni and T.O. Nelson (eds) *Metacognition and Cognitive Neuropsychology*: 139–59. Mahwah, NJ: Lawrence Erlbaum Associates.

Dasen, P.R. (1972) Cross cultural Piagetian research: a summary, *Journal of Cross Cultural Psychology*, 3(1): 23–40.

De Corte, E. (1990) Towards powerful learning environments for the acquisition of problem-solving skills, *European Journal of Psychology of Education*, 5(1): 5–19.

Department for Education and Employment (1999) *Raising Aspirations in the 21st Century: A Speech By The Rt Hon David Blunkett, Secretary Of State For Education And Employment 6th January 2000*. London: DfEE Publications.

Department for Education and Employment (2001) *Learning and Teaching: A Strategy for Professional Development*. London: DfEE Publications.

Department for Education and Skills (2001) Framework for teaching English: years 7, 8 and 9, at www.standards.dfes.gov.uk

Department for Education and Science (1982) *Mathematics Counts: Inquiry into the Teaching of Mathematics in Schools* (Cockroft Report). London: HMSO.

Donaldson, M. (1978) *Children's Minds*. Glasgow: Fontana.

Duncan, J. (2001) Attention, relevance and the prefrontal cortex. Paper delivered at the British Psychological Society Annual Conference, Glasgow, 30 March. Address: MRC Cognition and Brain Sciences Unit, Chaucer Road, Cambridge. Email: john.duncan@mrc-cbu.cam.ac.uk

Dweck, C.S. and Bempechat, J. (1983) Children's theories of intelligence: consequences for learning, in S.G. Paris, G.M. Olson and H.W. Stevenson (eds) *Learning and Motivation in the Classroom*. Hillsdale, NJ: Lawrence Erlbaum Associates.

Eames, D., Shorrocks, D. and Tomlinson, P. (1990). Naughty animals or naughty experimenters?, *British Journal of Developmental Psychology*, 8: 25–7.

Edwards, D. and Mercer, N. (1987) *Common Knowledge – The Development of Understanding in the Classroom*. Milton Keynes: Open University Press.

Ekman, P. and O'Sullivan, M. (1991) Facial expression: methods, means and moues, in Feldman, R.S. and Rime, B. (eds) *Fundamentals of Non-verbal Behaviour*. Cambridge, UK: Cambridge University Press.

Epstein, H.T. (1986) Stages in human brain development, *Developmental Brain Research*, 30: 114–19.

Epstein, H.T. (1990) Stages in human mental growth, *Journal of Educational Psychology*, 82: 876–80.

Feuerstein, R., Rand, Y. and Hoffman, M. (1979). *The Dynamic Assessment of Retarded Performers: The Learning Potential Assessment Device, Theory, Instruments and Techniques*. Baltimore: University Park Press.

Feuerstein, R., Rand, Y., Hoffman, M. and Miller, M. (1980) *Instrumental Enrichment: an Intervention Programme for Cognitive Modifiability*. Baltimore: University Park Press.

Flavell, J.H. (2000) Developing intuitions about the mental experiences of self and others. Paper presented at the Meeting of the Jean Piaget Society, Montreal, Canada, June.

Flavell, J.H. (1979). Metacognition and cognitive monitoring, *American Psychologist*, 34(10): 906–11.

Flavell, J.H. and Wellman, H.M. (1977) Metamemory, in R.V. Kail and J.W. Hagen (eds) *Perspectives on the Development of Memory and Cognition*: 3–33. Hillsdale, NJ: Lawrence Erlbaum Associates.

Fusco, E.T. (1983) The relationship between children's cognitive level of development and their response to literature. Unpublished PhD dissertation, Hofstra University.

Gallagher, J. and Reid, K. (1981) *The Learning Theory of Piaget and Inhelder*. California: Wadsworth.

Gardner, H. (1993) *Frames of Mind*, 2nd edn. New York: Basic Books.

Goldin-Meadow, S., Wein, D. and Chang, C. (1992) Assessing knowledge through gesture: using children's hands to read their minds, *Cognition and Instruction*, 9(3): 201–19.

Goswami, U. (1998) *Cognition in Children*. Hove: Psychology Press.

Greenhough, W.T., Black, J.E. and Wallace, C.S. (1987) Experience and brain development, *Child Development*, 58: 539–59.

Grice, H.P. (1975) Logic and conversation, in P. Cole and J. Morgan (eds) *Syntax and Semantics*, Vol. 3: Speech Acts. New York: Academic Press.

Grouws, D.A. and Schultz, K.A. (1996) Mathematics teacher education, in J. Sikula (ed.) *Handbook of Research on Teacher Education*, 2nd edn: 442–58. New York: Macmillan.

Guba, E.G. and Lincoln, Y.S. (1994) Competing paradigms in qualitative research, in N.K. Denzin and Y.S. Lincoln (eds) *Handbook Of Qualitative Research*. London: Sage.

Hamaker, A., Jordan, P. and Backwell, J. (1997) An evaluation of a two-year cognitive intervention for Key Stage 4 students in the UK, Journal of Design and Technology Education, 3(1): 26–33.

Hamers, J. and Csapó, B. (1999) Teaching thinking, in J. Hamers, J. Van Luit and B. Csapó (eds) *Teaching And Learning Thinking Skills*. Lisse: Swets & Zeitlinger.

Hamers, J.H.M. and Overtoom, M.Th. (1997) *Teaching Thinking In Europe: Inventory of European Programmes*. Utrecht: Sardes.

Hamers, J., Van Luit, J. and Csapó, B. (1999) *Teaching and Learning Thinking Skills*. Lisse: Swets & Zeitlinger.

Hargie, O., Saunders, C. and Dickson, D. (1994) *Social Skills in Interpersonal Communication*, 3rd edn. London: Routledge & Kegan Paul.

Harland, J., Kinder, K. and Hartley, K. (1995) *Arts in their View: A Study of Youth Participation in the Arts*. Berkshire: NFER.

Hart, K. (ed.) (1981) *Children's Understanding of Mathematics: 11–16*. London: John Murray.

Hartman, H.J. (1998) Metacognition in teaching and learning: an introduction, *Instructional Science*, 26(1–2): 1–3.

Hogan, D. and Tudge, J. (1999) Implications of Vygotsky's theory for peer learning, in A.M. O'Donnell and A. King (eds) *Cognitive Perspectives On Peer Learning*, Mahwah: Laurence Erlbaum Associates.

Howe, A.C. (1996) Development of science concepts with a Vygotskian framework, *Science Education*, 80(1): 35–51.

Hudspeth, W.J. and Pribram, K.H. (1990) Stages of brain and cognitive maturation, *Journal of Educational Psychology*, 2: 861–4.

Hutchby, I. and Wooffitt, R. (1998) *Conversation Analysis*. Cambridge: Polity Press.

Inhelder, B. and Piaget, J. (1958) *The Growth of Logical Thinking from Childhood to Adolescence*, London: Routledge & Kegan Paul.

Inhelder, B. and Piaget, J. (1964) *The Early Growth of Logic in the Child*. London: Routledge & Kegan Paul.

Johnson, D.C. (ed.) (1989) *Children's Mathematical Frameworks 8–13: A Study of Classroom Teaching*. Windsor: NFER-Nelson.

Johnson, D.W. and Johnson, R.T. (1979) Conflict in the classroom: controversy and learning, *Review of Educational Research*, 149: 51–61.

Johnson, D.W. and Johnson, R.T. (1994) Collaborative learning and argumentation, in P. Kutnick and C. Rogers (eds) *Groups in Schools*: 66–86. London: Cassell.

Johnson, J.S. and Newport, E.L. (1993) Critical period effects in second language learning: the influence of maturational state on the acquisition of English as a second language, in M.H. Johnson (ed.) *Brain Development and Cognition*. Oxford: Blackwell.

Johnson, M.H. (1997) *Developmental Cognitive Neuroscience*. Oxford: Blackwell.

Joyce, B. and Showers, B. (1995). *Student Achievement through Staff Development*, 2nd edn. New York: Longman.

Kelly, G.A. (1955) *A Theory of Personality: The Psychology of Personal Constructs*. New York: Norton Library.

Kelly, S.D. and Breckinbridge-Church, R. (1997) Can children detect conceptual information conveyed through other children's non-verbal behaviours?, *Cognition and Instruction*, 15(1): 107–34.

Kendon, A. (2000) Language and gesture: unity or duality?, in D. McNeil (ed.) *Language and Gesture*: 47–63. Cambridge, UK: Cambridge University Press.

Kite, A. (2001) *Developing Children's Thinking* Research in Education No. 28. Scottish Council for Research in Education (www.scre.ac.uk).

Klauer, K.J. (1989) Teaching for analogical transfer as a means of improving problem-solving, thinking and learning, *Instructional Science*, 18: 179–92.

Kline, M. (1986) *Mathematics and the Search for Knowledge*. Oxford: Oxford University Press.

Kohlberg, L. (1966) A cognitive developmental analysis of children's sex-role concepts and attitudes, in E.E. Maccoby (ed.) *The Development of Sex-differences*: 52–173. Stanford: Stanford University Press.

Kontos, S. and Nicholas, J.G. (1986) Independent problem-solving in the development of metacognition, *Journal of Genetic Psychology*, 147: 481–95.

Kuhn, D. (1993) Science as argument: implications for teaching and learning scientific thinking, *Science Education*, 77(3): 319–37.

Kuhn, D. (1999) A developmental model of critical thinking, *Educational Researcher*, 28(2): 16–46.

Kuhn, D. (2000) Theory of mind, metacognition and reasoning: a life-span perspective, in P. Mitchell and K.J. Riggs (eds) *Children's Reasoning and the Mind*: 301–26. Hove: Psychology Press Ltd.

Kuhn, T.S. (1962) *The Structure of Scientific Revolutions*. Chicago: University of Chicago Press.

Kyllonen, P.C. and Christal, R.E. (1990) Reasoning ability is (little more than) working memory capacity?!, *Intelligence*, 14: 389–433.

Lerman, S. (1996) Intersubjectivity in mathematics learning: a challenge to the radical constructivist paradigm?, *Journal of Research in Mathematics Education*, 27(2): 133–50.

Light, P., Sheldon, S. and Woodhead, M. (1991) *Learning To Think*. London: Routledge.

Lipman, M., Sharp, M. and Oscanyan, F. (1980) *Philosophy in the Classroom*, 2nd edn. Philadelphia: Temple University Press.

Logie, R.H. (1999) Working memory, *The Psychologist*, 12(4): 174–8.

Lucangeli, D., Galderisi, D. and Cornoldi, C. (1994) Transfer effects after metacognitive training, *Learning Disabilities, Research and Practice*, 10: 11–21.

Ma, L. (1999) *Knowing and Teaching Mathematics: Teachers' Understanding of Fundamental Mathematics in China and the United States*. Mahwah, NJ: Lawrence Erlbaum Associates.

McGuinness, C. (1990) Talking about thinking: the role of metacognition in teaching thinking, in K. Gilhooly, M.T.G. Keane, R.H. Logie and G. Erdos (eds) *Lines of Thinking*: 301–12. London: John Wiley and Sons.

McGuinness, C. (1999) *From Thinking Skills to Thinking Classrooms: A Review And Evaluation Of Approaches For Developing Pupils' Thinking*, research report no. 115. Department for Education and Employment, Norwich, Her Majesty's Stationery Office.

McNeil, D. (1995) *Hand and Mind*. Chicago: The University of Chicago Press.

McNeil, D. (ed.) (2000) *Language and Gesture*. Cambridge, UK: Cambridge University Press.

Meloth, M. and Deering, P. (1999) The role of the teacher in promoting cognitive processing during collaborative learning, in A. O'Donnell and A. King (eds) *Cognitive Perspectives On Peer Learning*. Mahwah, NJ: Lawrence Erlbaum Associates.

Miles, M.B. and Huberman, A.M. (1984) *Qualitative Data Analysis: A Source Book of New Methods*. Thousand Oaks: Sage.

Moss, E. (1990) Social interaction and metacognitive development in gifted preschoolers, *Gifted Child Quarterly*, 34: 16–20.

Mueller, N. (1996) Teddy bear's picnic: four-year-old children's personal constructs in relation to behavioural problems and to teacher global concern, *Journal of Child Psychology and Child Psychiatry*, 37(4): 381–9.

National Advisory Committee on Creative and Cultural Education (1999) *All our Futures: Creativity, Culture and Education*. London: DfEE Publications.

Newman, D., Griffin, P. and Cole, M. (1989) *The Construction Zone: Working for Cognitive Change in School*. Cambridge, UK: Cambridge University Press.

Nisbet, J. (1993) The thinking curriculum, *Educational Psychology*, 13(3 and 4): 281–90.

Nuthall, G. (1999) Learning how to learn: the evolution of students' minds through social processes and culture of the classroom, *International Journal of Educational Research*, 31(3): 141–256.

O'Donnell, A.M. and King, A. (1999) *Cognitive Perspectives On Peer Learning*. Mahwah, NJ: Laurence Erlbaum Associates.

Papetti, O., Cornoldi, C., Pettavino, A., Mazzoni, G., and Borkowski, J. (1992) Memory judgements and allocation of study times in good and poor comprehenders, in T.E. Scruggs and M.A. Mastropieri (eds) *Advances in Learning and Behavioural Disabilities*, Vol. 7: 3–33. Greenwich: JAI.

Pascual-Leone, J. (1976) On learning and development, Piagetian style, *Canadian Psychological Review*, 17(4): 270–97.

Pascual-Leone, J. (1988) Organismic processes for neo-Piagetian theories: dialectic causal account of cognitive development, in A. Demetriou (ed.) *The Neo-Piagetian Theories of Cognitive Development: Towards an Integration*. Amsterdam: North-Holland.

Peel, E.A. (1971) *The Nature of Adolescent Judgement*. Great Britain: Granada Publishing.

Perkins, D.N. and Saloman, G. (1989) Are cognitive skills context bound?, *Educational Researcher*, 18(1): 16–25.

Piaget, J. (1930) *The Child's Conception Of Causality*. London: Routledge & Kegan Paul.

Piaget, J. (1933/2000) Commentary on Vygotsky's criticisms of *Language and Thought of the Child* and *Judgement and Reasoning in the Child*, *New Ideas in Psychology*, 18: 241–59.

Piaget, J. (1976) *The Grasp of Consciousness: Action and Concept in the Young Child*. Cambridge, MA: Harvard University Press.

Piaget, J. (1995) *Sociological Studies*. London: Routledge.

Piaget, J. and Inhelder, B. (1974) *The Child's Construction Of Quantities*. London: Routledge & Kegan Paul.

Piaget, J. and Inhelder, B. (1976) *The Child's Conception Of Space*. London: Routledge & Kegan Paul.

Plomin, R. (2001) Genetics and behaviour, *The Psychologist*, 14(3): 134–9.

Pout, L. (2001) Unpublished MA thesis, University of Liverpool.

Ravenette, A.T. (1975) Grid techniques for children, *Journal of Child Psychology and Child Psychiatry*, 16: 79–83.

Rich, J. (1972) *Interviewing Children and Adolescents*. London: MacMillan Press Ltd.

Rogoff, B. (1991) The joint socialization of development by young children and adults, in P. Light, S. Sheldon and M. Woodhead (eds) *Learning To Think*. London: Routledge.

Sacks, H. (1995) Lectures, Fall 1964 to Fall 1965, in E. Jefferson (ed.) *Lectures on Conversation*, Vol. 1 and 2: 3–230. Oxford: Blackwell.

Sacks, H., Schegloff, E.A. and Jefferson, G. (1974) A simplest systematics for the organisation of turn taking for conversation, *Language*, 50: 696–735.

Salmon, P. (1988) *Psychology for Teachers*. London: Cassell.

Schegloff, E.A. (1991) Conversation analysis and socially shared cognition, in L. Resnick, J.M. Levine and S.D. Teasley (eds) *Perspectives on Socially Shared Cognition*: 150–71. Washington: American Psychological Association.

Schön, D.A. (1983) *The Reflective Practitioner: How Professionals Think in Action.* New York: Basic Books.

Schwanenflugel, P.J., Stevens, T.P. and Carr, M. (1997) Metacognitive knowledge of gifted children and non-identified children in early elementary school, *Gifted Child Quarterly*, 41(2): 25–35.

Shayer, M. (1993) Piaget: only the Galileo of cognitive development? Comment on Niaz and Lawson on genetic epistemology, *Journal of Research in Science Teaching*, 30(7): 815–18.

Shayer, M. (1999a) Cognitive acceleration through science education II: its effect and scope, *International Journal of Science Education*, 21(8): 883–902.

Shayer, M. (1999b) *GCSE 1999: Added-value from Schools Adopting the CASE Intervention.* London: Centre for the Advancement of Thinking.

Shayer, M. and Adey, P. (1981) *Towards a Science of Science Teaching.* Oxford: Heinemann Educational.

Shayer, M. and Beasley, F. (1987) Does instrumental enrichment work?, *British Educational Research Journal*, 13: 101–19.

Shayer, M. and Gamble, R. (2001) *Bridging from CASE to Core Science.* Hatfield: ASE Publications.

Shayer, M. and Wylam, H. (1978). The distribution of Piagetian stages of thinking in British middle and secondary school children II: 14- to 16-year-olds and sex differentials, *British Journal of Educational Psychology*, (48): 62–70.

Shayer, M., Demetriou, A. and Pervez, M. (1988) The structure and scaling of concrete operational thought: three studies in four countries, *Genetic, Social and General Psychological Monographs*, 114(3): 309–375.

Shayer, M., Johnson, D.C. and Adhani, M. (1999) Does 'CAME' work? Report on Key Stage 3 results following the use of Cognitive Acceleration in Mathematics Education, CAME Project in Years 7 and 8. Proceedings of the British Society for Research into Learning Mathematics Conference, St Martin's College, Lancaster, 5 June.

Shayer, M., Küchemann, D.E. and Wylam, H. (1976) The distribution of Piagetian stages of thinking in British middle and secondary school children, *British Journal of Educational Psychology*, 46: 164–73.

Shayer, M., Wylam, H., Küchemann, D. and Adey, P. (1978) *Science Reasoning Tasks.* Slough: National Foundation for Educational Research.

Smith, L. (1996) The social construction of rational understanding, in A. Tryphon and J. Vonéche (eds) *Piaget-Vygotsky: The Social Genesis of Thought.* Hove: Psychology Press Ltd.

Sternberg, R.J. (1998) Metacognition, abilities and developing expertise: what makes an expert student?, *Instructional Science*, 26(1–2): 127–40.

Stigler, J.W. and Stevenson, H.W. (1991) How Asian teachers polish each lesson to perfection, *American Educator*, 15: 12–47.

Swanson, H.L. (1990) Influence of metacognitive knowledge and aptitude on problem-solving, *Educational Psychology*, 82(2): 306–14.

Thomas, L.F. and Harri-Augstein, E.S. (1985) *Self-organized Learning.* London: Routledge.

Tishman, S., Perkins, D.N. and Jay, E. (1995) *The Thinking Classroom: Learning and Teaching in a Culture of Thinking.* Boston, MA: Allyn and Bacon.

Towse, J., Hitch, G. and Hutton, U. (1998) A re-evaluation of working memory capacity in children, *Journal of Memory and Language*, 39: 195–217.

Tryphon, A. and Vonéche, J. (1996) *Piaget-Vygotsky: The Social Genesis Of Thought.* Hove: Psychology Press Ltd.

van der Veer, R. and Valsiner, J. (1991) *Understanding Vygotsky: A Quest for Synthesis*. Oxford: Blackwell.

van der Veer, R. and Valsiner, J. (1994) *The Vygotsky Reader*. Oxford: Blackwell.

Vygotsky, L.S. (1978) *Mind in Society*. Edited by M. Cole, V. John Steiner, S. Scribner and E. Souberman. Cambridge, Mass: Harvard University Press.

Vygotsky, L.S. (1979) The genesis of higher mental functions, in J.V. Wertsch (ed.) *The Concept of Activity in Soviet Psychology*. Armonk, NY: M.E. Sharpe.

Vygotsky, L.S. (1986) *Thought and Language*. Edited by Alex Kozulin. Cambridge, Mass: MIT Press.

Wadsworth, B.J. (1996) *Piaget's Theory of Cognitive and Affective Development: Foundations of Constructivism*. London: Longman.

Wegerif, R., Mercer, N. and Dawes, L. (1999) From social interaction to individual reasoning: an empirical investigation of a possible socio-cultural model of cognitive development, *Learning and Instruction*, 9(6): 493–516.

Wigan Education Authority (1989) *The Arts in Wigan Schools: A Policy Statement*. Wigan: Wigan Education Authority.

Wood, T. and Turner-Vorbeck, T. (1999) Developing teaching of mathematics: making connections in practice, in L. Burton (ed.) *Learning Mathematics: From Hierarchies to Networks*. London: Falmer Press.

Woolfolk, A.E. and Brooks, D.M. (1983) Non-verbal communication in teaching, in *Review of Research in Education*, Vol. 10: 103–49. Washington: American Educational Research Association.

Yackel, E. and Cobb, P. (1996) Sociomathematical norms, argumentation and autonomy in mathematics, *Journal for Research in Mathematics Education*, 27(4): 458–77.

# INDEX

Page numbers in *italics* refer to tables.